# Privatisation Performance in Major European Countries Since 1980

# Privatisation Performance in Major European Countries Since 1980

*Motasam Tatahi*



palgrave
macmillan

First published 2006 by
PALGRAVE MACMILLAN
Houndmills, Basingstoke, Hampshire RG21 6XS and
175 Fifth Avenue, New York, N.Y. 10010
Companies and representatives throughout the world.

PALGRAVE MACMILLAN is the global academic imprint of the Palgrave Macmillan division of St. Martin's Press, LLC and of Palgrave Macmillan Ltd. Macmillan® is a registered trademark in the United States, United Kingdom and other countries. Palgrave is a registered trademark in the European Union and other countries.

ISBN-13: 978–0–230–00484–9 hardback
ISBN-10: 0–230–00484–9 hardback

This book is printed on paper suitable for recycling and made from fully managed and sustained forest sources.

A catalogue record for this book is available from the British Library.

A catalog record for this book is available from the Library of Congress.

10 9 8 7 6 5 4 3 2 1
15 14 13 12 11 10 09 08 07 06

Printed and bound in Great Britain by
Antony Rowe Ltd, Chippenham and Eastbourne

# Contents


*List of Tables* viii

*Acknowledgements* xv

**1 Introduction** **1**

**2 Public versus Private Ownership: Theory and Performance** **10**

Introduction 10
Property rights theory 13
A critical assessment of property rights theory 17
Public choice theory 23
A critical assessment of public choice theory 26
The Austrian school of economics 28
A critical assessment of the Austrian school of economics 31
The principal–agent theory 34
A critical assessment of the principal–agent theory 38
The new synthesis 44
The new political economy 44
New institutional economics 45
The neo-Austrian school of economics 45
A critical assessment of the new synthesis 46
Conclusion 48

**3 Literature Review of Public and Private Ownership: Strengths and Weaknesses** **52**

Introduction 52
Historical overview of privatisation 56
Empirical studies 60
The relative performance of state-owned and privately owned firms 60
The most significant empirical studies 63
Empirical studies on privatisation 68
The most significant empirical studies 71

A critical assessment 76
Conclusion 79

**4 Why Factor Analysis? 82**

Introduction 82
The neo-classical approach 85
Total factor productivity 86
Critiques against the neo-classical total factor productivity approach 86
Insider critiques 86
The Cambridge critique 89
The main criticisms 91
Defining different aspects of factor analysis 92
Practical procedure 94
Conclusion 96

**5 Results from the Empirical Study: Part I 97**

Introduction 97
The type-one factor analysis 100
Austria 101
Belgium 104
Bulgaria 106
Denmark 109
Finland 111
France 113
Germany 117
Italy 118
The Netherlands 121
Norway 123
Poland 126
Portugal 128
Sweden 131
The UK 131
Total-country analysis 135
Conclusion 138
Appendix: notes on the data sources 139
Exchange rates 142

**6 Results from the Empirical Study: Part II** **143**

Introduction 143
The type-two factor analysis 146
  Privatisation performance 146
The type-three factor analysis 148
  Method one 148
  Method two 149
  Method three 153
  Method four 155
Type-four factor analysis 158
  Sweden (Concentration) 159
Conclusion 161

**7 Summary and General Conclusions** **163**

*Bibliography* 170

*Index* 184

# List of Tables


| | | |
|---|---|---|
| 3.1 | Market value, sales and profits of the 34 largest, publicly traded, privatised firms | 59 |
| 5.1 | List of companies based on their ownership | 100 |
| 5.2(a) | Descriptive statistics for 4 mixed companies, Austria 1988 | 101 |
| 5.2(b) | Descriptive statistics for 2 mixed companies, Austria 2000 | 102 |
| 5.2(c) | Descriptive statistics for 51 private companies, Austria 1998 | 102 |
| 5.2(d) | Descriptive statistics for 47 private companies, Austria 2000 | 102 |
| 5.2(e) | Descriptive statistics for 15 state companies, Austria 1998 | 102 |
| 5.2(f) | Descriptive statistics for 11 state companies, Austria 2000 | 103 |
| 5.3 | Company performances: Austria | 103 |
| 5.4(a) | Descriptive statistics for 5 mixed companies, Belgium 1998 | 104 |
| 5.4(b) | Descriptive statistics for 2 mixed companies, Belgium 2000 | 104 |
| 5.4(c) | Descriptive statistics for 59 private companies, Belgium 1998 | 104 |
| 5.4(d) | Descriptive statistics for 65 private companies, Belgium 2000 | 105 |
| 5.4(e) | Descriptive statistics for 36 state companies, Belgium 1998 | 105 |
| 5.4(f) | Descriptive statistics for 53 state companies, Belgium 2000 | 105 |
| 5.5 | Company performances: Belgium | 106 |
| 5.6(a) | Descriptive statistics for 60 mixed companies, Bulgaria 1998 | 106 |
| 5.6(b) | Descriptive statistics for 104 mixed companies, Bulgaria 2000 | 107 |
| 5.6(c) | Descriptive statistics for 171 private companies, Bulgaria 1998 | 107 |
| 5.6(d) | Descriptive statistics for 300 private companies, Bulgaria 2000 | 107 |

| | | |
|---|---|---|
| 5.6(e) | Descriptive statistics for 109 state companies, Bulgaria 1998 | 107 |
| 5.6(f) | Descriptive statistics for 196 state companies, Bulgaria 2000 | 108 |
| 5.7 | Company performances: Bulgaria | 108 |
| 5.8(a) | Descriptive statistics for 6 mixed companies, Denmark 2000 | 109 |
| 5.8(b) | Descriptive statistics for 43 private companies, Denmark 1998 | 109 |
| 5.8(c) | Descriptive statistics for 44 private companies, Denmark 2000 | 109 |
| 5.8(d) | Descriptive statistics for 17 state companies, Denmark 1998 | 110 |
| 5.8(e) | Descriptive statistics for 30 state companies, Denmark 2000 | 110 |
| 5.9 | Company performances: Denmark | 110 |
| 5.10(a) | Descriptive statistics for 6 mixed companies, Finland 1998 | 111 |
| 5.10(b) | Descriptive statistics for 8 mixed companies, Finland 2000 | 112 |
| 5.10(c) | Descriptive statistics for 56 private companies, Finland 1998 | 112 |
| 5.10(d) | Descriptive statistics for 117 private companies, Finland 2000 | 112 |
| 5.10(e) | Descriptive statistics for 48 state companies, Finland 1998 | 112 |
| 5.10(f) | Descriptive statistics for 75 state companies, Finland 2000 | 113 |
| 5.11 | Company performances: Finland | 113 |
| 5.12(a) | Descriptive statistics for 7 mixed companies, France 1998 | 114 |
| 5.12(b) | Descriptive statistics for 7 mixed companies, France 2000 | 114 |
| 5.12(c) | Descriptive statistics for 250 private companies, France 1998 | 114 |
| 5.12(d) | Descriptive statistics for 313 private companies, France 2000 | 114 |
| 5.12(e) | Descriptive statistics for 243 state companies, France 1998 | 115 |
| 5.12(f) | Descriptive statistics for 280 state companies, France 2000 | 115 |

| | | |
|---|---|---|
| 5.13 | Company performances: France | 115 |
| 5.14(a) | Descriptive statistics for 67 mixed companies, Germany 1998 | 116 |
| 5.14(b) | Descriptive statistics for 52 mixed companies, Germany 2000 | 116 |
| 5.14(c) | Descriptive statistics for 259 private companies, Germany 1998 | 116 |
| 5.14(d) | Descriptive statistics for 231 private companies, Germany 2000 | 116 |
| 5.14(e) | Descriptive statistics for 174 state companies, Germany 1998 | 117 |
| 5.14(f) | Descriptive statistics for 177 state companies, Germany 2000 | 117 |
| 5.15 | Company performances: Germany | 118 |
| 5.16(a) | Descriptive statistics for 3 mixed companies, Italy 1998 | 118 |
| 5.16(b) | Descriptive statistics for 4 mixed companies, Italy 2000 | 119 |
| 5.16(c) | Descriptive statistics for 37 private companies, Italy 1998 | 119 |
| 5.16(d) | Descriptive statistics for 45 private companies, Italy 2000 | 119 |
| 5.16(e) | Descriptive statistics for 30 state companies, Italy 1998 | 119 |
| 5.16(f) | Descriptive statistics for 41 state companies, Italy 2000 | 120 |
| 5.17 | Company performances: Italy | 120 |
| 5.18(a) | Descriptive statistics for 5 mixed companies, the Netherlands 1998 | 121 |
| 5.18(b) | Descriptive statistics for 5 mixed companies, the Netherlands 2000 | 121 |
| 5.18(c) | Descriptive statistics for 45 private companies, the Netherlands 1998 | 121 |
| 5.18(d) | Descriptive statistics for 64 private companies, the Netherlands 2000 | 122 |
| 5.18(e) | Descriptive statistics for 40 state companies, the Netherlands 1998 | 122 |
| 5.18(f) | Descriptive statistics for 51 state companies, the Netherlands 2000 | 122 |
| 5.19 | Company performances: the Netherlands | 123 |

| | | |
|---|---|---|
| 5.20(a) | Descriptive statistics for 14 mixed companies, Norway 1998 | 124 |
| 5.20(b) | Descriptive statistics for 33 mixed companies, Norway 2000 | 124 |
| 5.20(c) | Descriptive statistics for 63 private companies, Norway 1998 | 124 |
| 5.20(d) | Descriptive statistics for 101 private companies, Norway 2000 | 124 |
| 5.20(e) | Descriptive statistics for 43 state companies, Norway 1998 | 125 |
| 5.20(f) | Descriptive statistics for 66 state companies, Norway 2000 | 125 |
| 5.21 | Company performances: Norway | 125 |
| 5.22(a) | Descriptive statistics for 19 mixed companies, Poland 1998 | 126 |
| 5.22(b) | Descriptive statistics for 33 mixed companies, Poland 2000 | 126 |
| 5.22(c) | Descriptive statistics for 173 private companies, Poland 1998 | 126 |
| 5.22(d) | Descriptive statistics for 215 private companies, Poland 2000 | 127 |
| 5.22(e) | Descriptive statistics for 148 state companies, Poland 1998 | 127 |
| 5.22(f) | Descriptive statistics for 172 state companies, Poland 2000 | 127 |
| 5.23 | Company performances: Poland | 128 |
| 5.24(a) | Descriptive statistics for 5 mixed companies, Portugal 1998 | 129 |
| 5.24(b) | Descriptive statistics for 5 mixed companies, Portugal 2000 | 129 |
| 5.24(c) | Descriptive statistics for 47 private companies, Portugal 1998 | 129 |
| 5.24(d) | Descriptive statistics for 46 private companies, Portugal 2000 | 129 |
| 5.24(e) | Descriptive statistics for 8 state companies, Portugal 1998 | 130 |
| 5.24(f) | Descriptive statistics for 9 state companies, Portugal 2000 | 130 |
| 5.25 | Company performances: Portugal | 131 |
| 5.26(a) | Descriptive statistics for 33 mixed companies, Sweden 1998 | 132 |

| | | |
|---|---|---|
| 5.26(b) | Descriptive statistics for 37 mixed companies, Sweden 2000 | 132 |
| 5.26(c) | Descriptive statistics for 379 private companies, Sweden 1998 | 132 |
| 5.26(d) | Descriptive statistics for 375 private companies, Sweden 2000 | 132 |
| 5.26(e) | Descriptive statistics for 344 state companies, Sweden 1998 | 133 |
| 5.26(f) | Descriptive statistics for 338 state companies, Sweden 2000 | 133 |
| 5.27 | Company performances: Sweden | 133 |
| 5.28(a) | Descriptive statistics for 110 private companies, the UK 1998 | 134 |
| 5.28(b) | Descriptive statistics for 100 private companies, the UK 2000 | 134 |
| 5.28(c) | Descriptive statistics for 90 state companies, the UK 1998 | 134 |
| 5.28(d) | Descriptive statistics for 100 state companies, the UK 2000 | 134 |
| 5.29 | Company performances: the UK | 135 |
| 5.30(a) | Descriptive statistics for 228 mixed companies, total countries 1998 | 136 |
| 5.30(b) | Descriptive statistics for 298 mixed companies, total countries 2000 | 136 |
| 5.30(c) | Descriptive statistics for 1,743 private companies, total countries 1998 | 136 |
| 5.30(d) | Descriptive statistics for 2,063 private companies, total countries 2000 | 136 |
| 5.30(e) | Descriptive statistics for 1,345 state companies, total countries 1998 | 137 |
| 5.30(f) | Descriptive statistics for 1,599 state companies, total countries 2000 | 137 |
| 5.31 | Company performances: total countries | 137 |
| 6.1 | Samples for type-two factor analysis: comparison between state-owned and privatised companies | 143 |
| 6.2 | Samples for type-three factor analysis | 144 |
| 6.3(a) | Type-two factor analysis for 52 privatised companies, 1998 | 147 |
| 6.3(b) | Type-two factor analysis for 56 privatised companies, 2000 | 147 |

| | | |
|---|---|---|
| 6.3(c) | Type-two factor analysis for 58 state companies, 1998 | 147 |
| 6.3(d) | Type-two factor analysis for 54 state companies, 2000 | 147 |
| 6.4 | Type-two factor analysis: company performances | 148 |
| 6.5(a) | Type-three factor analysis for 52 privatised companies, 1998, method 1 | 149 |
| 6.5(b) | Type-three factor analysis for 56 privatised companies, 2000, method 1 | 149 |
| 6.6 | Type-three factor analysis, method 1: company performances | 150 |
| 6.7(a) | Type-three factor analysis for 228 mixed companies, 1998, method 2 | 150 |
| 6.7(b) | Type-three factor analysis for 298 mixed companies, 2000, method 2 | 150 |
| 6.7(c) | Type-three factor analysis for 785 private companies, 1998, method 2 | 151 |
| 6.7(d) | Type-three factor analysis for 2,107 private companies, 2000, method 2 | 151 |
| 6.7(e) | Type-three factor analysis for 1,345 state companies, 1998, method 2 | 151 |
| 6.7(f) | Type-three factor analysis for 1,599 state companies, 2000, method 2 | 152 |
| 6.8 | Type-three factor analysis, method 2: company performances | 152 |
| 6.9(a) | Type-three factor analysis for 228 mixed companies, 1998, method 3 | 153 |
| 6.9(b) | Type-three factor analysis for 298 mixed companies, 2000, method 3 | 153 |
| 6.9(c) | Type-three factor analysis for 1,785 private companies, 1998, method 3 | 154 |
| 6.9(d) | Type-three factor analysis for 2,107 private companies, 2000, method 3 | 154 |
| 6.9(e) | Type-three factor analysis for 1,345 state companies, 1998, method 3 | 154 |
| 6.9(f) | Type-three factor analysis for 1,599 state companies, 2000, method 3 | 155 |
| 6.10 | Type-three factor analysis, method 3: company performances | 155 |
| 6.11(a) | Type-three factor analysis for 228 mixed companies, 1998, method 4 | 156 |

6.11(b) Type-three factor analysis for 298 mixed companies, 2000, method 4 156
6.11(c) Type-three factor analysis for 1,785 private companies, 1998, method 4 156
6.11(d) Type-three factor analysis for 2,107 private companies, 2000, method 4 157
6.11(e) Type-three factor analysis for 1,345 state companies, 1998, method 4 157
6.11(f) Type-three factor analysis for 1,599 state companies, 2000, method 4 157
6.12 Type-three factor analysis, method 4: company performances 158
6.13(a) Type-four factor analysis for 33 mixed companies, 1998 Sweden (Concentration) 159
6.13(b) Type-four factor analysis for 39 mixed companies, 2000 Sweden (Concentration) 159
6.13(c) Type-four factor analysis for 379 private companies, 1998 Sweden (Concentration) 160
6.13(d) Type-four factor analysis for 368 private companies, 2000 Sweden (Concentration) 160
6.13(e) Type-four factor analysis for 344 state companies, 1998 Sweden (Concentration) 160
6.13(f) Type-four factor analysis for 343 state companies, 2000 Sweden (Concentration) 161
6.14 Type-four factor analysis: company performances, Sweden 161

# Acknowledgements

I convey my sincere gratitude to my supervisor Professor Ben Fine, who has always provided me with timely and well-focused guidance. His analytical insights, comments and suggestions have enabled me to improve the overall quality of this work and for that I am much indebted to him.

Special thanks go to all my friends who have lent me their support in idiosyncratic but crucial ways. Various forms of support from them remain my debts for life.

# 1
# Introduction

Privatisation as an extensive programme emerged in western European countries at the beginning of the 1980s, as governments seeking cost reductions turned to the private sector to provide services that would ordinarily have been provided by governments. This withdrawal of state involvement in industry, which came to be known as 'privatisation', takes place through a number of policy initiatives. The most common is a change from public to private in the ownership of an enterprise (or part of an enterprise). Alternatively, public enterprise may remain in existence while privatisation takes place without transfer of ownership of assets. Falling into this category are liberalisation involving deregulation of controls on entry, price, output and profit, as well as the adoption of a commercial approach, whereby the provision of a good or service moves from the public to the private sector, but with ultimate responsibility for providing the service remaining with the government, frequently referred to as 'contracting-out'.

In what is now a very extensive literature on the relationship between public and private sectors as well as on privatisation and its various aspects, the question of comparison between public and private firms' performance and privatisation performance remains open. The aim of this thesis is to investigate public and private sector performance alongside privatisation performance. It has been over 20 years since the beginning of intensive privatisation programmes in the UK, and other European countries subsequently adopted similar policies beginning in the early 1980s; there is thus adequate in principle evidence available to make such an investigation possible. The questions regarding public and private firms' performance and privatisation performance which this volume aims to answer may be summarised in the following three points:

1. Does the available evidence support the idea that private and privatised firms outperform state-owned firms?
2. Is ownership an influential aspect of corporate performance, as claimed by the many theories in favour of privatisation?
3. Is competition a significant phenomenon in determining corporate performance?

Central to these questions is the fundamental issue of the method used to measure corporate performance, given that different economic theories have suggested different methods. Moreover, our findings suggest that the issue of method has not been sufficiently addressed by theories in favour of privatisation, a point that will be examined in more detail in Chapter 2. The absence of a generally accepted method of measuring corporate performance has led to contradictory results in the comparison between public and private sector performance, including privatisation performance, according to empirical studies, which are covered in Chapter 3.

State involvement with the market and with the operation of public enterprises, as documented in the literature, is justified in various ways, notably preventing 'market failures'; establishing firms in those areas where the country has a dynamic comparative advantage; and intervening in circumstances where the capital market is incomplete or undeveloped, or in projects that require large capital initially, as, for instance, in cases requiring large infrastructural investment, or where there are macroeconomic considerations. It seems that privatisation and market liberalisations are used as a replacement for the role government might otherwise take to deal with market failure. Such measures are taken in the name of the improvement of the economy as a whole through the superiority of market forces.

A comparison between the private and public sectors and the effect of privatisation on the index of the shift in property relations might well show that privatised companies have many more opportunities to be involved in the rest of the economy (Fine, 1997a). Public sector firms have a completely different economic role to that of similar firms in the private sector: they do not compete with private companies, or try to promote situations in which the private sector is given greater opportunities for development. The adjustment from public to private ownership will result in the abandonment of those restrictions as well as in a complete reversal of strategic goals in favour of profitability (Fine, 1997a). This process is also directed by globalisation, which requires relatively small public sectors compared to private sectors, because private sectors provide more opportunity for investment and profit-making. It is inevitable during the adjustment process to a greater market economy that making industrial policy in the new situation, with relatively small public sectors, is even more difficult (Fine, 1997a).

Positive views of privatisation point to a number of benefits resulting from its adoption. Because privatisation undermines the role of the unions, it permits a tough labour policy, which deals with the problems caused by inefficient workers and thereby makes controlling employment levels much easier. It also permits the public sector economy to become familiar with 'the enterprise culture' as well as with the mechanism of the marketplace, leading to the rationalisation of asset portfolios and the strategic reorganisation of investment. This in turn leads to improvement of the company's balance sheets, introducing sensitivity and product quality improvement while providing adequate facilities for merging as required by the economics of international competition. Furthermore, since public managers and politicians act in favour of each other, issues such as wage levels, investment plans, borrowing requirements and restructuring projects are assumed to be resolved by this internal relationship. Privatisation supposedly breaks up this relationship and introduces a more efficient process of decision-making.

A final argument in favour of privatisation identifies a number of financial benefits to the policy. Firstly, the sale of public enterprises results in the removal of their capital investment programmes from the public sector accounts; consequently, public sector borrowing is reduced. Secondly, it has been argued that private companies have more direct and faster access to the international capital market than public companies do. Thirdly, privatisation contributes to the growth of the stock exchange, and can widen the capital market by bringing in many new investors. Fourthly, privatisation helps minimise the commercial risk and therefore reduces economic problems for the government in different periods, especially when the market is volatile or in recession. It seems, however, that the above principle does not apply to private companies. As Vickers and Wright (1989: 8) argue, 'it should be pointed out that such rescue operations have not been restricted to the public sector, and nationalisations have often been precisely the result of bailing out private firms in dire financial difficulty'.[1]

The expansion of the public sector prior to the oil crises at the beginning of the 1970s led to a higher proportion of gross national product (GNP) spending in the public sector. This provided goods for which there is always extra demand, for instance, in education and health care. Extra demand for public goods also generates criticism and dissatisfaction. The argument of whether and how the public sector can allocate resources in the way that consumers can be satisfied remains open (Clarke, 1993). Moreover, it has become apparent that bureaucracy in the public sector has caused inefficiency and inflexibility. As far as managerial behaviour is concerned, there is supposed to be a tight link between the management of public sector enterprises and the government; this opens the way to political interference, and thus to further difficulties in strategic planning. Difficulties have mounted when governments involved in public industries face external constraints on further borrowing. Responding to these difficulties, governments have undertaken a series of reforms in order to improve public sector performance, including measures such as limitations on the amount of money pumped into public sector industry, limitations on employment levels, introduction of assessments of staff and organisations as well as costs and outputs, and introduction of a competitive base for performance indicators and performance measurements (Clarke, 1993).

However, in order to understand privatisation in greater depth, it is necessary to view it from a number of different angles. Privatisation, the act of handing down an economic activity from one party to another, involves a much deeper adjustment than one concerned only with the redistribution and redefinition of property rights. For example, it is generally believed that privatisation leads to an expansion in share ownership through the sale of a governmental economic activity to shareholders. What happens in reality seems to be the exact opposite. Much empirical evidence suggests that privatisation actually results in a further consolidation of economic power and an increased concentration of corporate ownership.

[1] It has been argued that selling state assets provides money for the government to run public sector requirements as well as reducing large budget deficits. This may true for a short period, but not in the longer term. As Vickers and Wright (1989: 8) stress, 'it should be noted, however, that asset sales improve short-term cash flow in a once-and-for-all manner: in general they do not enhance a government's long-term net worth, and may even cause it to deteriorate if profitable assets are sold off too cheaply'.

From this, it can be concluded that privatisation should be analysed with an eye to the close relationship between economic and political power. On the one hand, the number of shareholders increases sharply, while on the other, there is a further consolidation of economic power in the hands of huge corporations, which demand much greater flexibility in employment laws and much less power for trade unions. This shows how privatisation, which may begin with the aim, for example, of economic efficiency, actually results in an extension of political power, which affects a far wider range of the members of society.

From the consumers' point of view, the primary concern in relation to privatisation and its broader macroeconomic impact has always been what happens to quality of service, that is, whether prices remain unchanged and whether or not the scope of service declines. In order to respond to these public concerns, governments have deployed a range of remedies, from establishing regulatory committees to a policy of subsidies to the privatised industries. Whether such responsive policies succeed in meeting the consumers' demands remains an open question. However, the conflict between regulator and regulated has a greater impact on consumer benefits. There is no doubt that the regulated will resist all regulations that limit their power to make decisions in different areas. This resistance on the part of the regulated has limited the room for manoeuvre of the regulators. In addition there are legally defined matters, such as the level of investment, training, employment, and so on, over which regulators have very limited power. It has to be concluded that privatisation adjustment involves a process in which suppliers have increasing freedom over their decisions, while consumers have less.

In the two decades or so since the first intensive privatisation programme by the British government, it has become clear that the success of any privatisation programme depends to a large extent on economic and political preconditions. The comparison between the processes of privatisation in different European countries shows clearly how privatisation performances can differ as a result of variations in the economic and political preconditions. As Vickers and Wright (1989: 49) point out, 'simple comparisons of the efficiency and effectiveness of private sector and public sector management cannot readily take account of their very different objectives. This fact confounds comparative assessments of public and private sector efficiency.'

Another important point is who may benefit directly from privatisation. Some financial institutions can make enormous amounts of money by arranging the sale of assets including their commissions. Their political advisors also benefit, specifically in terms of their salary as directors of previously publicly owned companies. Conyon's study (1995) clearly demonstrates that directors' salaries have jumped upwards sharply compared to their salaries before privatisation. What we can conclude from this very determined effort toward privatisation is that privatisation has been a very specific point in the conflict between those who benefit from the implementation of this process, and those who are forced to accept demotion. There is also an issue of loss of confidence among civil service employees when the public sector is perceived to adopt private sector norms, which may have significant consequences: where public sector employees see the process of adjustment as not likely to work in their favour, and thus do not expect work conditions to improve, inefficiencies may rise substantially (Fine, 1997b).

Privatisation as an economic adjustment is also inextricably bound up with ideology. This ideological involvement raises a wider range of issues, from casting doubt on the legitimacy of government to public service ethics (Fine, 1997b). The expectation that the private sector will perform much more efficiently than the public sector has led to the adoption of private sector norms in the public sector. Whether this is helpful or not in enhancing the efficiency of the public sector is, however, a matter for debate. As Hague (1996: 200) stresses, in most of the market economies, the efficient and profitable sectors are dominated by private firms, whereas the public sector is left with activities which are socially unavoidable but economically non-profit-making and unattractive, such as health care, food provision, housing, and education for the poor. Due to this monopolisation of profitable enterprises by the private sector and the imposition of economically less viable functions on the public sector, the comparison between the two becomes relatively unjust.

Heald (1983: 298) describes privatisation as 'an umbrella term for many different policies loosely linked by the way in which they are taken to mean a strengthening of the market at the expense of the state'. Privatisation, then, is not a single determinate policy, but encompasses a range of variant policies. In addition, neo-liberalism has attached itself to the policy of privatisation, with the object of lowering taxation and inflation, cutting back on public involvement in industry and on more restrictive budgetary macroeconomic policies, changing labour market policies by increasing 'flexibility', squeezing the size of public administration and abandoning subsidiary policies to different industries. It must be added that massive technological advances have eased the entrance to natural monopoly in several industries (such as telecommunications) for the private economic agent, while economic crisis in other industries (particularly rail transport, coal and steel) has undermined governments' economic activities (Vickers and Wright, 1989).

The question may arise of why privatisation has become such a widespread policy. The answer to this may not be straightforward. Some might point to the policy shifts towards a right-wing laissez-faire policy such as that associated with Thatcherism and Reaganism at the expense of Keynesianism/welfarism. However, the emergence into prominence of this neo-liberal perspective may not be sufficient to explain the wider adoption of the policy, especially for those who seek objective explanations in terms of market domination. As Fine (1997a: 373) points out, 'more secure grounds for explaining the emergence of privatisation are to be found in the shifting conditions under which the accumulation of capital has been occurring'.

In relation to this approach, three factors should be emphasised. The first is concerned with the production process of the restructuring of capital, which has changed in terms of the internationalisation of production, with implications for state ownership. New technology has caused the old divisions between various sectors of the economy to break down. This leads to a new era in the relation between the public and private sectors, in which the former seems increasingly to be confined and restricted compared to the latter, as Fine argues (1989, 1990).

The second point relates to the effects of globalisation and new technology, which have revolutionised the financial sectors. From the emergence of this global process and its strength, it would appear that privatisation both gives and takes benefits at the same time. In a more and more competitive environment, which increasingly promotes the financial sector, privatisation seems to have a significant role.

The final and the most noticeable point in explaining the rise of privatisation is to be found in the relationship between capital and labour. The implementation of the privatisation process involves reorganisation and restructuring of the balance between these two parties. As a result, the balance has shifted in favour of capital, at the cost of much higher levels of unemployment. Privatisation and its effects cannot be ignored in enhancing the flexibility of the labour market, shifting the balance in favour of capital and resulting in significantly weakening labour.

The theoretical literature on privatisation suffers from different shortcomings. As Fine (1997a: 14) emphasises, the theoretical literature on privatisation is sorely limited in its ability to address the issue with which it is concerned. This is not simply a matter of omission that can be corrected. The whole approach is deficient for its undue generality, for being exclusively concerned with static conditions of resource allocation and efficiency as opposed to the dynamics of industrial change, and for its lack of socioeconomic, political and historical content. The reasons for this lie in part in the attempt to impose previously developed theory on a host of very different circumstances.

This observation suggests that the theoretical literature on privatisation cannot offer an effective explanation for this economic adjustment in every circumstance. The general direction of existing theories, and particularly their failure to take into account the process of historical change, inevitably undermine the reliability of the theoretical literature on privatisation. Not surprisingly, the low standard of existing theoretical work has provided the opportunity for theories such as the new political economy, the new industrial economics, and neo-Austrian theory to assert the benefits of the privatisation process, with no significant intellectual opposition.

This volume, by contrast, will engage directly with the empirical and theoretical issues arising in relation to the privatisation process, in order to answer the questions raised in this introduction. Chapter 2 presents a review of the theoretical literature on privatisation, with particular attention to the treatment given by various theoretical approaches to the issue of measuring corporate performance. Theories to be considered are the property rights school, the public choice school, the principal–agent theory, the Austrian school of economics, and the new synthesis, comprising the new political economy, the neo-Austrian school of economics and the neo-institutional economics. Each of these approaches has concentrated on some particular aspect of the relationship between public and private sector.

Chapter 3 provides a literature review of empirical studies on the relationship between public and private sector and privatisation, focusing mainly on the most well known studies. The discussion will be methodological, and will consider how the studies are conducted, what criteria have been used for measuring corporate performance, and what the results show.

Chapter 4 offers a critique of the conventional method of measuring corporate performance, total factor productivity, outlining various problems with this method, and summarising some of the criticisms that have been made of the neo-classical school with which this method is associated. It then proposes as an alternative the method known as factor analysis, arguing that this method is more suitable and presents, in principle, fewer problems in measuring corporate performance. Factor analysis looks at the correlation between the different variables involved, searching out systematic patterns. Today it can be undertaken easily using the assistance of the Statistical Package for the Social Sciences (SPSS) programme, which is widely used in other social sciences, such as psychology and sociology. This chapter will therefore explain and justify our decision to use factor analysis in our investigation of the outcomes of privatisation. It will also give a more general outline of the research method and process, which gives particular emphasis to local difference. The research is based on an exploration of the privatisation experience in several different European countries, each with its own particular economic structure and dynamic, and these need to be investigated separately. Furthermore, each sector of the economy differs from others in terms of its finance, markets, international position, technological prospects, political context, and so on. Thus I intend to avoid drawing any conclusions that might disregard these factors. My aim in looking at the privatisation experience in various European countries is not to find a general theory or explanation, but to analyse the effects of privatisation in different contexts.

Chapters 5 and 6 are devoted to the discussion of the investigation results, derived from factor analysis of different types. Type-one factor analysis, in Chapter 5, compares the performance of public and private companies of 14 European countries for two years, 1998 and 2000. Calculations are carried out for each country for the two years, and at the end of this section a cross-country analysis presents the combination of results for the countries involved for the two years. Type-two factor analysis, in Chapter 6, looks at privatisation performance by comparing the performance of public and privatised firms for the same two years, 1998 and 2000. The type-three experiment, in Chapter 6, examines the characteristics of variable ownership by adding some new parameters to the main variables. The last type of factor analysis, again in Chapter 6, investigates the effect of competition on corporate performance by adding a new variable called, concentration. It is confined to Sweden. Finally, the main findings and conclusions are summarised in a brief closing chapter.

# 2
# Public versus Private Ownership: Theory and Performance

## Introduction

This chapter's aim is to examine theories of the relationship between the public and private sectors. The main purpose is to draw out the empirical implications of theory for assessing the performance of private versus public enterprises. As a general procedure, their strengths and weaknesses will be discussed. Specifically, the aim is to find out whether and how they are useful for measuring corporate performance.

A dramatic change has occurred in industrial policy in most European countries from the beginning of the 1980s. The change has led to a significant shift towards private ownership in many different industrial sectors. Also, a new era has begun in the relationship between the private and the public sectors. Minimising the size of the public sector and reducing the role played by the state in the economy have become policy goals for most governments in nearly all parts of the world. In order to implement this movement, privatisation has played a significant role.

Privatisation is not a simple matter of transferring ownership from the public to the private sector. This simplistic view is misleading and does not take into account many aspects of this type of economic action (Veljanovski, 1987).[1] The emphasis on privatisation and the theoretical

[1] As Veljanovski (1987: 77) stresses from his own property rights perspective, 'privatisation involves much more than simple transfer of ownership. It involves the transfer and redefinition of a complex bundle of property rights which creates a whole new penalty–reward system which will alter the incentives in the firm and ultimately its performance.'

benchmark for its legitimacy and usefulness have changed from that of the early 1980s. Current thinking has moved from a position in which differences in performance derive solely from differences in ownership to one that considers the measurement of performance irrespective of ownership. An increase in market competition has been regarded as more important than change in ownership for improving performance and efficiency (Cook and Kirkpatrick, 1995). Empirical studies purport to show that market competition is the catalyst for economic efficiency that is to be achieved under either public or private ownership (Millward, 1988).

What is revealed by this simple shift in understanding of the determinants of public/private sector is that ownership as such is not the only important factor but, by the same token, why is only one further factor – competition – considered? Of course, regulation, whether of private or public, was soon to follow. But why stop here rather than adding each and every factor that may or may not contribute to economic performance over and above that of ownership (itself liable to be too crudely seen as the simple dichotomy of public and private, with many different forms within each of these broad categories)?

This all suggests that a deeper point is involved, and the theory of public/private sector performance inevitably depends upon a more general stance on economic theory – a conception of how the economy functions ranging from methodology at one extreme to which factors are included or excluded at the other. Consequently, the treatment of public/private sector performance is liable to be generally influenced by prevailing economic theory. At the time that privatisation came to the fore as a policy in practice, the new information-theoretical approach to microeconomics was also emerging. Indeed, as in many other areas, privatisation has served as a convenient application for the theory of market imperfections and asymmetric information. It becomes a principal–agent problem as Fine (1997a: 8) stresses, 'privatisation proved a natural application, even though such factors are far from being its sole nor most important determinants'.

Further, quite apart from privatisation being interpreted within the current fashions attached to economic theory, there is an influence in the opposite direction. Privatisation itself offers a topic to be addressed and so does its experience in practice as it evolves. Thus two main features have characterised the whole issue of privatisation. As Fine (1997b: 376–7) stresses:

> first, the issue of privatisation has been interpreted within the existing fashions of the discipline. This has involved the new microeconomics

> and industrial economics around transaction costs, property rights and informational imperfections and asymmetries. Second, the literature has tailed upon market developments as they have arisen in sequence with the progress of privatisation itself ... what to privatise, how to privatise, and how to regulate.

Subsequently, the privatisation literature, which focuses on the redefinition and redistribution of property rights, has been taken a step further to investigate the actual results of privatisation. Fine (1997a: 15) argues that from its own perspective, 'this is nothing other than the exercise of those newly formed property rights'.

If the performance of public versus private sector performance is to be understood, the theoretical framework for doing so is crucial. Before looking at empirical studies on relative performance my objective is to concentrate on several economic theories that favour the private sector and privatisation. The purpose is to take out from the theory the likely implications for measurement of performance. In other words, I shall investigate how those theories are applicable in practice for evaluating relative performance. What are the implications of the theory for outcomes and how might they be measured?

To illustrate more precisely, for instance, the mainstream economics traditionally points to the efficient resource allocation through the price mechanism, whereas neo-Austrian economics points to the freedom of entrepreneurship as the most effective way for enhancing performance of the economy as a whole. How these approaches can be useful for measuring economic performance is an important question.

We examine the latter approach alongside the property rights theory, the public choice theory, and the principal–agent theory, as well as the 'new synthesis', which is comprised of the new political economics, the new institutional economics and the neo-Austrian school of economics. The main goal as mentioned is to evaluate them for their implications for measuring economic performance.

All these theories generally favour private ownership and view state ownership as inefficient, especially in a competitive market. To summarise broadly, the property rights school emphasises the role of ownership; private ownership is believed to improve corporate performance through incentives, and market phenomena are seen as disciplinary mechanisms for allocating resources efficiently. The public choice school emphasises the idea that the public sector acts against the public interest and efficiency – while the private sector is controlled by market discipline, the public sector serves the interests of managers or politicians.

Principal–agent theory, on the other hand, emphasises the relationship between the principal shareholders and the agent (company managers) and tends to claim that the latter can be made to work more favourably on behalf of the former. In the presence of market discipline the Austrian school of economics stresses the role of the entrepreneurial factor in the market, and relaxation of any barriers is believed to improve entrepreneurs' behaviours. According to the new synthesis, creating greater competition is assumed to be more important than ownership. The new political economy sees government activities in markets as inducing rent seeking behaviour. The neo-Austrian school stresses individual behaviour as a dynamic phenomenon. The new institutional economics divides institutions into market and non-market institutions; it separates the internal organisation of a firm from its external market relations and further asserts that since the economic agent cannot have adequate information for decision-making, non-market institutions cannot behave optimally.

As a generalisation, it can be concluded that the different theories offer plenty of opportunity for empirical investigation, while difficulties in measurement of comparative performance in practice remain unsolved. Yet the problem of how to measure relative performance has rarely been taken forward on the basis of the theories. My findings emphasise how those theories that favour the private sector and support privatisation policy have scarcely broached their implications for measuring corporate performance.

The rest of this chapter is organised as follows. In the second section, the property rights school is discussed in detail. The main features of the theory are presented in order to give a broad picture. Its strengths and weaknesses and specifically its implication for measuring corporate performance are examined closely in a separate subsection. The same procedures are used for evaluating the other theories. The public choice school, the Austrian school of economics, the principal–agent theory and the new synthesis are discussed in successive sections. Each section has a subsection in which the critical points of each school will be discussed as in the property rights section. The last section will be devoted to concluding remarks in which a brief summary of the main points, our critical assessment, and its implications for the next chapters will be presented.

## Property rights theory

The argument of property rights theorists is that differences in performance between private and public firms depend on their ownership arrangements. In other words, various forms of property ownership give rise to different economic incentives and in the end to different economic results. As Furubotn and Pejovich (1972: 1138) argue, 'different property rights assignments lead to different penalty-reward structures and, hence, decide the choices that are open to decision makers'.

The property rights school puts much emphasis on methodological individualism and the role of individuals as the source of decision-making. Individuals as a unit make decisions instead of firms or any other organisations or institutions. They are viewed as seeking maximum utility while the prevailing system of property relations imposes limitations. According to the property rights theorists, who owns a resource is not as important as who has the right to use the resources. In a general form, this refers not only to the right to use material things, but also to so-called human rights, that is, the rights of voting, freedom of speech and freedom of religion. As Pejovich (1990: 27) points out: 'the property-rights definition applies to all rights of an individual vis-à-vis other people'.

The following elements of the right of ownership are the most important subcategories of property rights: the right to use an asset, the right to have suitable returns from the asset, and the right to change that asset's form or its substance. The last element seems to be an important part of the right of ownership. It implies that the owner has the rights to transfer all or some of the rights in the asset to others at mutually agreed terms. It asserts that the right of ownership is an exclusive right, but it is not an unrestricted right as it is subject to legal limitations. Thus exclusivity and transferability are the main characteristics of ownership by which the owner is free to choose what to do with an asset, subject only to limitations of the law. A combination of the owners' rights, utilisation of that property and the acceptance of the consequences of any given decision, will create incentives for the owner to seek the best use for assets. Therefore, the resources will move to their highest-valued uses under private ownership, which provides adequate incentives for those actions.

How these considerations apply to the real world, in the case of a joint-stock company, for example, is an open and important question. Modern economic activity is nowadays based on cooperative activities, and the efforts of the individual are part of overall efforts made by all participants. As a result, compensation is not easily determined on an individual basis. Adding to this, because it does not come about via a single or singular action, measurement of corporate performance faces a multitude of difficult problems. In such a complex situation, the role played by individuals is impossible to determine (Tittenbrun, 1996).

In order to deal with such measurement problems it is necessary to explore certain property rights further, especially the right to be a residual claimant, the right to revise employee conditions of work, or, more simply, to hire and fire, and the right to sell these rights. Regarding revision of employees' conditions in the modern corporation, however, a sensitive reward system has to be introduced to encourage the cooperating employees to put in optimal productive efforts. This brings an acute need for introducing a monitoring system by which it would be possible to discourage shirking. The question that arises is what happens if the monitor self shirks? The only person one can expect not to shirk is the owner of the firm.

In modern corporations, ownership is typically dispersed among many shareholders. Individual owners incur high costs in monitoring managerial decisions, which enforce residual-maximising behaviour. This reduces the ability of smaller shareholders to control managerial behaviour, even though the managers' decisions affect the shareholders' wealth. As a result, managers might, and in some cases will, pursue their own interests at the expense of the owners' interests. The greater the dispersion of ownership, the greater the managers' opportunity to pursue own welfare.

But property rights proponents argue that there are several effective ways to offset those kinds of behaviour. One way is competition among managers of different companies, leading to a hidden monitoring system, managers monitoring managers themselves. Moreover, the capital market also acts as a second outsider to monitor managerial decisions. If a manager's decisions are inappropriate, it will lead to lower profits, lower share prices and the threat of takeover bids, all of which are to the detriment of the manager. Inside the company, because the overall performance of the firm is the initial priority, higher-level management is interested in checking shirking by lower-level management. Lower managers, on the other hand, are also motivated to monitor upper-level managers because if the company performs well, the success of the firm will increase the chance of their own success, vis-à-vis new managerial posts outside the company. A second way is forming incentive payment based on the corporation's profits.

A third way involves diversification of labour and duties. In the owner-manager company one person is dealing with a wide range of duties and it is unlikely that he or she will have sufficient competence to fulfil all duties in an efficient way. In contrast, a modern company distributes duties among competent staff so that each duty is handled expertly. Finally, the saleability of shares combined with knowledge of various company past records and expected future share prices can provide adequate material for an appropriate investment decision (Alchian, 1977).

These factors can create discipline, which in turn safeguards anticipated behaviour of managers. Alchian (1977: 231) stresses this guarantee as 'Managers can move to new jobs; and they compete for jobs by superior performance on present jobs.' Hence the system encourages them to put in much effort to seek a high return for shareholders since that, in turn, increases their own value for the managerial post in the labour market. As a result, market control is a powerful disciplinary force for inefficient managers. These economic forces are strong enough to protect both the shareholders' wealth and the tendency for resources to seek their highest-valued uses. Pejovich (1990: 64) stresses that 'the bundle of property rights in a corporate firm provides some powerful incentives for top management to pursue policies and decisions that tend to maximize the firm's market worth'.

These arguments can be interpreted as an economic rationale for privatisation and against nationalised companies. The form of ownership can make a difference for economic performance. The reason is that private ownership introduces a system of incentives that do not apply to public enterprises. The basic difference is that ownership rights allow the private owner to sell shares, while the public owner is unable to do so (Alchian, 1977). This brings about two fundamental results. On the one hand, takeovers in the public sector become impossible and, on the other, there is no possibility of specialisation regarding different areas of work among owners.

The property rights theory believes that ownership of public property is a compulsion on individuals. Moving from one community to another involves acquiring new shares in public ownership without paying for it. This kind of ownership does not exist under private ownership. Because property in public enterprises is not transferable, issues such as the capitalisation of future value based on current decisions and residual claimants must be ruled out. Increases in value of public assets are dispersed throughout the community, and at the same time enhanced profitability and cost reductions in a public enterprise could be refunded to the public through tax reductions. Other phenomena relevant to public enterprises can be pointed out, such as: each person's wealth and his own activity have a much weaker relationship to public ownership which leads to a weaker incentive to monitor the behaviour of decision-makers in public enterprises; competition for managerial jobs is much weaker than in privately owned corporations; and efficiency incentives for public enterprise managers are assumed to be weaker because there is no link between their compensations and financial performance. As a consequence, managers of those firms have greater opportunity for shirking than managers of private companies (Zeckhauser and Horn, 1989). Hence, when an enterprise is owned by the entire society, no individual member has the incentive to take care of it and inefficiency is an inevitable consequence.

Thus the property rights analysis of public ownership comes to the conclusion that public enterprises are less economically efficient than private enterprises. Forms of ownership lead to differences in the rewards–penalties systems. Inefficiency will arise when property rights are dispersed and motivation is diminished across individuals. Even though there is a similar divergence between ownership and management in the modern corporation, that does not lead to any major change in the performance of private enterprise. The problem of how shareholders are able to monitor management in a large corporation can be resolved by introducing other phenomena.

### A critical assessment of property rights theory

Important questions regarding shareholder ownership are whether shareholders own the company in reality or are only lenders of money to an economic activity, and which comprises the higher risk. Can having the right to sell your shares at any time and the right to dividends after a period of time be regarded as ownership of the company? One could consider that, because they have the right to vote, shareholders are owners. What happens in reality is that daily routine decisions are made by managers, not by the shareholder, and important policies will be decided in the shareholders' meeting. Those shareholders who have acquired a large number of shares have the greatest effect on which future policies are going to be implemented. It is obvious that smaller shareholders have little or no effect on decisions regarding the future of the company. Demsetz (1967: 358–9) puts forward the idea that

> Effective ownership, i.e., effective control of property, is thus legally concentrated in management's hands ... shareholders are essentially lenders of equity capital and not owners ... What shareholders really own are their shares and not the corporation. Ownership in the sense of control again becomes a largely individual affair. The shareholders own their shares, and the president of the corporation and possibly a few other top executives control the corporation.

Whether this is true or not can be investigated further by raising the question, what are the differences between the owners of bonds issued by government or by any financial institutions and the smaller shareholders as far as the ownership is concerned? Showing clearly that there are no differences between these two types of owners, Alchian and Demsetz (1972: 789) write that

> instead of thinking of shareholders as joint owners, we can think of them as investors, like bondholders ... If we treat bondholders, preferred and convertible preferred stockholders, and common stockholders and warrant holders as simply different classes of investors ... why should stockholders be regarded as 'owners' in any sense distinct from the other financial investors?

This can be counted as a significant reason why smaller shareholders have limited incentive to monitor managerial behaviours.

Who owns the public enterprises – the government or the public as whole – is unknown. This uncertainty can be seen in the statement made by Nutter (1974: 222):

> If an abstract entity such as the state is to be called the owner, then government must be the concrete agency charged with trusteeship. Government will be ... responsible to some group of persons for whom it is acting as agent, and it will presumably be responsive at least indirectly to their interests. Ultimately, then, the persons controlling government are the effective owners of state-owned enterprises, while government or some part of it serves as manager.

The concept of what comprises public ownership is also another ambiguity as far as the property rights argument is concerned. It is assumed that the public at large owns this kind of property. While it might be clear that what is called publicly owned differs from area to area, only the enterprises which are owned by the central government can be counted as owned by the whole public of a particular country. However, different enterprises owned by local authorities are also assumed to be publicly owned, although any benefits or losses resulting from those enterprises will presumably remain restricted to the public from those areas, not the entire population of the whole country.

The ambiguities and inconsistencies are not restricted to those areas only; 'mixed' enterprises offer a case in point. Where can they be located in the relation between public and private ownership? Can the degree of participation be the main criterion? Is not such a procedure a mechanical procedure?

Similarities between public and private enterprises cannot be ignored; they exist in many different ways. It has been one of the main arguments in favour of large privately owned corporations that the risk will be diversified among shareholders. In the case of publicly owned companies, if the owner is the public, then the risk will be diversifiable much more so among taxpayers (taken as the shareholders). Hence, why the latter has little incentive to monitor management compared to the former is an open question. Sappington and Stiglitz (1987: 567) argue that

> many similarities exist between the everyday operation of public and private enterprise in practice ... Neither congressmen nor minority shareholders directly control the daily activities of an enterprise that is, in principle, under their control. Instead, oversight of the firm's operation is delegated to a commission or board of directors.

The outlook of the property rights school is that private ownership is important for better performance. It has been concluded that if managers in manager-controlled firms seek their own objectives then such firms will perform less well compared to owner-controlled firms. In contrast, Monsen et al. (1968) conducted an investigation of 72 corporations among 500 of the largest industrial firms in the United States and found that owner-controlled firms are more efficient than shareholder companies for allocating resources, as manifested in a much better return on shareholders' equity. In a study by Bothwell (1980), owner-controlled firms had better results than shareholder companies. In a study of a single industry, of 1,406 banks, Glassman and Rhoades (1980) found that owner-controlled banks are more profitable than manager-controlled ones.

These findings do not support the property rights theory and the empirical evidence available declares results inconsistent with the theory's claims. However, in the property rights literature, these findings are attributed to the failure of internal and external control forces, which are deemed to diminish managerial discretion.

According to the property rights literature, compensation to managers based on the wealth of the shareholders provokes the optimal effort by the former on behalf of the latter. However, matters are not that simple. Dividends seem to be more interesting for shareholders, yet capital gains and share options are said to be the most effective mechanism for inducing management to run the firm effectively. However, freeriding by managers may not be eliminated by mechanisms like share option schemes, profit-sharing systems and other related systems (Williamson, 1970). The performance of the firm is a function of many different factors. The management only controls some of those factors and others will only be indirectly reworded or even excluded from sharing in the gains available (Tittenbrun, 1996). Different ways have been used to determine compensation to executives. One is by sales. However, both reported profits and equity market values are considerably more important than sales in the determination of executive compensation. Even if there were a positive relationship between profits and executive rewards or between compensation and sales, that does not undermine the possibility that managerial objectives diverge from shareholders' goals. The research published in *The Economist* (1992b: 21), based on a study of 459 major US companies, dismisses the relation between executive compensation and total returns to shareholders.

It has been argued that share options give managers an incentive to put in optimal effort for achieving the company's long-term success, and, therefore, the wealth of its owners. But many factors beyond the control of the manager (that is, bull markets, inflation, takeover bids, and so on) play a role, which can bring 'unearned' gains. On the other hand, unlike normal shares, executive share options are a one-way street; you can win with them but cannot lose according to the rules applied to incentive arrangements in general (Thackray, 1983).

Figures published in *The Economist* (1992b: 22) show that in 1981 the average chief executive was paid about 15 times more than a factory worker ($315,000 versus $21,300). Ten years later, chief executives of the 500 largest US corporations earned a total average annual pay of $2 million (including the estimated value of stock options), which is approximately 85 times the pay of the average factory worker. This gap has thus widened over time even though much research shows a negative correlation between the number and value of incentive schemes and the company's performance (*The Economist*, 1992b). A related question which may arise is, what relationship is there (if any) between the gains to controllers (shareholders) and job occupiers (managers) as far as stock performance is concerned? A lower turnover of management should be expected in those companies that have performed poorly. But factors other than shareholders' gains and companies' performance play significant roles determining managerial compensations.

What happens in reality, regarding the effects of the market for executives, is in contrast to the claim made by property rights proponents.

Chief executives of other companies (who dominate the board's compensation committee) set the payment for the company's chief executives. A self-propelled mechanism is set as *The Economist* (1992a: 15) indicates: 'most non-executive directors are themselves executives in other firms and they are only too happy to raise the pay of their peers, as they are part of the same job market and therefore stand to benefit from generous benchmarks for their "market price" '.

The role of competition among managers claimed in the property rights literature is another point of consideration. The claim is that managers compete for promotions and new higher position jobs by giving outstanding performance in their present jobs. Anders' study (1992) of 220 large companies shows that the average chief executive has stayed in office for at least six and a half years; while according to some other studies, the normal length of time in office is ten years. Hence the empirical evidence does not support the above claim unless it is by fear of dismissal.

The mechanism of takeover is assumed to be the last solution if incentive systems failed to motivate managers to maximise the wealth of shareholders. The argument is that the threat of takeover will lead to a removal of management that is unsuccessful in using assets efficiently. It is known that if assets have been poorly managed there is always a threat of takeover by some outsider (in privately owned companies, but not in publicly owned companies). Moreover, since the market for corporate control is independent of the character of the product market, property rights proponents stress that the absence of competition in product markets may not lead to a different quality of management in monopolistic markets as compared with competitive markets. How these arguments can be applied to the exceptional economic performance of companies in Japan and Germany is an open question. Herman (1981: 100) proposes an idea which seems to be closer to reality. He believes that the takeover threat is more probable when an enterprise has made quicker profits than normal, in opposition to predictions of the property rights proponents. This may lead to 'quick gains at the expense of risk-taking and longer-term investment'. Hence the likelihood of takeover may work in the opposite direction, and the manager may have an even greater interest in increasing his personal satisfaction at the expense of the shareholders.

Privatisation does not necessarily free the treat of takeover. The introduction of 'golden shares' as a form of corporate control by the government itself, limits on the size of individual shareholdings and regulation of companies all tend to reduce the risk of takeover. As Bos

(1991: 59–60) confirms:

> the raider knows that he too will be regulated after executing a successful takeover. Therefore the regulated firms are not attractive candidates for a takeover. Profits will be low even after takeover, while divestiture typically will be legally forbidden. Since the privatised utility knows it is not a good target for potential raiders, there is no takeover threat and consequently no influence on productivity.

The claim that the takeover mechanism will lead to efficiency improvement is dismissed by available evidence regarding mergers. Cowling et al. (1980) found no signs of efficiency improvement due to mergers in nine major cases. Lower-cost operations as an indicator of efficiency were not found by Barnes (1985), in a comparison study of before and after mergers.

The property rights school's argument is that if the stock market is efficient, then share price will be an efficient tool for monitoring purposes. Vickers and Yarrow (1991a: 115) confirm that share price 'can be used in contracts between shareholders and manager – remuneration packages may include stock options, for example – and it might have further incentive effects via the managerial labour market'. What can be concluded is that the property rights approach puts more weight on the disciplinary function of the market for corporate control and fails to realise the state's ability to monitor. This role is explicitly expressed by Bailey (1987: 141): 'the constraints on public managers are certainly greater than on private managers. The constraints of labour, the press, and the citizenry hold public managers to a higher standard of accountability than private managers.'

Summing up, this analysis shows many weaknesses of the property rights theory in (1) claims of superiority of privately owned firms versus publicly owned firms, and (2) in the policy recommendation that privatisation will lead to greater efficiency. In property rights literature, ownership is given a substantially greater weight for determining performance than organisational characteristics such as type of leadership and cultural factors. The property rights theory's emphasis on ownership alone fails to acknowledge other important concepts relevant to performance, such as information asymmetry, the effect of various economic incentives, the variety of contracts, differences relevant to public/private ownership, particular conditions or characteristics that might cause public institutions to perform well, and ambiguity of goals. As Starr (1989: 29) stresses, the property rights approach 'takes the market as the standard for judging value and finds public institutions deficient because they fail to measure up to that standard (e.g., their "shareholders" cannot sell stock)'. Another criticism is that human socialised actions are undermined by the individualistic property rights approach. The theory remains silent about how corporate performance should be measured. No attention has been given to this despite the fact that the theory is about a comparative study of public and private sectors.

## Public choice theory

Some of the economic literature regarding privatisation is more focused on the comparative economic efficiency of the public and private sector (Parker, 1998). A school of thought that has specifically concentrated on this aspect is called the public choice school. The assumption is that public sector activities are assumed to be less efficient than those in the private sector because state economic agents are maximising their own goals instead of the objectives of social welfare. Additionally, state industries are managed poorly and conflict among participants is inevitable because there are no integrated strategically operating goals. As a consequence, disruptive political interventions in management, the presence of rent-seeking groups (notably trade unions) and financial failure cannot be separated from state-owned enterprises. It has been argued that, generally speaking, inefficiency can be attributed to the ideological and political motives for government ownership of firms. These motives lead to behaviour that sustains political involvement in their management.

The fundamental reason for government intervention in the market is as a result of market failure associated with monopoly, externalities, public goods, and so on. The rationale behind the conventional welfare economics of the public interest or nationalisation of industries should be seen in that regard. Such a view results in assuming the following: that the main concerns for public managers are public interests; that they will then act to fulfil those interests; that their behaviour can be monitored by the public or by the government; and that public managers can be controlled by different principles than citizens, politicians and civil servants.

The theory of public choice, like the property rights analysis, provides the rationale for privatisation. As Linowes (1990: 83) reveals: 'much of the intellectual inspiration of the contemporary privatisation movement in the United States has been derived from the writings of the Public Choice school'. It involves an extension of orthodox neo-classical analysis to politics rather than a theory of property rights as such. The public choice school focuses on managerial behaviour in public enterprises. Hence a major consideration is determining the public managers' objectives or motives. Public managers, in contrast to private managers, are concerned with gross revenue as distinct from profits. These revenues are expected to derive from selling products to the consumers and from getting subsidies from the government. Such behaviour inevitably brings about an increase of output beyond the profit-maximising level. According to the theory, what public enterprises do is to equalise the marginal social benefit of the last unit produced to actual marginal cost of production. As a result, public enterprises are inherently inefficient.

It has been argued that output goals in the public sector leads to overinvestment. A lower interest rate at a discount cost available to the managers of state firms can predispose the public managers toward using more capital (Niskanen, 1968; De Alessi, 1969). According to the public choice school, pressures on the part of the government cannot remedy this distortion because politicians, who are in office for a limited period, cannot have long-term plans regarding public enterprises and their managements. This concentration on the short-term results in non-optimal behaviour of public managers.

The state enterprise is assumed to occupy a double monopoly position, one with regard to their position in the market and another with respect to their position in attaining government support. Furthermore, public managers can strengthen their bargaining position and present their own performance favourably because of exclusive access to information (Downs, 1967).

The position of the managers in public enterprises can be strengthened by other phenomena like asymmetry of information and the citizen's limited power to monitor managers of state firms. Individual citizens have limited scope for action. In contrast, special groups such as trade unions are given more opportunity to act freely gain through rent-seeking. According to Sunstein (1990: 70): 'In this context, rent-seeking might be defined as the dissipation of wealth through efforts to redistribute resources by way of politics, rather than the production of wealth through markets.' The public sector has become overmanned, overpaid and underworked with the help of trade unions. Rent-seeking is the source of inefficiency as resources are wasted in pursuit of these rents.

In the public choice literature, Fiorina and Noll (1978) present another model in which the relation between the government and public firms is seen differently. The assumption is that politicians have power over managers to dictate decisions about pricing, investment, employment, and so on. The aims of the politicians are to satisfy their local constituents and secure their own political gains. Moreover, conflict over policy often occurs because profit maximisation is not the main criterion and the government body is not a single entity, but consists of a number of politicians with different objectives. As Rees (1989: 23) confirms:

> [the government] consists of a number of politicians and administrators with different priorities or emphases, which they give to the various objectives. The balance of power may shift among members of this group, or its composition may change as a result of elections, political reshuffles, career changes, and so on. As a result the implicit weights given to the various objectives ... may change quite sharply over time.

It is assumed that government uses the public firms as instruments to achieve various political goals. It can be an attempt to reduce unemployment or other goals such as regional development and subsidised goods or services. The named objectives may not be consistent with the economic goals of public enterprise in the short or long run and may weaken performance. However, political motives can be achieved even if commercial success and efficiency are sacrificed. As authors like Cook and Kirkpatrick (1988a: 12) believe, 'the most common cause of inefficiency in the public enterprise sector is political interference'. Whether managers of public enterprises try to maximise their own power or politicians do the same through their own electoral interests, the end result is assumed to be inconsistent with efficient performance.

It is clear that the public choice viewpoint, like the previous school of thought, maintains very strong views about public ownership. Nationalisation is unfavourable since it will reduce aggregate profitability. Therefore, private enterprises, which perform efficiently, are preferable to public enterprises. This conclusion provides a convincing economic case for privatisation. Privatisation will lead to change in economic prospects and will allow profit-maximising entrepreneurs to be the main source of economic performance. Operational efficiency is guaranteed, leading to lower production costs. Political pressures to redirect the enterprise's activities at the expense of market efficiency will be eliminated. Large subsidies and other special economic considerations will be minimised and the search for ways to reduce costs will no longer be necessary. All these remedies lead to enhanced economic performance.

## A critical assessment of public choice theory

There are many examples of government involvement in the economy and concern for economic conditions that reveal how those actions have been necessary for the economy as a whole. Governments from many of the EU countries – specifically, Sweden and Austria – have worked to safeguard employment and improve working conditions. The governments of Finland and France have given much attention to regional policy, and the governments of Sweden, Finland and France have tried to impose economic policies to rebuild state-owned enterprises in order to compete on an international level. Adding to this list, in Germany in the 1960s, government economic policy was based on an expectation that state firms should compete against private firms with the aim of enhancing operating efficiency (Parker, 1998).

The objectives for state enterprises differ substantially from private ones (Parker, 1998). State enterprise objectives are often multiple and change from time to time. Hence it is very difficult for this management to follow consistent and long-term business strategies, whereas this may not be so for private enterprises. Additionally, it is true that a change in government or a change in ministry has a direct effect on the economic policy agenda (Parker, 1998). These restrictions and these characteristics of state enterprises differ from the private sector and need to be accessed differently.

The following questions therefore arise in response to the public choice approach. What is the consequence of government intervention and why does it always lead to distortions of the economy? Do interventions from governments substantially affect the performance of enterprises (private or public)? Parker (1998) points out that many examples can be found to show that political intervention has led to loss-making activities in state industries in Europe. But whether this profit reduction has led to social welfare reduction is unknown. A clear example given by Parker is government intervention in the UK and France in order to control prices or safeguard jobs.

The public choice school of thought claims that if adequate systems of control and monitoring do not exist, then self-interested managers of public enterprises are able to freeride without paying attention to whether government ministers or the voters agree with their actions. This is a strong assumption, which in basic form refers to human behaviour. A lot of research and many different experiments dismiss the idea that individuals act only in favour of their own interests. In an experiment conducted by Martinez-Vazquez (1981) on how income groups voted, they found that the voters consistently voted against their self-interest and in favour of the poor. A similar result has been found by Marwel and Ames (1981) in testing a freerider hypothesis. Taken with the statement by Starr (1987: 31) that 'the whole point of "government by discussion" is to discover and express common interests not easily voiced or achieved in private sphere; the public choice approach simply does not comprehend this preference-shaping function of political democracy'. These findings lead to the conclusion that people are capable of sacrificing their narrow self-interest and acting in favour of the collective or public interest. This refutes the public choice view that preferences are fixed in favour of self-interest.

The public choice view of public enterprises is comprised of different elements such as 'easy access to funds', 'subsidiary sectors', and so on; in the end it considers the public sector as a sector of 'excess of output' and 'excess of inputs'. This accusation is not supported by empirical evidence, as Dunleavy (1991: 212) clarifies: 'in experimental studies very few decision makers ... the role of bureaucrat maximise without limit'. Referring to the latter, the claim is that higher capital–labour ratios are supposedly characteristic of the public sector. Some studies (for example, that by Borcherding et al. (1977)) support this claim, while others (such as that by Cram and Zardkoohi (1978)) reject this. Hence, it can be stated that the empirical evidence regarding 'excess of input' is inconclusive.

Another assumption, which is made by this school of thought, is that the public sector is run inefficiently. Whether this is correct or not, it should not be ignored that the public sector is not the same across all countries and it does not remain the same within a country through time. Many public enterprises were established after the Second World War by governments throughout Europe. Empirical evidence has shown that public enterprise was efficient in countries such as Germany, Austria, France and Sweden in the period of the post-war boom. Adding to this, Starr (1990: 112) points to an inverse aspect rejecting the above claim: 'it cannot explain the variations over time or across societies. If the influences on budget were always one sidedly in favour of expansion, spending should have grown rapidly even in those periods which it has not.'

Policy recommendations of privatisation for enhancing economic performance made by the public choice school, as with the property rights school, are dismissed by many economists. Cook and Kirkpatrick (1988a: 190) argue that 'these changes are not conditional on privatisation: internal reform of public enterprise is an alternative option for realising the same gains'. The post-privatisation period can make a clear case against many charges made by the school that favour the private sector over the public sector. Privatisation might officially mean no more pressures from specific groups or subsidises to a particular sector, but experience has shown that privatised firms can press for government aid via different forms, such as tax benefits, regulatory protection, and so on, just as public enterprises did. Goldring (1993: 28) makes this point, which opposes that made by the public choice school in favour of privatisation:

> privatised industries are not genuinely private. On Tuesday the prime minister was answering questions about water prices in the south-west. What on earth have local water prices to do with the prime minister? ... it demonstrates that privatised industries are unfree to run as normal businesses.

In another statement, Tanoira (1987: 56) very precisely claims that 'privatisation is less likely to be seen as a means for eliminating the enormous subsidises received by SOEs [state-owned enterprises], than as a means for transferring the protection of the state to the private (in other words, not-so-private) firms'.

This theory, like the previous theory, does not address the issue of measuring corporate performance. Most of the attention has been devoted to the relationship between public enterprise managers and politicians; it asserts the superiority of the private over the public sector without addressing how to measure corporate performance.

## The Austrian school of economics

What Hayek (1984: 135) stressed about 'true individualism' seems to be useful in forming a clear picture of the Austrian school of economics' fundamental idea. He believed that 'true individualism' should be distinct from 'the properly collective theory of society' as well as 'the rationalistic pseudo-individualism', which is that the combined effects of individualism lead to the establishment of many institutions without prior planning. He stressed that this view of individualism is the only proper method for economic theory. Furthermore, he pointed out that any institutions which do not result from individual actions are merely susceptible to being a 'spontaneous social product' like the market, money and others that are more efficient than actions based on 'economic plans' or parliamentary law (Hayek, 1984: 137).

The accidental actions of isolated individuals can coalesce at some point and the outcomes are much more efficient because these actions are grounded in their private interests. This point contradicts the statement that individual private interest has important implications as far as the role of government and state industries in the economy is concerned. Public enterprises are said to be inferior to private enterprise. Hayek (1984: 137), clearly believes so in stating that 'the design theories necessarily lead to the conclusion that social processes can be made to serve human ends only if they are subjected to the control of individual human reason ... true individualism believes on the contrary that if left free, men will often achieve more than individual human reason could design or foresee'. Deliberate arrangement and the role of governments ought to take place in a way that does not disrupt spontaneous actions. Thus the characteristic role of government is described by Hayek (1989: 112) as 'being not to produce any particular services or products to be consumed by the citizens, but rather to see that the mechanism which regulates the production of those goods and services is kept in working order'. It can be concluded that any interference by the government other than in performance of the above duty is seen to disrupt the benefits of the market. This result is argued to be inevitable, since the spontaneous actions of individuals conform to a unique system based on specific information of a particular subject. The system will be destroyed by any exogenous actions, which are based on different, generally lesser knowledge and different purposes.

Besides individualism, subjectivism is another basic point in the Austrian view. As O'Driscoll and Rizzo (1985: 1) explain, the contents of the human mind, and hence decision-making, are not rigidly determined by 'external events': individual actions result from different interactions in mind which are independent of the events that happen externally. This viewpoint has different implications for economic theory such as: the unpredictability of human action, the uncertainty in the market, the dynamic conception of time, market competition and its effect on the discovery or learning process, and the decentralisation of private knowledge. The concept of the imperfect predictability of human action implies a dynamic view of time, which is shared in both real and subjective views about time. This view differs from the conventional view of neo-classical economics in which time is the image of space, which can then be transformed into a static category, while changes are viewed as a succession of discontinuous states. This view of time follows other concepts, such as uncertainty and the characteristics of an individual, to arrive at the concept of entrepreneurship, which occupies an important part of the Austrian school of thought.

This new concept related to the market context means presenting new discoveries and creating new possibilities, which have not yet been introduced by other market participants. This view differs again from neo-classical economics, which sees decision-making as 'using known available resources in the most efficient manner to achieve given purpose' (Kirzner, 1976: 118). However, the Austrian school of thought holds a completely different view, with Hayek (1984: 257) presenting decision-making as 'a capacity to find out particular circumstances'. Entrepreneurs are seen to be primarily searching for new profitable opportunities and trying to exploit emerging profit opportunities. In this context, the role of price becomes an important element as a guide for entrepreneurs. Price provides all-important information for profit maximisation, as Hayek (1984: 56) illustrates: 'most of the information which the capitalist entrepreneurs have consists of prices determined in a competitive market'.

Prices are further seen to be the product of competition. The latter gives entrepreneurs the opportunity to discover new ways of production through which they are able to exploit the circumstances and make through unconventional means profits (Hayek, 1989). Price information, competition and adequate incentive through profit-making will lead to dispersed knowledge. The latter is viewed as essential to effective decision-making in the Austrian view. The process is like a chain, starting from competition and resulting in decentralised knowledge through price as a medium. As a consequence, all economic agents have the same opportunity to obtain the general knowledge possessed by others. Hence competition is seen to lead to a discovery or learning process.

The Austrian school's views on the characteristics of the market carry a critical view of public enterprise. The claim of discovery through competition is restricted by the role of public ownership. Nationalisation rules out the role that can be played by new entrants, and the role of profit. The role of entrepreneurship will be limited and capacity for change and innovation are undermined (Littlechild, 1989). Free capital movement, which is conventional in the case of private ownership and which shifts capital from one line to another in seeking a higher level of return, will be restricted by introducing public ownership. Public enterprises have limited ability to learn from failure because the threat of bankruptcy and the role of uncertainty and profit have been excluded as a spur to innovation.

The Austrian position is that rational economic choice should be based on broad knowledge, specifically about prices. This, in turn, requires a competitive market in order to obtain adequate information. But competition requires private ownership if it is expected to be a source of innovation and a learning process, as Moldofsky (1989: 18) stressed, so that 'individuals be free to act and dispose of their property while using their knowledge of their circumstances of time and place as they see fit, in order to gain access to more and better knowledge than would be possible with less freedom of action'. Market competition provides enough knowledge for economic agents to know about consumers' tastes, consumers' willingness to pay, and different methods for production, and so on. This knowledge leads resources to be reallocated efficiently, cheaper products to be produced and lower prices to be maintained (Hayek, 1984). Accordingly, privatisation acts so that competition is introduced and higher efficiency and responsibility to consumer demands are reached (Littlechild, 1986a).

### A critical assessment of the Austrian school of economics

An important proposition made by the school concerns the role of competition as part and partial of the market mechanism. But how to examine competition empirically is an open question even to Hayek (1984: 255) who stresses that competition 'can never be tested empirically'. Furthermore, the argument presented by the Austrian school is that those who participate in the market can systematically learn from their experiences, leading their actions to become increasingly coordinated. On the other hand, the Austrian methodology is all about spontaneous action by human beings and claims that indeterminacy is inherent to changes in human knowledge. These two arguments demonstrate tension within the school's theory (Kirzner, 1976). Thus it is a controversial point among the proponents of the school whether entrepreneurial actions based on discovering new opportunities move in parallel with the market process towards continuous discovery and increasing coordination or not. Kirzner sees the process moving towards equilibrium, while Littlechild (1989: 32) has another view: 'if a market participant acts on the basis of a perceived opportunity that turns out not to exist, he may further discoordinate the market'.

Subjectivism, which is also one of the main pillars of the Austrian school theory, requires more attention in terms of policy implications, especially those related to privatisation recommendations. The question of how methodological subjectivism can be reconciled with policy statements arises. The subjectivist point of view is that different policies are a matter of individual preferences. A valid question is how efficiency can be achieved when the preferences of a variety of different individuals are taken into account (Kirzner, 1976). Moreover, it is obvious that some people are in favour of privatisation and some are against it. Many people may prefer nationalisation and more equally distributed income to unemployment. A question arises as to why privatisation is the policy recommended from a subjectivism point of view since it is known that many do not prefer the policy. Does it not show a conflict between methodological subjectivism and policy recommendation?

Hodgson (1988: 121) points to another defect of subjectivism related to human consciousness and knowledge. He believes that 'we cannot hope to create a conceptual framework capable of handling vast quantities of information on our own' with a subjectivist point of view. If that is the case, subjectivism seems to be a barrier to conscious decision-making and individuals who are able to learn from each other and affect each other do not offset this defect. Hodgson (1988: 237) again presents the idea that 'it is wrong to assume that all knowledge is individual in character'. Some information (often information about the location of other information) is necessarily centralised and institutionalised (for example, telephone directories). It is doubtful that the 'decentralised market can provide an effective signalling device for all information and all activities in a complex economic system'. Subjectivism and its defects seem to be endless. O'Driscoll and Rizzo (1985: 20) ask this question: 'How can individuals acting in the world of everyday life unintentionally produce existing institutions or, more generally, the overall patterns of social interaction?' Related to this, Hayek (1984: 135) presents the idea that 'the spontaneous collaboration of free men often creates things which are greater than their individual minds can ever fully comprehend'. How these types of action are relevant to the subjectivist assumption is unknown. Social relations are much more complex and much broader than could fit with a notion about separate individual actions and inter-subjective relations. Furthermore, social relationships include individuals, but it does not mean that they are aware of everything. For example, consumer and suppliers come to a relationship in the market but a lot of information about both sides of the action remains unknown to each side. These defects can cast a shadow over the validity of subjectivism as a proper explanation for social and economic relationships.

One basic question to consider is whether the individual action is the only action that can influence others in a social and economic manner. Hodgson (1988: 71) totally disagrees and points to the fact that 'the socio-economic and institutional environment has a significant effect on the kind of information we receive, our cognition of it, or preferences, and thereby much of our behaviour'. However, if such social influences on individuals do exist, then the whole 'methodological individualism' is suspect. Thus the 'individualist' label can only survive if human actions can be referred to as spontaneous and indeterminate.

The Austrian view on ownership is worth considering. Those who are sympathetic to the Austrian approach point to private ownership as the only way by which entrepreneurs can act purposefully to find better ways of production with lower cost. Hodgson (1988: 268) believes that 'there is no obvious relationship between the pattern of private or public ownership, on the one hand, and the fertility of these conditions, on the other'. Hence private ownership might not be the only effective form of ownership, as believed by the Austrian view. Furthermore, private ownership is not a sufficient condition for achieving optimal efficiency and providing a circumstance in which the entrepreneur can act optimally. As Hodgson (1988: 268) stresses, other conditions must exist, such as 'the type and level of social culture, the level of technical and general education, and the material and institutional supports for entrepreneurial activity'.

What the Austrian school sees about common ownership, as distinct from private ownership, conforms only to the form of state ownership. Tittenbrun (1996: 100) claims that 'the Austrian fail to notice that their criticism of common ownership really only applies to state ownership'. However, state ownership is just one form of common ownership. Many group ownerships also exist which entrepreneurs may join voluntarily to pursue their own interest. As Jasinski (1991: 18) points out, 'group ownership seems to be compatible with market economy as long as there are many groups, independent of each other, and individuals have a choice of whether to join them or not'. The Austrian view about ownership remains limited and one-dimensional and fails to see all social phenomena.

The Austrian unilateral focus on the characteristic of entrepreneurship seems to inhibit recognition of decision-making and the whole process of production. It ignores the fact that it is common for workers to get involved in decision-making in capitalist countries such as Japan or in western Europe. Hodgson (1988: 237) also notes that the Austrian approach 'is silent about the real process of production'. Since capitalism today involves huge multinational corporations, the individual today differs from the individual of early capitalism. The characteristics of entrepreneurs have changed and take many different forms ranging from the characteristic of managements to an activity as a union worker. Modern corporations, financial market institutions and financial intermediaries all bring about the separation of owners and managers and involve many different players and wider ranges of economic agents which do not fit within the confined meaning of ownership in the Austrian view. As a result, the Austrian view has limited applicability to today's way of production and the process of decision-making.

The Austrian argument about information is another point of confusion. The argument is that privatisation will release the information required for efficient decision-making. Rowthorn and Chang (1991: 4–5) argue that this is not always the case: 'the information provided by the market is normally the result of product market competition and not private ownership'. Confining efficiency to private ownership is another misleading argument by the school; there are many examples showing that public enterprises have succeeded in acting efficiently, especially in the post-war era in different European countries such as Germany, Austria and Sweden.

The Austrian approach argues that privatisation increases competition and competition creates price information by which economic agents make better decisions which leads to superior outcomes. However, competition can exist without privatisation taking place (Tittenbrun, 1996) and price signalling is not always effective. Examples can be found where the price of a particular product has signalled wrongly to the investors and they have lost a lot of money. Obviously, if prices always signalled correctly then there would not be any losers in the market, which is clearly not the case. Additionally, from a microeconomic point of view it has been argued that, because markets are inherently incomplete and there are many public goods as well as externalities, the external costs and benefits cannot be reflected in market prices (Tittenbrun, 1996). How price alone can reflect all needed information, as anticipated in the Austrian view, is doubtful.

How to measure corporate performance has not been considered by the Austrian school of economics. The public sector has been critically compared to the private sector without addressing how corporate performance should be measured.

## The principal–agent theory

The principal–agent theory is about recognition of diversity between control and ownership in both public and private shareholder companies. It is expected that managers pursue their own objectives, which can be different from those of shareholders or the voting public. Suitable incentives should be introduced in order to convince managers to act in favour of company owners rather than their own interest. Other phenomena, such as a system of monitoring, and a system of pressure and sanctions, should exist to encourage the managers to respect the contract. The fact that different systems of monitoring are used in the public and private sectors has drawn much attention.

The principal–agent arguments are based on several points. Firstly, if a private firm performs badly profitability will fall. Secondly, falling profitability results in the shareholders selling their shares at low prices. Thirdly, the possibility of takeover will be activated. Finally, the threat of bankruptcy will lead managers to put more effort into running the firm more efficiently (Singh, 1971). This discipline is assumed to be lacking in public enterprise. Since public enterprises are often monopolies, customers have no other option for preference. In addition, public enterprises are protected from the threat of bankruptcy and takeover. Because they do not belong to the capital market and there is no efficient control forcing them to operate efficiently, they remain inefficient (Yarrow, 1989).

The principal–agent theory views public enterprises as problematic as far as performance is concerned. It supposes that the general public is the principal and government ministers are the public's agents, while in the next step the latter become the principals of the enterprises' managers. More fundamentally, the theory assumes a public enterprise is characterised by the obligation to maximise some social welfare. This in turn is comprised of consumers' and producers' surpluses. The role of the government in this context is significant. There is no doubt of the government's willingness to enhance economic efficiency, for political motives if no other. Governments have enough incentives to act in favour of the public interest. For example, lower prices of a product produced by a public firm give a good image of the current government. However, incentives are very limited. Both the voters (when dealing with the government) and the government ministers (when dealing with public enterprise managers) suffer from considerable information asymmetries. The voters cannot monitor the government ministers, and their powers to impose something on the government ministers are very limited. Additionally, because collecting information is not cost-free and no voter is willing to pay for information, the government ministers are free to take any decisions without serious burdens.

Apart from this, it is assumed that governments do not act strategically to obtain maximum internal efficiency because of political motivations. The government actions have a variety of effects on individuals as well as on different groups. For instance, a cost reduction may adversely affect the work of a public enterprise directly, but the benefit of lower prices spreads over all people of that country. From a cost-benefit analysis, it can be shown that the benefits and costs of decisions made by governments do not affect everyone in the same way. So instead of voters as a whole, some groups of people who belong to a certain class of society may have adequate incentive to monitor government decisions. These groups, unlike the voters as a whole, are assumed to have the ability to affect government decisions. Given the further assumption that the government acts politically rather than to pursue social objectives, the government neglects the reduction of costs in the interest of some social groups. Another source of added costs is frequent intervention by ministers in the process of managerial decision-making and the high levels of bureaucracy in the public sector. All these show that the system of monitoring and control of public enterprises is relatively weak compared with private sector disciplines.

Applying the principal–agent problem to the operation of public enterprises, it is obvious that a public enterprise is run by someone who does not own the enterprise. Hence careful operation of business and efforts to improve efficiency are not expected. This problem would be solved if an efficient monitoring system existed. However, since information cannot be perfect about managerial behaviours, and managers still know more about the job, the actual results may not be satisfactory. Because monitoring of public enterprise managers falls to the government as the agent of the public, it will be difficult for the public to monitor the government as agent. This is because they do not anticipate that the government puts in enough effort monitoring public enterprise managers (Yarrow, 1989). Privatisation would eliminate the inefficiency inherent to public ownership by breaking this relationship between the public and ministers, and between ministers and managers, and by providing a direct relationship between the principal and the agent (Yarrow, 1989). However, it should be noted that the need for dual monitoring is not limited to public enterprises; private firms also suffer from this problem if they are not run by owner-managers (Yarrow, 1989).

Contrary to the public enterprises, large privately owned companies with diffused shareholders are assumed to maximise the expected return. The company's managers are acting optimally because they believe their efforts affect the company's growth and their incomes are a function of that growth. However, individual shareholders may have the same problem as the individual has in his or her relation with the public firm. They cannot effectively monitor the managers, for the same reason, as is the case with public enterprises. The difference this time is assumed to be the transferability of property rights. Unlike public ownership, shareholders have the right to sell their shares if they are not satisfied with the company's performance. If undue selling occurs, then the share prices will be depressed, showing managerial failure to maximise profits. As a result, the possibility of a hostile takeover will arise. This potential threat is supposed to act as an effective device stimulating managerial behaviour in favour of their own shareholders. Thus the takeover threat is the most important proposition of the principal–agent theory; it highlights the superiority of private ownership over public ownership and the importance of the market in corporate control.

The potential threat of bankruptcy is assumed to be another superiority of private ownership over public ownership. The argument is that the manager of a public firm does not act optimally because public firms are not threatened with bankruptcy. This is not the case in a privately owned company where any careless behaviour from the managers will activate the threat of bankruptcy. However, the threat of bankruptcy is effective only when a company faces intense competition and a lower level of demand conditions (Iordanoglou, 2001).

A competitive industry is required as a precondition for private firms to maximise their profits without abusing market power and to help allocative efficiency to take place.[2] Competition, which is given the most attention by the theory's writers, is therefore assumed to occupy the main role in the trade-off between private and public ownership. Caves and Christensen (1980) stress that competition should be seen as a great enhancement improving internal efficiency regardless of the company's ownership. If the level of cost is given, then public enterprises are supposed to be more efficient in terms of allocative efficiency, as long as they pursue social welfare instead of profit maximisation. However, whether the gains from internal efficiency are greater than the gains from allocative efficiency is the main trade-off between the private and the public sector (Iordanoglou, 2001). For principal–agent theory, the superiority of private ownership over public ownership is an initial starting point and leans towards a policy of privatisation. Further, the enhancement of allocative efficiency of non-competitive industries does not necessarily need public ownership. In some cases, the public's interest can best be achieved by privatisation plus regulation. Otherwise,

[2] Internal efficiency depends upon the costs of a firm for a given level and composition of output. Allocative efficiency depends upon the firm's level and structure of output (and the corresponding level and structure of prices) given its cost structure.

in a normal situation with no monopoly power in place, private ownership, which is not subject to regulation, is the best guarantee of superior internal efficiency (Iordanoglou, 2001).

### A critical assessment of the principal–agent theory

A critical assessment of the principal–agent theory, which asserts the superiority of private ownership over public ownership, is a very difficult task. Firstly, a direct comparison seems to be impossible when the two types of owned companies do not exist in the same line of activity. Most public enterprises in the majority of countries occupy a monopoly or sub-monopoly position. Hence it is an open question how the relative detail of economic activities of both types of owned companies can be calculated. Even if both types of owned companies coexist in the same industry, many problems of assessment still remain resolved.[3] Secondly, if increasing returns to scale are to be considered then the size of the companies and other dimensions of the outputs of the companies under comparison must be carefully taken into account. Thirdly, the argument is that if managers are given enough incentives, then they will act in favour of the companies' owners. Such a prospect can only be justified in the presence of information asymmetry between the owners and managers of the companies. Finally, in terms of efficiency, ownership seems to be less important than other factors such as competition or regulation.

The study by Borcherding et al. (1982: 5), which concentrated on municipally supplied versus privately supplied service industries with higher levels of labour intensity (cleaning services, fire protection, refuse collection and slaughterhouses), shows that the privately owned companies generally operated with lower cost structure than the publicly owned companies. Another conclusion of the study is that competition had a positive effect on the public firms' performance. By contrast, a study by Pescatrice and Trapani (1980) that concentrates on the electrical utility industry, which is capital intensive rather than labour intensive, indicates that the public firms operated with lower unit cost than their private opponents. They also concluded that the rate of technical progress was faster in public firms than in private companies. In contrast to this finding, Morgan (1977) found that, in the water utility sector of the US, the private firms had lower costs than

[3] For example, for a proper comparison of private electricity companies, their output dimensions must be controlled for differences in the size and nature of regions served, and differences in quality such as security of supply.

public firms. Millward and Parker (1983: 258) conclude that 'There is no systematic evidence that public enterprises are less effective than private firms.'

These findings do not support the general conclusion drawn by the theory's authors that publicly owned companies are less efficient than privately owned companies independent of the type and characteristics of the industry under consideration. Where labour is intense and smaller-sized firms dominate, the privately owned activities have clear cost efficiency. On the other hand, in the case of capital-intensive companies such as utility companies and transport industries the mixed results do not provide enough room for generalisation.

With regard to the main arguments emphasised by the theory's proponents, I shall concentrate on empirical evidence showing whether private or public firms perform relatively better or worse in order to indicate the validity of the theory's propositions. One of the points highlighted by the theory's proponents is the existence of the takeover threat facing privately owned companies if they perform poorly. The assumption is that if profitability declines, the takeover threat will potentially increase (Iordanoglou, 2001). But Singh (1992a) found a negative relationship between profitability and the probability of takeover threat. Surprisingly, his finding shows that many companies that recorded excellent profitability are taken over rather than those with negative profitability.

The takeover threat, if valid, has to work regardless of the size of the firm. If the takeover threat declines when the size of firms increases, then the mechanism of the takeover threat will work in favour of the managers' interests instead of being an effective device for controlling managerial behaviours. Singh again shows that larger-sized companies are at significantly less risk of being taken over than smaller and medium-sized ones. He also concludes that large inefficient firms are much safer than smaller efficient firms in terms of the takeover threat.

Hostile takeover bids are different across countries; for example, the stock markets are less open to such behaviour in countries such as Germany than in the UK and the US (Parker, 1998). In most European countries, privatisation has taken place with clear restrictions on foreign investment. Governments from different countries have tried to impose restrictions by creating different policies such as retaining golden shares or the majority of shares, finding domestic investors for newly privatised companies and imposing a specific policy (for example, foreign investors cannot hold more than 20% of privatised companies' shares).

Theses types of restrictions can be found in many different countries in Europe, such as the UK, France, Italy, Austria, Sweden and Belgium (Parker, 1998). The elimination and restriction of takeover bids can refute the validity of the principal–agent theory's main argument for the superiority of private firms over public firms.

Another important point concerns the post-takeover period. If the takeover is a potentially effective mechanism then we should see an improved performance when the takeover occurs. Regardless of whether accounting data on profitability or the share price performance is used as a measurement, a lot of studies show no improvement has occurred after takeover has taken place. Cowling et al. (1980) emphasise that, with some exceptions, the performance of many companies has not improved sufficiently after mergers have taken place. Cosh et al. (1980), on the basis of a slightly different methodology and different measures of profitability, found weak support for the thesis that mergers had a positive effect on performance.

This finding again undermines the validity of the takeover deterrent. However, the most significant evidence, which undermines the effectiveness of the takeover threat, is the outstanding performance of the Japanese and German economy after the Second World War. Their bank-dominated system, in contrast to the stock market-based system, has been successful without being based on hostile takeovers (Iordanoglou, 2001).

Whether managers are risk-evaders or risk-takers is a concern of the theory's authors, but the worry is expressed through the idea that shareholders cannot monitor the managerial efforts. Whether higher or lower levels of risk are taken by the managers can be more important than whether managers have efficiently acted to reduce costs or not. What the proponents of free markets claim is that private sector managers, at least in the Anglo-Saxon world, do not normally take higher-risk decisions (Iordanoglou, 2001). Furthermore, it has been argued that because asymmetric information occurs, company managers and financial market operators prefer a short-term investment rather than a long-term one and pursue higher rates of return from a risky project (Iordanoglou, 2001). The latter pursuit is comprehensible for several reasons: managers are trying to satisfy shareholders, their rewards relate to short-run share price movements rather than stock market value and the fear of takeover bids can be a stimulating point forcing managers to pursue short-termism. If so, it can be concluded that short-termism and, at the same time, excessive higher risk are consistent with the private companies of shareholder diffusions. Furthermore, the pursuance of short-term investments instead of long-term investments can be a source of market failure.

The theory's view about public enterprise consists of two main points. The first point is that the individual (consumer or taxpayer) has no incentive to acquire costly information about ministerial economic decisions since the individual cannot put pressure upon the ministers. Because of that, as a second point, ministers and public servants may have enough room to pursue their own objectives. Whether these two claims are valid or not is an open question. Public enterprise outputs are used by a variety of customers. Apart from individual users, industrial users of those products as inputs are highly concerned about any decisions taken by public enterprise authorities and these industrial users may be willing to pay for costly information. Thus, the above claim about the users and their motives remains unsatisfied. Furthermore, even individual users are usually members of different organisations that may have power to influence government decisions and thus avoid freerider problems. Hence the claim that ministers have enough room for manoeuvring remains very limited.

Another strong assumption made by the theory's writers is that private enterprises have a substantially better system of control over managerial decisions and the speed of adjustment is systematically faster in private enterprises than it is in public enterprises. These claims are very general and ignore a lot of differences among sectors and their position in the national economy. Differences among countries in terms of their economic, institutional and political structure are substantial. Furthermore, as Iordanoglou (2001) argues, many western countries have established different bodies for controlling public enterprises; in many cases they have succeeded in influencing the strategic decisions made by public enterprise managers. Those bodies have played an important role in disclosing much information about public enterprise circumstances and their positions in terms of the economic point of view; hence it does not seem to be less efficient than the conventional control in private sector enterprises. Furthermore, Iordanogolu (2001) claims that there is no clear evidence to show that the speed of adjustment is systematically slower in public enterprises than in private ones. Finally, it is important to highlight that the current government in office should have strong incentives to monitor public enterprise managers and guard against any fluctuation in prices and the quality of output produced by public enterprises in order to maintain a good image among electors for the sake of future elections. This also can work as a substantial device to stimulate government efforts to manage public enterprise economic activities.

Another point that is argued by the principal–agent writers is that the public enterprises can never go bankrupt and they are well protected by the government. First of all, as Aharoni (1986) argues, the public enterprises can go bankrupt in the form of 'liquidation'. Furthermore, as far as the larger firms are concerned, the protection would be the same for both public and private enterprises from the government point of view. All the experience so far has demonstrated this claim. Aharoni (1986) again presents some examples (Chrysler of the US, Volkswagen of Germany, and many more), which show how governments have tried to rescue large firms in critical situations regardless of ownership. These examples challenge the claim that 'soft budget constraints' exist only for public enterprises, with private firms being excluded. One cannot ignore the evidence that, in order to preserve employment, governments from different countries have tried to give a hand to those private firms that are found in a situation of bankruptcy.

It can be concluded that the main propositions made by the theory's authors have a lot of defects that cast a shadow over the validity of the theory. The superiority of the private sector over the public sector cannot be proven by general propositions that ignore structural differences in each sector and economical and institutional differences from one country to another. The reality is that there is no guarantee that privatisation brings about efficiency. There is also no guarantee that dispersed shareholders have the ability to monitor managerial behaviour since such monitoring is not cost-free (Vickers and Yarrow, 1988).

In terms of monitoring, it must be recognised that public enterprises have different agencies such as ministers, public enterprise agencies and public holding companies watching them. All of those are responsible for the performance of public enterprise. More collective action will take place in those public enterprises; therefore fewer problems may arise. This kind of official monitoring is more effective than monitoring through shareholders; therefore public enterprises are more efficient than private enterprises in that regard (Chang and Singh, 1993).

One of the points that is highlighted by the principal–agent theory concerns different levels of delegation, and the assumption is made that public enterprises suffer from an excess of levels. Ministers, local authorities and public enterprises managers all represent different levels of delegation, which is assumed to have negative effects on the performance. It is claimed that privatisation will bring about a reduction in the levels of delegation involved in the management of an enterprise. There are several important points that should be mentioned with regard to this claim. Firstly, the level of delegation is a function of the size of the firm, whether the firm is a public or private one. Secondly, there is no standard way of assigning the levels of delegation. The matter varies from firm to firm, sector to sector and country to country; Dertouzos et al. (1989: 97) point out that a Japanese firm has fewer levels of delegation than an American firm. Finally, whether privatisation can always reduce the level of delegation is doubtful. For example, the levels of delegation may well be increased when a firm has been purchased by a foreign firm.

The claim that public managers are seeking their own interest is again suspicious. There are a lot of clear examples in non-democratic countries like Taiwan and Korea that show how public enterprises operate efficiently without proper control from the public or principals: 'we think preferences are often endogenously formed, so that bureaucrats and PE managers may to a large extent put public interest first if they operate in an environment where they are required' (Chang and Singh, 1993: 53).

The idea that the capital market disciplinary system, called the 'exit' system, is the only efficient system for controlling firms is dismissed by many economists (see Stiglitz, 1985). As Chang and Singh (1993) believe, the 'voice' system, which is a way of complaining against bad performance by different parties such as customers or disciplinary agents, may work more efficiently than the 'exit' system. This is particularly so in the case of a monopoly private firm (Chang and Singh, 1993). How the share prices can work as a good disciplinary mechanism is doubted by Cosh et al. (1990). They argue that the role of speculation, and the volatility of stock market prices, can undermine the role of the stock market as a disciplinary mechanism. To extend the idea further, the stock market may impact on firm behaviour and investment decisions in a negative way by encouraging managers to pursue short-term gains rather than long-term investments (Cosh et al., 1990).

The policy recommendation of privatisation brought forward by the principal–agent approach gives priority to the market discipline as a virtual system. As Littlechild (1986a) emphasises, market discipline can work through forces of competition and the takeover mechanism ensuring efficiency. The ability of the market system to work efficiently has been undermined even by proponents of the market. Theories like the freerider problem, transaction costs, and so on, reject the idea that the market may work efficiently for corporate control (Chang and Singh, 1993). Experience suggests that, as a disciplinary mechanism, the takeover threat may work in a completely different way from that theorised.

The takeover may work in an opposite fashion since powerful firms may desire to take over smaller profitable firms in their sector to establish an empire in order to avoid being taken over themselves.

Again, this theory has not addressed the issue of measuring corporate performance. The relationship between principal (shareholders) and agent (managers) has been analysed and the private sector, which is disciplined by market characteristics, is assumed to be much more efficient than the public sector. The latter claim has been maintained by the theory, while the issue of measuring corporate performance has been ignored.

## The new synthesis

The collapse of the post-war boom and, in the intellectual area, the collapse of Keynesianism and the idea of the welfare state system (which was not able to resolve the issue of ownership and the relationship between the state and the market) can be counted as significant reasons for the appearance of what Fine (1990) has called the 'new synthesis' about privatisation. These events provided enough room for the new synthesis to be introduced with emphasis on how to deal with potential market failure, how property rights can be defined and utilised, the notion of asymmetric information and the effects of transactions cost. Fine (1997a: 8) stresses that,

> interestingly, the ways in which it has evolved can be seen as pulling in opposite directions in terms of conclusions about the relative merits of forms of public and private ownership ... the scope of market failure has been considerably widened. It now includes issues such as how property rights are defined and utilised, informational imperfection and asymmetries, and the effects of transactions costs.

Market failure, and the expansion of its domain, highlight again the controversial role of the state and its responsibilities. The 'new synthesis' can be categorised as comprising three different schools of thought: 'new political economy', 'new institutional economics' and 'neo-Austrian'.

### The new political economy

The new political economy highlights the role of the state in terms of rent-seeking and remarks that state interventions cause the economy to move away from a perfectly competitive environment, stimulating economic agents to seek advantage in a wasteful and possibly illegal way.

This view of rent-seeking, which is a static theory of distortion from market efficiency, emphasises that inefficiency in the market is not sustainable without costs (Fine, 1997b: 380). Any economic intervention by the state, in this view, refers to rent-seeking behaviour under any circumstances.

### New institutional economics

The new institutional economics divides market from non-market institutions and sees the internal organisation of the firm as separate from its external market relations. In this theory, the economic agent cannot obtain all available information; hence the market transactions are not costless. As a result, non-market institutions such as the state and the internal organisation of large corporations or non-market collective action occur spontaneously; only individuals can engage in optimising behaviour (Fine, 1997b: 381). Principal–agent problems fall into this category: asymmetric information prevents agents from monitoring principals' actions adequately.

### The neo-Austrian school of economics

The neo-Austrian school of economics, unlike the new political economy school and the new institutional economics, is primarily concerned with the dynamics of the market economy in the context of an uncertain and changing world. Issues such as the notion of equilibrium and formal mathematical modelling, which are important within the other two schools, are ignored. Instead, decentralised decision-making is given greater attention. In a dynamic world of change and uncertainty, individual economic agents have extensive opportunities to obtain adequate information and allocate resources effectively or to develop new methods of production.

The Austrian school emphasises the role played by individual entrepreneurial initiative in a dynamic way of change rather than a static context in the market for allocating resources efficiently. However, the school's adherence to laissez-faire does not sweep away its antagonistic differences with monetarists and their emphasis on neo-classical foundations. Furthermore, Austrian supporters of laissez-faire try to downplay the significance of monopolistic behaviour in the market; this is in contrast to the neo-classical framework, which stresses the static deadweight loss of monopoly. For the Austrian school, new innovations take place through monopoly profits, and a competitive environment through entry to the various sectors of activity is the guarantee of progress (Fine, 1990).

Each of these three new schools has its own feature. The neo-Austrian is highly supportive of laissez-faire, and hence it has become very useful support for policy-making. The new institutional economics and the new political economy, despite having critical views of government, are less influential in neo-liberal policy-making. However, they have succeeded in forming themselves into the new orthodoxy (Fine, 1990). All schools are in favour of privatisation and see the adjustments from the public to the private sector as a significant movement for enhancing the performance of the economy as a whole. What can be concluded about these three elements in the new-founded syntheses is that, firstly, there are many similarities in the way that points are emphasised and points are ignored. Secondly, each of these, by highlighting one particular aspect (for example, rent-seeking behaviour, institutional forms and their role, and the characteristic of an individual agent and its impact on economic development) shows the desire for a more active role for the market as opposed to the state. Finally, for both the new political economy and the new institutional economics, emphasis is placed upon market failure and the possibility of regulatory failure in contrast to the beginning in view of the other in the old public sector economics.

### A critical assessment of the new synthesis

It can be concluded that the new synthesis shifts the balance in favour of the market and undermines state economic activities (Fine, 1997b). The new political economy and the new institutional economics emphasise the notion of market failure, supplemented by the notion of regulatory failure, as the most important point. These problems take precedence over ownership as such, although privatisation has become more forward with its progress in practices (Fine, 1997b: 382).

The second important point that is highlighted by the proponents of the new synthesis is that the market and its phenomena have potential abilities to resolve any distortions in the market and it regulates itself automatically. The intervention of the state is only necessary to provide enough room for competition by relaxing regulations and any barrier to entry into a particular sector. The perspective behind this idea is that consumers will be better off if there are more competitors in the market. This is a quantity theory of competition, which was criticised by Weeks (1981). The question of whether more competition in the market is beneficial or not depends mainly on very controversial assumptions like the abandonment of externalities, decreasing returns to scale and partial equilibrium.

The third point, which is related to the previous one, is that the new synthesis has altered the way industrial economics is conceived. The previous approach, under the name 'structure conduct-performance' (SCP), has been undermined by the notion of an equilibrium in which economic agents are able to affect the choices of conduct and structure in a competitive way. As a result, the new industrial economics, as opposed to the old one, reduces the range of factors under consideration to those explanatory variables that can be readily modelled (Fine, 1997b). This reduction causes the remaining model to be very formal and sophisticated. Such models do not always point to the benefits of competition. Moreover, those variables that are excluded can have substantial effects on industrial performance (Fine, 1997b).

Fourthly, an industrial policy at any particular time and in any particular country may not be applicable at other times and in other countries. An industrial policy has its own rationale in particular circumstances. This includes broader issues like trade, R&D, skills, finance for industry, vertical integration, small business provision of infrastructure, and so on. However, the new synthesis authors have reduced this broader insight to competition, regulation and ownership (Fine, 1997b).

The fifth point about the new synthesis deals with a situation in which there is no competition in the market and hence a competitive equilibrium output cannot be expected. A regulatory body is charged to constrain prices and consequently barricade excessive profits, and to monitor the level of quality and access of provision to consumers. The new synthesis assumes that there is a considerable distinction between artificial and natural monopoly. The former requires relative industrial policies and a regulatory body in order to create a competitive environment, while the latter does not. In practice, there are few cases to show how a regulatory body could not prevent a monopoly power from charging higher prices.

The next defect of the new synthesis is its inability to consider broader social and economic conditions. Its narrow insight leads to a very confined view about all economic and social actions and their outcome. For example, two methods can be used to explain the process of privatisation and its consequences. The first method, which is used by the new synthesis writers, is superficial and considers the process as a very simple adjustment from one owner to another. The second method tries to see the complexity of the issue and to extract major economic and social outcomes, and asserts that privatisation cannot be a simple shift to exercise property rights. It should be seen that the public sector involves a political process subject to a broader social interest. In contrast, the private sector is mainly responsive to market conditions and to private property rights. Even if both sectors are subject to competition and regulation, it is hard to anticipate that private sectors can conform to the way that public sectors respond politically in favour of broader social interests. The new synthesis, by concentrating primarily on competition and regulation with ownership as a secondary issue, is unable to realise the broader consequences of these issues. It is a failure of the new synthesis that it does not see the historical aspects of nationalised industries, their dynamic phenomena and their broader impact (Fine, 1997b).

As the final point, the theory suffers from a number of different aspects. Firstly, the theory seems to be a universal theory that deals only with microeconomic issues and without regard for macroeconomic issues like unemployment, inflation, and so on. Secondly, it makes no distinction between regulation of public firms and regulation of private firms, while both differ in terms of their objectives and processes. Thirdly, it does not recognise that regulators have very limited power over issues such as wage differentials, employment levels, R&D, skills and training of the workforce, and so on, in contrast to prices and profits, which they do directly affect. All these aspects, to some extent, may have direct effects on people's daily lives; for example, their right to basic utilities (Fine, 1997b).

The new synthesis, like the previous theories, has not made specific suggestions as far as corporate performance and its measurement are concerned. The private corporation is seen as superior to public enterprise without due regard to measurement issues.

## Conclusion

There are several different schools of thought behind privatisation, each of which addresses one particular aspect of the matter. It is worth emphasising that these schools, unlike the recent application of their theories, date as far back as 1870. Thus schools of thought on privatisation can be divided into two categories based on when they emerged. The first category consists of the Austrian school, the property rights school and the public choice school. The second category, which refers to recent ideas, is comprised of the principal–agent theory, the new political economy, the neo-Austrian school of economics and the new institutional economics.

The property rights analysis of public ownership leads to the conclusion that public enterprises are less economically efficient than private enterprises. Thus forms of ownership generate different rewards/penalties.

Generally, the more dispersed property rights are, the less motivated their holders will be to use their assets efficiently. Moreover, according to the property rights school, the separation of ownership and management, which is characteristic of the modern corporation, does not lead to any fundamental change in the performance of private enterprise. It acknowledges that shareholders in a large corporation are not able to monitor management as closely as a manager-owned company, but asserts that there are other factors at work in the modern corporation that compensate for this.

The public choice perspective, like the theory of property rights, holds very strong views about public ownership. The fact that 'public enterprises necessarily perform less efficiently than private enterprises' (Starr, 1989: 31) provides an influential economic case for privatisation. Privatisation allows profit-maximising decision-making to take place. Under public ownership, political motives, which lead to large subsidies and other concessions, are much more important than cost efficiency. Key public officials and ministers may pursue higher goals than operational efficiency leading to a higher cost of production. By contrast, privatisation frees an enterprise from the burden of political interference and non-market criteria, thus limiting politicians' ability to redirect the enterprise's activities in order to promote their personal agenda or to yield to short-term political pressures at the expense of market efficiency. This clarifies the objectives of the enterprise and leads to the enhancement of economic performance.

The Austrian school points to the fact that continual changes over time in tastes, techniques, available resources, prices, plans and expectations require that individuals (economic agents) be allowed to arrange their property as they see fit, in order to gain access to more and better knowledge than would be possible with less freedom of action (Moldofsky, 1989). The welfare of economic agents is improved in a competitive market which allows them to learn what consumers want, how much they are willing to pay, what factors and methods of production are available, and so on. This process continuously ensures that resources are reallocated to new preferable uses in the best possible way. The competitive market provides an environment in which products will be produced by someone who can do so more cheaply than anybody who does not produce it, and that each product is sold at a lower price (Hayek, 1984). The competitive market, whose foundation is price and shared economic knowledge, can generally only exist in the context of private ownership. It follows that privatisation, via the introduction of competition, will improve efficiency and sensitivity to consumer demand, with a better quality and range of goods and services (Littlechild, 1986b).

Principal–agent theory also views critically the state-owned enterprises. It asserts that, in the case of public enterprises, there is no efficient mechanism by which the principals (the public) can control the actions of their agents (officials). Thus they are deemed inefficient. In general, the agents (government officials) pursue their own goals in a world of information asymmetries, incomplete contracts and the absence of clear objectives. If the reverse were the case, then the ownership would be a problem and agents could have acted according to contracts. Moreover, because the incentive is weak and unrelated to the profit motive in state enterprises, agents have no enthusiasm to achieve the highest efficiency level (Bos, 1991). In contrast, private ownership sets a precise restriction on the managerial behaviour by linking it to expected future profits. If profits are expected to decline, it will squeeze share prices and increase takeover bids. Large shareholders clearly know the consequences of poor managerial performance; hence they have enough incentive to motivate managerial behaviours. More importantly, because managerial salaries in the private sector are linked to profit, stock options and bonuses, while in the public sector they are tied to fixed salary scales, the managerial motives will differ leading to different effort and outcomes.

The new political economy sees rent-seeking behaviour from government intervention into the market. It also sees these interventions as destroying a perfectly competitive environment. The new institutional economics sees the internal organisation of the firm as separate from its external market relations. It also sees that the economic agent has limited power to obtain all available information and that market transactions are not cost-free. Non-market institutions cannot act optimally, but individuals can. The neo-Austrian school of economics, unlike the two other schools, sees the market economy as a dynamic phenomenon in an uncertain and changing world. Individual economic agents are assumed to be the main source of decision-making; that decision-making is based on all the information and knowledge they are able to obtain.

The most important conclusions that can be extracted from the study of these three newly founded schools of thought are:

1. The characteristic of the new ownership is much more important than the role played by competition and regulation.
2. Private sector economy and, in this regard, privatisation, are much more favourable than public sector economy.

All the above schools are in favour of privatisation and see the adjustments from the public to the private sector as a significant movement for enhancing the economy as a whole.

The literature is mainly devoted to the relation between state and market and between public and private sectors with the assumption that each of these opposes the other. It perceives that the market and private sectors are more favourable than the state and public sectors. These subjective roles for the market and the private sector reduce the important role played by the state and the public sector in the economy. It is assumed that the role of the state and the public sector undermine the role of the private sector and limits economic development as a whole. Such a view inevitably has led to overgeneralising the role of privatisation. As a result, there is pressure for privatisation in principle, even if the allocation of those same resources to the further improvement of the public sector would result in a better outcome from a social perspective. Of course, when resources are limited, the public sector is employed to produce those commodities and services that are neglected by the private sector because the production initially requires a huge amount of capital or it is perceived by the private sector as unprofitable.

Apart from analysing the strengths and weaknesses of all those schools of thought, the main purpose of this chapter was to determine whether they have any recommendations for measuring corporate performance. What was discussed emphasises that those theories do not have any suggestions for measuring corporate performance. They have concentrated on the relationship of public and private sector without addressing how corporate performance should be measured. Each of them evaluates a particular aspect of those sectors, with their sympathies for the private sector made apparent, but they do not advocate how to measure the superiority of the private sector compared with the public sector. This defect casts a shadow over those theories' legitimacy and usefulness as theoretical benchmarks for any economic action.

# 3
# Literature Review of Public and Private Ownership: Strengths and Weaknesses

## Introduction

Having examined the various privatisation theories in the previous chapter, I now move on to review empirical case studies on public and private enterprises, making comparisons and determining their strengths and weaknesses. A review of the literature on the relationship between public and private enterprise and their relative performance that followed the wave of privatisation shows an enormous number of works in this field. The number of publications increases sharply if government and consultancy papers as well as books are added. Fine (1997a: 376) reports that more than 3,000 articles have been found in academic journals over the previous few years.

The British privatisation programme, which started in 1980, can be counted as the first major experiment in moving from public to private ownership. It is claimed with a certain measure of pride that privatisation has been the UK's most successful recent export, and many other countries, whether developed, developing or transitional, have followed the UK's lead. On this basis, most empirical studies have appeared in the wake of privatisation beginning in 1980 in the UK and then afterwards in other countries. The related economic issues – for instance, the economics of regulation – emerged at a later stage.

In most empirical studies, the leading emphasis is upon economic efficiency. It has been argued that the private sector is generally more efficient than the public sector. The latter is deemed to be inefficient because it faces no threat of bankruptcy or takeover, and it has no private shareholders to be satisfied and to serve as an external disciplinary force. Therefore, managers in public enterprises will pursue their own preferred goals. On the other hand, managers in private firms have an incentive to allocate resources efficiently to the extent that they face market mechanisms. The private sector supposedly derives its strength from the neo-liberal idea that the market is the best mechanism for allocating resources (Fine, 1997b).

The belief that public firms are less efficient than private has in part been motivated by, or at least has been used to justify, the appearance of privatisation programmes around the world. It also has influenced debate over economic and industrial policy. The empirical studies published in recent decades can be categorised as either those that focus on the relative performances of public versus private enterprises or those that concentrate on the performance of the privatised enterprises.

For the former, the most important international surveys are those of Borcherding et al. (1982), Millward and Parker (1983) and Boardman and Vining (1989, 1992). These surveys reveal different results. For instance, Millward and Parker (1983) conclude that the empirical evidence does not support the idea that public firms exhibit higher cost than private firms. On the other hand, the surveys by Borcherding et al. (1982) and Boardman and Vining (1992) confirm that private enterprises are more efficient than public enterprises. Other authors have looked at the relationship between public and private sector from a variety of angles or criteria. Significant authors are: Forsyth and Hocking (1980), Finsinger (1984), Faere et al. (1985), Foreman-Peck and Waterson (1985), Sappington and Stiglitz (1987), Laffont and Tirole (1991), Hartley and Hooper (1992), De Fraja (1993), Boycko et al. (1994, 1996), Hart et al. (1997) and Dewenter and Malatesta (1998).

Studies of privatised industries can be divided into two subcategories. One consists of those studies that focus on the UK. The second subcategory covers studies in other countries or studies that include both the UK and other countries. Some studies on the UK experience have focused on the effects of privatisation on productivity growth; for instance: Bishop and Kay (1988), Dunshire et al. (1991), Haskel and Szymanski (1993), Bishop and Thompson (1992) and Martin and Parker (1995). International studies include: Galal et al. (1992), Kikeri et al. (1992), Ramanadham (1993), Megginson et al. (1994), Ehrlich et al. (1994), Galal et al. (1994), Newberry and Pollitt (1997), Anderson et al. (1997), Dewenter and Malatesta (1998) and Frydman et al. (1998a).

A number of difficulties arise with the empirical work on public and private enterprise performance. Firstly, most studies use accounting data like output per employee, sales per asset, and so on. Secondly, the data are analysed at firm level. Thirdly, studies of the relative performance of public and private firms are usually based on cross-sectional data. With respect to the use of accounting data at the firm level, it is significant how inputs and outputs are measured. The issue of evaluating efficiency and performance is more complicated in the case of non-manufacturing industries because quantities and quality of service output are difficult to measure consistently. Moreover, allocating costs to a particular service output is often impossible. The second problem concerns the selection of variables, which results in eliminating some variables believed to have less effect on the final outcome. However, there is always the risk that this is not the case in practice.

Empirical studies on the performance of public versus private enterprises and privatised companies compound a wider set of issues: their methodologies, their criteria for measuring performance, their data set, the reasons given for different behaviours of public and private enterprises, and so on. It should be emphasised that a particular study may differ from the others in terms of any of the above issues. Some studies, for instance, might try to compare the performance of public and private enterprises that are operating in the same sector. Some might use cross-sector or cross-country approaches. Costs of operation might be used as a criterion for measuring performance in one study, while productivity or any other indicator might be chosen in another. The data set might cover all types of costs, or some simplifications might be made in order to ease investigation. However, whatever the criteria by which performance is assessed, the reasons given for the outcome for relative efficiency, for example, may be associated with one or other explanatory factor, whether measured or not, as in appeal to the incentive structure, for example.

In general the literature assessing relative performance tends to favour the private sector. In assessing performance, it often assumes without question that the same criteria should be used whether the company is private or public. Furthermore, the criteria used are generally those developed for the private as opposed to public sector performance. The issue is even more significant when investigating performances of different companies in different countries, where the rationale for the public sector might vary. Moreover, the theory of individual performance puts much emphasis on the complexity of the market process, whether for public or private sector, whereas the empirical literature suggests simple relationships between economic variables on a purely technical level. This is an inconsistent approach that has been characteristic of many economists. How the gulf between theory and measurement is bridged in evaluating corporate performance is an important feature of the literature.

It has been observed that assessing the performance of privatisation, especially in the industrialised countries, involves a tendency among policy-makers to ignore detailed monitoring and evaluation of those enterprises which have been privatised (Cook and Kirkpatrick, 1995). The monitoring and evaluation are deemed to be less important if private sector companies operate in a 'competitive' environment; that is, one in which there are appropriate independent institutions marketing the same product. But such sales competition is not the only means by which firms compete.

The various empirical studies will be assessed against the background of these general observations. In doing so, I will examine several aspects presented above: the methodology, the criteria for measuring performance, the data set, the reasons given for behaviour of public and private enterprises arising out of discussion from the previous chapter and, lastly, which type of enterprise, public or private, performed better. Moreover, I will examine the studies in the light of the theories that were examined in the previous chapter. Do the reasons given for behaviour of public or private enterprises refer to those theories? This gives a broader insight into those theories and their usefulness for empirical studies. Are the studies weak in implications for empirical measurement? This is important because most studies rate performance without regard to underlying theory and do not distinguish between theories.

The main results are as follows. The overview of empirical studies reveals that many studies suffer from methodological problems and in many others the criteria for measuring corporate performance are not always appropriate to both sectors. In most studies the greatest attention is devoted to the data and the technical problems of measurement. They tend to concede that the problems involved led to the subjective resolution of inconsistencies. In most studies, not much care has been taken to relate the empirical measurement to some theory of performance. Whilst primarily focused on empirical studies, occasional reference is made to the non-empirical literature as it points to variables that should be measured in assessing performance.

In this light the chapter is organised as follows. In the second section, a historical overview of changes in the balance between public and private enterprise is presented. It is noted that the British privatisation programme has led to much pressure being placed upon developing and transitional countries for immediate and universal privatisation of public assets as a way out of their economic problems. Since the beginning of the new era it can be emphasised that the balance between the two sectors has shifted towards the private sector, especially in developed countries.

In the third section, empirical studies on the relative performance of public and private enterprise are reported. Each study is assessed around some aspect of the relationship between public and private sectors. The conclusion as to which sector has performed better, the reasons given, the theoretical framework that is referenced, the methodologies of the studies, and the data set will be examined.

In the fourth section, I look at privatisation performance. Many empirical studies have been conducted following the wave of privatisation beginning in 1980. Each study can be placed into one of two categories. The first consists of those studies that compare company performance before and after privatisation. The second approach is based on the comparison of privatised companies and those companies that have remained under state control. A procedure identical to the previous section is used to evaluate these studies in terms of theory, method, data, explanatory factors given and the relationship between these.

The studies surveyed are gathered together and assessed in the fifth section, where they are shown to be subject to criticism. The concluding remarks are devoted to a summary of the findings and the main problems to be resolved across those studies proposing to measure corporate performance.

## Historical overview of privatisation

Before modern privatisation programmes by Margaret Thatcher's Conservative government in the UK in 1979, the first large-scale, ideologically motivated privatisation programme of the post-war era was launched by the government of the Federal Republic of Germany in 1961. A majority stake in Volkswagen was offered to small investors, and four years later an even larger number of shares in VEBA were offered. Despite initial success, the first cyclical downturn in stock prices forced the government to bail out many small shareholders (Megginson et al., 1994). A few non-European governments pursued privatisation during the 1965–79 period (Megginson et al., 1994). However, the Thatcher government's large privatisation programme is without question the most important historically. It also gave rise to a change in terminology from 'denationalisation' to the more appealing 'privatisation'. It was firmly established as a basic economic policy when British Telecommunications was publicly offered in November 1984.

The role of state-owned enterprises (SOEs) in the British economy was reduced to essentially nothing after the Tories left office in 1997 while over 10% of gross domestic product (GDP) was associated with the role of SOEs when the Tories took office 18 years earlier. The objectives set for the British privatisation programme were: to raise revenue for the state, to promote economic efficiency, to reduce government interference in the economy, to promote wider share ownership, to provide the opportunity to introduce competition, and to expose SOEs to market discipline (for more information see Menyah and Paudyal, 1996). However, a major objective mentioned by the Tory government was in deepening the national capital market (Menyah and Paudyal, 1996). Further, as Clarke (1993: 229) emphasises, 'Thus the objective of much of the Thatcher governments' intervention in the public sector was to use financial controls to extend Taylorism in the control of public sector workers: to centralise management control: and to replace locally provided public services by mass-produced commercial ones.'

The British privatisation programme in general has influenced many other industrialised countries to begin divesting SOEs through public share offerings. The French government of Jacques Chirac, which was in power from 1986 until 1988, privatised 22 companies (worth $12 billion). The Socialist government re-elected in 1988 did not renationalise the divested firms. Since 1993, the Socialist government itself has launched a new and even larger French privatisation programme. Among these, the largest ever French privatisation was launched, selling the $7.1 billion French Telecom in October 1997. Several other western European governments, including Italy, Germany, Spain, the Netherlands and the Scandinavian countries, have tried to follow suit during the late 1980s and early 1990s. These programmes typically relied on public share offerings to achieve privatisation.

Outside of western Europe, not only rich countries such as Japan and Canada, but many other countries, including China, India, Chile, Mexico, Brazil, Sub-Saharan Africa, South Africa, and the Soviet bloc countries of central and eastern Europe have tried to use the opportunities to sell large companies when market conditions were attractive, or when money was needed to plug budget deficits. Kikeri et al. (1992) disclose that, by 1992, more than 80 countries had adopted privatisation programmes. As a result, 2,000 SOEs in developing countries and 6,800 SOEs worldwide were transferred to the private sector (for additional details, see Campbell White and Bhatia, 1998, and Bowen, 1997).

According to Bortolotti et al. (1998) the role of state-owned enterprises in the economies of industrialized countries declined significantly from 1978 through to 1991. That role, which accounted for roughly 9% of GDP in the Organisation for Economic Cooperation and Development (OECD) countries in 1978, had declined to less than

7% ten years later. Since 1988 the SOEs' share of industrialised-country GDP has probably slipped below 5%. In the transition economies of central and eastern Europe, this role has fallen even farther because of mass privatisation programmes (see Blanchard and Aghion, 1996, and Pistor and Spicer, 1997). Meanwhile, during 1978–91, the role of SOEs actually increased in some developing countries to about 11% of GDP in 1991, which was slightly higher than their share in 1978 (Haggarty and Shirley, 1996). However, other evidence suggests that in developing countries there has been a decrease in state involvement in the economy through SOEs (World Bank, 1995).

As Table 3.1 shows, 75 of the Global 1000 and 29 of the Top 100 Emerging Market companies are privatised firms; thus it can be concluded that total world stock market capitalisation would today be substantially smaller if privatisation had not happened. Privatised companies account for 20.1% of the total capitalisation of the non-US companies on the combined Global 1000 and Top 100 Emerging Market lists. The four most valuable emerging market companies all are privatised firms, and former SOEs account for 36.6% of the Top 100 Emerging Market companies' total value.

Why have governments been so enthusiastically embracing privatisation? One answer could be that it is about raising money. Goodman and Loveman (1991) reveal that the worldwide total sales of SOEs had topped $185 billion by 1990, and Megginson and Netter (1998) claim that governments have raised over $660 billion just through share offerings and direct sales (excluding voucher privatisations) since 1977. On the other hand, the revenue obtained cannot be the sole reason that privatisation has become popular since it is apparent that the revenue received from share sales of highly profitable SOEs would be offset by lost profit remittances in the future. Hence, the deeper answer must lie elsewhere. Veljanovski (1990: xiii) observes that,

> having read a great deal of this literature I have reached the inescapable conclusion that, with some notable exceptions, very little has risen above the commonplace. One defect in much of the work stands out and requires comment. Privatisation is a complex process, which takes place in the commercial market place, and in the political market place ... one must examine the political and institutional context on an equal footing to the purely economic aspects.

This is the light in which to view the account of the empirical studies that follows.

| Company name | Country | Global 1000 rank[a] | Country rank[b] | Market value (US $ m) | Total sale (US $ m) | Total profit (US $ m) |
|---|---|---|---|---|---|---|
| Nippon Telegraph & Telephone | Japan | 8 | 1 | 130,911 | 63,665 | 1,081 |
| British Petroleum | United Kingdom | 26 | 2 | 85,283 | 70,870 | 4,600 |
| Deutsche Telekom | Germany | 32 | 2 | 73,640 | 37,891 | 1,853 |
| British Telecommunications | United Kingdom | 40 | 6 | 66,261 | 25,504 | 3,307 |
| ENI | Italy | 57 | 1 | 56,424 | 34,551 | 2,913 |
| France Telecom | France | 59 | 1 | 56,011 | 26,197 | 2,484 |
| Telecom Italia | Italy | 67 | 2 | 51,301 | 24,372 | 1,963 |
| Telefonica | Spain | 78 | 1 | 45,854 | 15,617 | 1,256 |
| Elf Acquitaine | France | 91 | 2 | 38,123 | 42,507 | 1,702 |
| VEBA | Germany | 116 | 10 | 32,686 | 42,667 | 1,576 |
| Volkswagen | Germany | 122 | 11 | 30,938 | 63,521 | 749 |
| Total | France | 127 | 6 | 38,345 | 31,939 | 1,272 |
| Gazprom | Russia | 128 | 1 | 32,906 | 20,462 | 1,456 |
| Telebras | Brazil | 129 | 1 | 32,759 | 13,739 | 3,390 |
| Telstra | Australia | 130 | 1 | 30,278 | 9,668 | 1,608 |
| Koninklijke PTT Nederland | Netherlands | 150 | 7 | 26,420 | 7,590 | 1,339 |
| Cable & Wireless | United Kingdom | 156 | 17 | 25,601 | 11,417 | 1,194 |
| Endesa | Spain | 164 | 4 | 24,950 | 8,475 | 1,102 |
| Singapore Telecommunications | Singapore | 189 | 1 | 21,499 | 2,952 | 1,127 |
| Hong Kong Telecommunications | Hong Kong | 190 | 1 | 21,440 | 4,522 | 2,197 |
| China Telecom | China | 199 | 1 | 20,676 | 1,871 | 599 |
| BG | United Kingdom | 204 | 21 | 20,246 | 7,012 | 820 |
| Rhone-Poulenc | France | 207 | 10 | 20,122 | 15,042 | 571 |
| Telefonos de Mexico | Mexico | 209 | 1 | 19,999 | 6,873 | 1,455 |
| Commonwealth Bank | Australia | 211 | 3 | 19,828 | NA | 1,391 |
| Societe Generale | France | 216 | 12 | 19,548 | NA | 1,021 |
| East Japan Railways | Japan | 221 | 18 | 18,995 | 18,142 | 510 |
| Banque Nationale de Paris | France | 231 | 15 | 18,214 | NA | 997 |
| Compagnie de Saint-Gobain | France | 239 | 16 | 17,603 | 17,898 | 939 |
| Repsol | Spain | 256 | 5 | 16,694 | 21,208 | 833 |
| Paribas | France | 261 | 17 | 16,327 | NA | 1,099 |
| Credito Italiano | Italy | 265 | 6 | 16,113 | NA | 274 |
| British Aerospace | United Kingdom | 266 | 27 | 15,918 | 11,850 | 695 |
| Electricidade de Portugal | Portugal | 268 | 1 | 15,785 | 3,132 | 510 |

[a] 'Global 1000 rank' refers to the company's global ranking based on market valuation.
[b] 'Country rank' refers to the company's relative position among those firms from their country on the Global 1000 list.

*Source*: Information is from Morgan Stanley Capital International, as reported in 'The *Business Week* Global 1000', *Business Week* (13 July 1998): 52–92.

## Empirical studies

### The relative performance of state-owned and privately owned firms

In the immediate post-Second World War period, western countries (outside the United States) adopted an economic policy which deeply involved the national government. The involvement consisted of regulating the national economy and industrial sector activities through exclusive state ownership. Until 1979 when the Thatcher government came to power, it was an obvious and commonly accepted belief that the government should control at least those sectors such as telecommunications, postal services, electric and gas utilities, airlines, railroads, state-owned banks and certain 'strategic' manufacturing industries such as steel and defence productions. Thatcher's government challenged this belief from a purely ideological point of view, and thereafter the other western countries' governments have tried to follow suit.

Since the beginning of this era, early empirical studies were in favour of at least the economic competitiveness of state ownership. Vickers and Wright (1989: 23) have suggested that 'The nature of competition in the relevant market emerges as an important factor, with private ownership appearing relatively more efficient in competitive conditions.' The studies done by Caves and Christensen (1980), Faere et al. (1985), Kay and Thompson (1986), Yarrow (1986), Vickers and Yarrow (1988), Bishop and Kay (1989) and Beesley and Littlechild (1989) are in favour of reforming SOEs through the introduction of more competition in order to achieve more efficiency; in the end, they all favour privatisation. However, in their empirical studies on public versus private sector efficiency, Martin and Parker (1997) suggest that the environment in which firms are operating is important. Public enterprises, for instance, are more efficient if there is little or no product competition. They conclude that the statement that privately owned companies are more efficient than publicly owned firms is questionable because another factor, the environment, is more important for economic efficiency then the ownership. Yarrow (1985b) stresses that product market competition and regulatory policies are more important for economic performance than ownership. However, whether these latter findings are reliable as far as the corporate performance is concerned seems to be doubtful.

Some economists have questioned whether these two types of ownership are comparable. Vickers and Wright (1989: 23) note that,

> In truth, however, there are great problems in comparing the performance of public and private enterprises, because the criteria for assessing performance are varied, and because their activities do not always overlap sufficiently to permit meaningful comparison. Furthermore, private sector management has a basic duty to maximise profits for shareholders, which is not the case with public sector firms which are frequently bound by other objectives: low profitability is not necessarily inconsistent with efficient management.

Many economists have first developed theoretical models and then provided empirical evidence to support the presented model. However, each model highlights only one aspect of the relation between public and private sector. Many authors have contributed to the movement towards markets; a leading figure among them is Frederich Von Hayek. His book *The Road to Serfdom* (1944), which opposes the welfare state and collectivism, may have had the most direct impact on policy-makers. Yergin and Stanislaw (1998) believe that his ideas were a theoretical benchmark for the policies recommended by Keith Joseph, and later Margaret Thatcher, that led to a market economy. Another influential economist is Kornai (1988) who criticises the role of the state in creating peculiar incentives and accuses the state enterprises of having 'soft budget constraints'. As a result, the government has difficulty in imposing financial discipline on SOEs.

Forsyth and Hocking (1980) conducted research on air services in Australia and tried to compare one public company with one private operator. Their results show very little difference in the airlines' performance. Finsinger (1984) conducted an investigation of 96 life insurance companies in Germany, of which 12 were public firms. He found that the average total costs of public enterprises are less than three-quarters those of private firms and that the operating costs of both parts (public and private) are similar. Faere et al. (1985) conducted research of 123 private and 30 electric utilities operating in the US market. They found that publicly owned utilities are slightly more efficient than privately owned companies. In contrast to this result, Foreman-Peck and Waterson (1985) found the opposite. Their experiment dealt with 171 local authorities and privately owned stations in the UK. The results show that publicly owned (the local authority sector) enterprises in this branch are less efficient on average than the privately owned.

Sappington and Stiglitz (1987) conducted a theoretical investigation of the choice between public and private provision of goods. They point out that the preference depends on the level of transaction costs, regardless of whether the goods and services are produced by government intervention or by private ownership under informational asymmetry. For privatisation they suggest different policies based on different circumstances. It may be that government ownership is more appropriate than private ownership. On the other hand, they find that it is not necessarily optimal to make government intervention easy, and that the government's promise not to intervene is more credible under private ownership than under public ownership. They found similarities rather than differences between private and public ownership in respect to performance incentives.

> Thus, once there is delegation of responsibility and an effective separation of ownership and management, there is dissolution of performance incentives under both public and private ownership. Whether the problem is more severe under one mode of organization or the other, remains an open question. The answer depends in part on how well performance can be monitored, how effective is competition, etc., in the two models. (Sappington and Stiglitz, 1987: 18)

The question of which form of ownership is more likely to promote social welfare is investigated by Laffont and Tirole (1991). They state that because the objective is different for managers of public enterprises (maximising social welfare rather than profit) the investment cost is suboptimal. However, the cost of private ownership is not so straightforward. The manager of a private enterprise must try to satisfy regulators, on the one hand, and shareholders, on the other. Hartley and Hooper (1992) set out to investigate whether the productivity of nationalised industries as a whole moves in the same direction as national trends in the UK for the years 1979–90. The results clearly show that the average annual productivity growth of nationalised industries (4.4%) was above both manufacturing (4.1%) and the economy as a whole (1.9%). De Fraja (1993), observing the principal–agent problems, looks at the degree of inefficiency when an optimal incentive contract is in place on both public and private owners. He concludes that because consumers' welfare is part of the government utility function, public ownership always results in a higher level of productive efficiency. The government will gain more if an increase in productive efficiency occurs. Therefore it should pay more for those gains.

Boycko et al. (1994, 1996), in two successive articles, have tried to show the inefficiency of public enterprises based on both the public choice school and the principal–agent theories. In their model, politicians and public enterprise managers are assumed to be cooperating to achieve their own goals. Politicians are interested in satisfying the voters and public managers are ready to cooperate with them in order to promote their own positions further. They conclude that inefficiency is inherent with the public sector activities and the best remedy is privatisation, which leads to substantial improvements of public enterprises.

Hart et al. (1997) looked at incomplete contracts and recommend private ownership over public ownership if lack of incentive and high costs are present. They argue that public and private provision of goods and services would usually result in similarly efficient results if complete and enforceable contracts were in place. However, incomplete contracts are usual in public enterprises, which bring about a lack of motivation for controlling costs and improving quality on the part of government managers. Privately owned enterprises do not suffer from this problem because their contracts are usually complete and enforceable. In the question of public versus private ownership and their relative performances, the same data are consistent with the property rights school and the public choice theory, as Faere et al. (1985: 97) point out:

> in terms of sources of scale inefficiency, 66% of the privately owned utilities exhibited decreasing returns to scale, whereas 80% of publicly owned utilities were at a point of increasing returns to scale, suggesting that privately owned utilities have over-expanded, whereas publicly owned utilities could benefit from further expansions.

In contrast, several studies come to another conclusion and show that government ownership did not necessarily result in poor economic performance. These studies are more in favour of state than private ownership and point to the fact that there is no unambiguously preferable form of ownership. The work by Kole and Mulherin (1997) is a clear example of this type.

## The most significant empirical studies

The relative performance of public versus private firms has been more extensively analysed than privatisation. The main international studies are by Borcherding et al. (1982), Millward and Parker (1983) and Boardman and Vining (1989, 1992).

Borcherding et al. (1982) studied more than 50 empirical pieces of research from the US, Germany, Australia, Canada and Switzerland, covering a wide range of industries airlines, railway services, banks and insurance companies, utilities, refuse collection, construction, and also some in the public services arena such as the fire brigade, hospitals and forestry. They focus on two main points as criteria for their studies: cost of operations, and the question of whether ownership is more important than creating competition.

What they found confirms that public firms have higher costs than private firms in comparable companies (that is, public firms are less productive or cost-efficient). In some cases, unit costs are similar where public firms are operating in fiercely competitive environments. Although three studies were found in which public firms are more efficient than private ones, the authors of the surveys are sceptical about those results and suggest that adequate control was not maintained for relevant variables such as quality. They further conclude that public firms are adopting innovations and cost-saving measures. This is due to the fact that their managers enjoy longer tenure periods than private managers, and it seems that voters rather than non-voters affect their decisions.

They evaluate this evidence as support for the 'property rights' approach on the grounds that those public firms are inefficient since in the public sector property rights are imperfectly defined. Moreover, it is more difficult to monitor the agents involved (that is, managers and bureaucrats). The 'public choice' approach is also examined by them. This examination is based on some results from De Alessi (1969) about managers in public firms who set out to improve their firms' growth rather than to maximise welfare. Despite this, overstaffing and overcapitalisation of firms are still the outcome. The excess of unit costs, which is linked to public firms, is likely to result from the public choice effects, like self-interested managers/bureaucrats and unionised workers extracting rents. However, the authors believe that higher costs are generated from transferring redistributed income. These transfers are the cost of having public firms. Contracting out to private providers cannot sustain this behaviour.

Boardman and Vining (1989, 1992) have looked at the efficiency of public and private firms. The first study examines the economic performance of the 500 largest non-US industrial firms in 1983. The second looks empirically at state versus private ownership of Canadian firms. They review 91 studies examining which type of firm, public or private, is more efficient and also whether competition in the market is more important than ownership in determining the degree of efficiency.

Industries which were examined are: electricity, refuse collection, water, health, airlines, railroads, banks and financial services, fire services and non-rail transits.

Their comparative approach uses four profitability ratios and two measures of X-inefficiency. The finding seems to emphasise that ownership is generally important even in those industries where a high degree of competition is present. Private firms generally perform better than public ones. However, if public firms are operating in a competitive environment, efficiency improvements are visible. As the previous study by Borcherding et al. (1982) suggests, some state-owned enterprises have outperformed private enterprises, but the authors stress that this is because no real competition existed in those industries, which included utilities, airlines, the railway and the health services. They concluded that this could not be used as a reliable measure for comparing the efficiency of public and private firms in a competitive environment.

Borcherding et al. conduct their empirical study on the property rights hypothesis including:

1. several measure of profitability and efficiency performance
2. variables for SOEs (state-owned enterprises), PCs (private companies) and MEs (mixed enterprises)
3. various measures that reflect the nature of regulatory/competitive environment.

Thus, performance is formulated as:

> Performance = *f* (mixed, state, assets, sales, employees, market shares, concentration, industry and country).

They use the 500 largest manufacturing and mining corporations in the world outside the United States, as compiled by *Fortune* Magazine in 1983. (In their 1992 study they use 1986 data on the 500 largest non-financial corporations in Canada as compiled by *The Financial Post* (1987).) They categorise ownership in the following way: state-owned enterprises (SOEs), mixed enterprises (MEs), cooperatives (co-ops) and private companies (PCs). They set dummy variables for the first three and make PCs the benchmark. Some modifications are made in order to look at the relative performance of SOEs and PCs in competitive environments. They also treat MEs like PCs except for the ownership aspect. Examples of PCs in the data set are Nissan, Nestlé, and Scottish and Newcastle breweries; examples of SOEs include British Cost Board, Vale do Rio Doce and Petroleos de Venezuela; and examples of MEs are British Petroleum, Canada Corporation and Volkswagen.

Two different types of dependent variables of profitability and technical efficiency are used to examine performance. The profitability is measured by utilising three criteria: return on assets (ROA), return on sales (ROS) and net income (NI). Two performance measures, related to technical efficiency or X-efficiency, are used: the log of sales per employee and the log of sales per asset. An equation with the log of asset per employee – the capital–labour ratio – as the dependent variable is estimated. Accounting rates of return are generally not equivalent to economic rate of return because of different methods of measuring depreciation. These include assets, sales, employees and a measure of international market share to reflect the competitive position of each firm. In actual fact, assets, sales and employees measure size, economies of scale and, to some extent, market power.

Also there is evidence that the choice of depreciation method is related to firm size. The market share is computed as the ratio of the firm's sales to the total sector sales of the 500 international firms in the data. To control the competitive/regulatory environment of the industry, they include concentration and dummy variables for each industrial sector and each country. The concentration is measured by a four-firm concentration ratio (the percentage of an industry's employees accounted for by the four largest firms in an industry). It is computed by country. They obtained data from *Fortune*, R.M. Whiteside, ed., 'Major Companies of Europe' (a series of printed sources of data on companies) and the OECD's Industrial Structure Statistic to determine concentration. For some firms it is impossible to construct a concentration measure. A dummy variable is deployed: 'one' is used when no concentration measure is available and 'zero' when there is.

Industrial classifications are assigned to each company in the sample. This initially results in 22 industrial categories; next, those categories with small frequencies are combined with the most similar large industrial category ultimately to give 15 industrial categories. A dummy variable is also included for each of the major industrialised countries in the sample: Italy, France, Canada, Germany, Britain and Japan. The variable corresponding to all other countries is omitted from the regressions.

The variable means and standard deviations are given in a table in that article broken down by ownership type (PC, ME and SOE) and for total sample. Based on the above evidence the authors emphasise that, as far as efficiency is concerned, ownership is the focal/main point rather than competition. Consequently, they criticise this idea that in those industries where no relevant market failures existed, privatisation is not necessary. They argue that those who support this idea emphasise two hypotheses incorrectly. Firstly, it is argued that private firms may not always have maximum efficiency levels, since executives may seek their own personal objectives control them. Secondly, public firms are viewed as efficient because they produce additional sociopolitical outputs that are not pursued by private firms.

In order to test the first argument empirically, the authors surveyed 31 papers in which the difference in efficiency between owner-controlled and manager-controlled private firms was examined. They indicate that efficiency levels are higher in owner-controlled firms. It does not mean that inefficiency resulting from managers pursuing personal agendas must necessarily be equal or higher to that of public firms. The presence of X-inefficiency in both private and public firms is worse when pressure on managers/executives is reduced. Furthermore, the evidence stresses that, if X-inefficiency exists in private firms, it does not necessarily reach the same levels as public firms. However, the authors have not answered the question of why 'the observed inefficiency of public firms is higher than private counterparts'. The second argument is that public firms are inefficient because they pursue desirable social outputs, which is seen by the authors as an excuse for the higher costs of those firms. If this hypothesis were true, it would be possible to assume that the social objectives cannot be achieved by contracting out to private firms.

Millward and Parker (1983) have reviewed the literature on North American companies where public and private firms coincide in electricity, water supply, transport and refuse collection as in Australia, Indonesia and Switzerland. They come to different conclusions from the two previous studies. They conclude that it is hard to find systematic evidence that public enterprises are less cost efficient than private firms. Furthermore, the view that wages are higher in public firms has not been widely supported. Also, differences between public and private firms emerge when price and profitability are a major concern. Some case studies show that public firms have lower prices and higher output levels. However, they emphasise that competition is a key factor for raising efficiency.

Both Borcherding et al. (1982) and Millward and Parker (1983) share the view that in a competitive environment private and public firms do not differ significantly in their economic performance. However, Boardman and Vining (1992: 218) dismiss this idea and argue that 'ownership does matter and there is strong evidence for superior private enterprise performance'. They also claim that even in competitive markets, private firms outperform public ones.

What these empirical studies suggest is that the statement 'private ownership has superiority over public ownership' is questionable. Vickers and Wright (1989: 23) express this idea clearly: 'The evidence does not support any general propositions about the superiority of private over public ownership or vice versa.'

## Empirical studies on privatisation

The World Bank and many other international institutions, as well as a large proportion of the literature, support the idea that privatisation has led to economic and social efficiencies and performance has improved substantially. As Yarrow (1986) acknowledges, the gains achieved without privatisation would have been difficult to sustain. This belief tends to strengthen the view that ownership is important for performance gains as the property right theorists argued.

On the other hand, many theoretical and survey articles predict that competition and deregulation are more important than privatisation (for example, Bishop and Kay, 1989, and Vickers and Yarrow, 1991a). Adding to this list, some studies were conducted to examine how deregulation and, in general, relaxation of the market can affect the performance before privatisation takes place. Pinto et al. (1993) look at the state sector reform that took place in Poland in 1990 over a period of three years. The reform consisted of the deregulation of prices, the introduction of foreign investment to many industries, and the tightening of monetary and fiscal policies. They conclude that hard budget constraints connected to tighter bank lending behaviour can lead to an improvement of performance. Li (1997) found a similar result by looking at the total factor productivity of 272 Chinese state-owned companies over the period 1980–89 and the impact of the economic reforms initiated in 1979.

The evaluation of the effect of privatisation is a very difficult task because it involves several serious methodological constraints (Cook and Kirkpatrick, 1995). The effect of privatisation also covers a broader range of issues from economical to social aspects. For these reasons the assessment can be based on different criteria. Measuring performance can be the most difficult part and there are a variety of methods. One method of assessment is based on the objectives set for the privatisation. A prime objective is the expansion of the private sector and the formation of a market-based economy. This expansion and formation has occurred almost everywhere that Margaret Thatcher established an economic renaissance in Britain. Although the claim that monetarism and privatisation have improved the British economy is open to debate, the privatisation in Britain was founded on purely capitalist reasons and not on the improvement of the British economy (Clarke, 1993).

Macro indicators can be used as criteria to evaluate privatisation performance. Whether privatisation increases government revenue or reduces budget deficits can be one measure of performance. Another indicator is privatisation's impact on investment, including foreign direct investment. A third indicator measures privatisation performance, this time at the micro level, by looking at the enterprise efficiency or profitability. Different criteria have been used to measure efficiency such as profit margin, profit–asset ratio, labour productivity, production and export data, and sales performance. The fourth indicator is to investigate performance in terms of social impact by measuring the level of employment, wages and associated work conditions. The social impact can also be measured by looking at labour redundancy, unemployment and redundancy payment, and related safety provisions as a result of privatisation. The final indicator can measure the impact of privatisation on economic welfare by employing a cost-benefit analysis.

For evaluating the performance of privatised enterprises, two approaches have been widely used. One approach compares the performance before and after privatisation. The second approach compares the performance of those enterprises that are privatised and those that remain under public ownership control. This latter approach presupposes both to be in a similar sector. Both approaches have their advantages and disadvantages, which lead to approximation rather than ideal models (Cook and Kirkpatrick, 1995).

Dunshire et al. (1991) have looked at average annual growth rates of labour and total factor productivity before and after privatisation of a number of British companies and compared these with national trends for four years. The findings reveal that British Aerospace (BAe), a nationalised company, showed a deteriorated performance, while Rolls-Royce, with the same position of ownership, performed much better at that time. They conclude that privatisation led to improvement in the performance of British Airways, BAe and National Freight, while Royal factories showed a reverse result.

The World Bank report (1992) assesses privatisation performance by using the before and after privatisation approach and comes to the conclusion that privatisation has had a positive effect on economic performance. The report points to the success in Latin America (Mexico and Chile), Jamaica, Africa (Nigeria), Asia (Malaysia, Korea) and developed countries (the UK, France, Japan and New Zealand). The main indicators used are welfare and its consequences resulting from privatisation using a cost-benefit analysis. Changes in welfare are represented by the net economic welfare as changes in consumer surplus and enterprise profits. Additionally, increases in investment, improvements in productivity, and output growth and diversification are used to show how economic welfare has improved by privatisation policy. For the case study 12 firms from four countries (Chile, Malaysia, Mexico and the UK) were chosen.

Newberry and Pollitt (1997) have examined restructuring and privatisation of the Central Electricity Board in 1990 using a social cost-benefit analysis. They use an unconventional method by comparing post privatisation performance with the performance result if privatisation had not happened. They conclude that privatisation caused a significant improvement in performance with a permanent cost reduction of 5% per year, equivalent to an extra 40% return on assets. Anderson et al. (1997) conducted an investigation asking what happens to the retail prices when privatisation takes place and what happens to newly privatised companies competing against other private firms in an imperfectly competitive market. They stress that the short-term result will differ from a long-term one. That is because when the disciplinary role of the SOE is abandoned it results in higher prices in the short-term. Hence privatisation in such circumstances is harmful. But the outcome differs in the long-term because the new entry into the industry will lead to a more competitive environment.

Dewenter and Malatesta (1998) have performed a comparable study using a different method. They look at the profitability, labour intensity and debt level of state firms in the 500 largest international companies in 1975, 1985 and 1995. The companies they chose differ from private firms in the same sample. The effect of the business cycle is also considered. They find the same result as the study by Anderson et al.

Frydman et al. (1998b) compare the performance of 128 privatised and 90 state-owned companies in the Czech Republic, Hungary and Poland during 1990–93. They point out that the nature of firms that are privatised and those that remain under control of the state are different; therefore many privatisation studies are misleading. Another reason for error is that in those studies data are not disaggregated sufficiently or controlled for sample bias. As a remedy they examine the average effects of privatisation depending on the ownership structure of the firms and, in order to control potential sample selection bias, they choose fixed-effect models of privatisation based on different control groups and control for the macroeconomic environment. They look at the rate of growth of revenue, employment, labour productivity and costs per unit of output. They find that, on average, privatisation leads to an improvement of performance with immediate increases in revenue and productivity and with no sign of employment effects.

### The most significant empirical studies

Bishop and Kay (1988) have conducted a survey on privatisation performance in the United Kingdom from 1979 to 1988. They conclude that most privatised industries have grown since privatisation. The growth of these industries is more than that of those industries that have remained in public ownership. However, the growth is more related to the nature of the industries concerned than to privatisation alone. Furthermore, those privatised firms that have improved their relative performance were also improving before privatisation.

Bishop and Kay's evaluation of performance is comprised of several factors: profitability margins, represented by return on capital employed; return on sales; employment, and total factor productivity in the UK public sector. Data that are used are based on company accounts and tables containing data from each factor for each company comparing data from 1979 (when the companies were privatised) and 1988. Using all these factors as criteria for measuring the performance of 12 privatised companies and five publicly owned companies, they emphasise that 'The significant improvement in the performance of remaining public sector (Companies under the government control) denies any simple views about the relationship between ownership and performance' (Bishop and Kay, 1988: 653). The main focus of this survey article is market failure and they believe that simply taking enterprises into the private sector does not resolve the problems of market failure.

Bishop and Thompson (1992) have examined the productivity growth over 20 years of the nine largest nationalised industries in the UK, some of them privatised during the 1980s. They find that the rate of productivity growth improved significantly during the 1980s compared with the decade before.

The technique used by Bishop and Thompson to examine productivity growth and public enterprise efficiency is based on Tonqvist's productivity index of growth rates of inputs and outputs. They point out that this procedure is an appropriate measure of technical change and includes efficient pricing mechanism in both input and output markets, constant returns to scale, and achievement of technical efficiency. Output data, labour productivity and total factor productivity over the period of two decades 1970–90 are compared. Changes in public enterprise regulation have been identified significantly as the main source for productivity growth.

Haskel and Szymanski (1993) have tried to conduct an empirical study on privatisation performance in the UK from a different angle. They argue that most agency-based privatisation models are based on the owner–manager relationship and ignore the labour market. However, they present a model of the manager–workforce relationship in order to explain employment and wages when firms are privatised, government objectives become more commercial and markets become liberalised. Their research is based on data over the period of 1972–88 on 14 UK companies which were state-owned enterprises in 1972. They find that changes toward commercial objectives have resulted in the fall of employment and that wages are slightly affected depending on the firms' market power. Wages will fall significantly if a firm loses its market power.

Regression analysis is employed by Haskel and Szymanski to estimate two different equations, one for employment and another for wages. The equations include dummies for changes in objectives. Changes resulting from privatisation, deregulation and liberalisation of markets are seen as the main cause of drastic changes in employment over the period of 1972–88. However, changes in wages are assumed to be a function of the firm's market power. They also criticise most models of privatisation for ignoring the labour market and considering just the agency problem between managers and owners.

Martin and Parker (1995) conducted an investigation on 11 privatised British companies over the period 1981–88 by using profitability, measured as return on invested capital; and efficiency, measured as annual growth in value added per employee hour. They find a variety of results. In some cases privatisation improved the performance of the firm and in many other cases it did not. They also made an adjustment for the business cycle and found some improvements in the outcome. Furthermore, they state that privatisation could improve the performance of some companies for just a short period while privatisation was occurring but not afterwards. In their opinion, a general conclusion cannot be drawn that privatisation can improve performance in every case.

In Martin and Parker's study, labour productivity growth is measured through comparing input and output volumes changes. Hick's neutral technical progress based on a logarithmic form is used to measure total factor productivity (TFP):

$$\log(TFP_t / TFP_{t-1}) = \log(Q_t / Q_{t-1}) - \sum_{t=1}^{4} \left[0.5(V_{it} + V_{i-1}) \log(N_{it} / N_{it-1})\right]$$

where Q is the output; *t* is the time; $V_i$ is share of input *i* in total expenditure; and $N_i$ is the amount of input *i* employed. Comparison is made between each organisation's productivity growth and that of the whole economy where it should be relevant to the manufacturing sector in a short period of four years. Perfect competition, constant return to scale and the absence of externalities are assumed. The adopted procedure is accepted despite their belief that the measuring processes introduce several different distortions. They point out: 'In sum, the method adopted for measuring total factor productivity provides a useful insight into changes in productive efficiency even though the results below need to be interpreted cautiously recognising the possibility of some input bias and output omissions' (Martin and Parker, 1995: 206).

Martin and Parker's conclusion is interesting, particularly in view of the methodology used. They observe that 'privatisation is not the only factor, and may not be the main factor, affecting performance ... mixed results seem to confirm that privatisation does not guarantee good performance' (1995: 216). They also stress that

> those organisations that operated in regulated markets do not seem to have performed noticeably better or worse than those operating in more competitive markets. The best performance overall was associated British Ports which won back business from other UK docks. The worst performer was Jaguar which also operates in a competitive market. (1995: 217)

Apart from UK studies, there are three main international studies on privatisation, by Megginson et al. (1994), Galal et al. (1992) and Ehrlich et al. (1994). Megginson et al. (1994) have conducted a comparative study by using the pre- and post- privatisation financial and operating performance of 61 companies from 18 countries – six developing and 12 developed – including 32 industries that privatised fully or partially during the period 1961–90. They emphasise that privatisation has led to an increase in the level of employment. Since the time that these changes have taken place, the firms' real sales, profitability, capital investment, spending, operating efficiency and workforces have increased.

The data collected are limited to those companies that were sold to the public through the issuance of shares. A sample of the firms is drawn from the World Bank listing of privatised firms. The impact of privatisation is examined by different performance criteria. Profitability, which is the first testable measure, is represented by return on sales (net income/sales), return on assets (net income/total assets) and return on equity (net income/equity). Operating efficiency is measured by sale efficiency (sales/number employed) and net income efficiency (net income/number employed). Capital invested is presented by capital expenditures to sales (capital expenditures/sales) and capital expenditures to assets (capital expenditures/assets). Output is measured by real sales (nominal sales/consumer price index). Employment is represented by total employment. Debt to assets ratio (total debt/total assets) and long-term debt to equity ratio (long-term debt/equity) are assumed to predict leverage. Dividends to sales (cash dividends/net income) represent payout as the last variable. Data from these quantifiable variables are collected in order to compare the pre-privatisation with the post-privatisation era. The mean and median of each variable are assumed to show what happened to the performance of each company. The fact that privatisation has led to such a significant improvement in the performance of those firms has been explained by the inefficiency of public enterprises and the fact that they are not market-oriented.

Galal et al. (1992) have examined a comparative study of 12 large firms from Britain, Chile, Malaysia, Indonesia and Mexico. They compare the actual post-privatisation performance with the predicted performance of those firms if they had remained under state ownership. They argue that this method allows a social welfare analysis to be achieved. They emphasise that, on average, the net welfare gain in 11 out of 12 cases are reached and that in no case did workers lose out. They also argue that the study has shown that ownership is significant and a privatisation policy is beneficial.

For each country they have used three companies taken from the fields of aviation, energy, telecommunications, transportation and shipping, and gambling. In fact they conducted three case studies for each country. The method that is used for calculating welfare gain is the same in all case studies. All of the data are presented in terms of both current and constant prices. They argue that 'constructing constant-prices time series' for all relevant variables provides a position from which to examine the performance of the enterprise. Two measures of performance are used: the first is total factor productivity (TFP), which is estimated by this equation:

$$TFP = \text{benefit/all costs} = X \,/\, (II + W + R + rk^{w} + rk^{f})$$

where $X$ is the value of output, $II$ is the value of intermediate inputs, $W$ is employee comparison, $R$ is factor rentals, $rk^w$ is the opportunity cost of working capital and $rk^f$ is opportunity cost of fixed capital.

The second measure of performance is obtained by a formula called public profitability.

Public profitability = (benefit – variable costs) / fixed costs = $(X - II - W - R - rk) / k^f$.

Public profit is calculated by this equation:

Public profit = $X - II - W - R - rk^w$.

The authors argued that TFP and public profitability capture only efficiency effects that accrue to the enterprise itself. From a social point of view, traditional consumer surplus should be measured in order to capture the impact of the enterprise's activity on consumers. Through this kind of procedure they attempted to calculate social welfare gains from selling public enterprises. They point out that a policy of divesting public enterprises will result in welfare gains because public enterprises are subject to inefficiency. However, the results of the study cannot be used as a predictive model, especially in very poor countries or in the former centrally planned economies.

Ehrlich et al. (1994) conduct a study on the international airline industry looking at the effects of ownership on productivity growth and cost reductions. They have concluded that the long-term effect of a change (that is, a shift from complete state to full private ownership) can lead to an improvement in the long-run annual rate of TFP growth by 1.6–2%. Additionally, the rate of unit cost can decline by 1.7% to 1.9%. In contrast, they expect the short-run effect of a change from state to private ownership on the TFP and cost levels to be ambiguous.

An endogenous model is used to test panel data on 23 international airlines of varying levels of state ownership over the period 1973–83. Econometric techniques are employed with some observations as follows:

1. The short-term effect of ownership changes is separated from long-term effects.
2. The estimated ownership effect is isolated from other factors that might affect the firm's level or rate of productivity growth (for example, market conditions and external technical factors).
3. Testing to the extent permitted by the data is performed.

Total factor productivity indices are also calculated as the ratios of total output and input indices. Dummy variables are included to capture the effects of regulatory changes. Also firm and country-specific variables are represented by dummy variables to capture the possible effect of country-specific technology levels and progress on the level and rate of cost decline. A cost function, which is consistent with the Cobb-Douglas technology, is used to estimate cost fluctuations over the specific period. They found that productivity growth and cost reduction are functions of ownership, proving the point that ownership plays a key factor in performance.

In summary, therefore, the bulk of existing empirical studies on ownership and performance focus on private and public firms' relative efficiency. They are based, in a majority of cases, on cross-sectional data without taking into account firm-specific and unobservable features that complicate and sometimes even invalidate the firm comparisons. This may be one of the reasons for the lack of systematic results arising from these studies. By contrast, studies analysing the effects of privatisation on the firm performance use time series data, which overcomes the problem of unobservable firm-specific effects. In general, these studies indicate that privatisation is positively associated with performance improvement. Difficulties arise, however, in distinguishing among the effects on efficiency that results from the change in ownership, the change in market competition and the change in the firm's regulatory framework.

## A critical assessment

It should be noted that comparing performance over a period of time as a method of measuring corporate performance (as was done in these studies) makes it difficult to determine how much of the improvement resulted specifically from privatisation.

The above empirical evidence shows tremendous achievements by privatised companies in some cases. These achievements are doubtless the result of maximising profit, developing new methods of production, expanding qualities and enhancing sales. However, it is understandable that some profitability procedures are now available which were not available under public ownership, such as increasing prices, selling assets, reducing manpower and abandoning services, which are not profitable. As Marsh (1991: 469) stresses, 'a common consequence of privatisation is increased prices to customers'. Clarke (1993: 217) puts the matter in a broader way: 'if they had abandoned their commitments to social responsibility, the former public corporations could have recorded higher profits by precisely these means at any time, though whether this would have benefited the wider economy or society is open to question'.

Matthews and Minford (1987) doubt the profitability of the privatised firms in the UK and ask for further enquiries in order to indicate where the extra profits came from. Hence the claim that privatisation leads to a consumer democracy with freedom of choice is an open question for further investigation that involves a comparison of price indices before and after privatisation. In this regard, Clarke (1993: 221) claims that 'in fact, consumer complaints increased markedly in almost all the privatised companies as consumers found they were paying more for services which often had been reduced'.

It is important to recognise that the public enterprise that is subject to privatisation must have been commercially profitable at least in the last period before privatisation took place; otherwise, it would not be attractive to buyers. Fine (1997b: 389) points out that 'in many ways, the industries' experience before privatisations can be described as a period of successful restoration to commercial viability. Something that has to occur in any case before the private sector would be willing to purchase them.' Thus the above empirical studies that makes comparisons before and after privatisation or that compare those companies that are privatised with those that remain under state control do not show the whole story. Even if collected data are chosen carefully and the results are interpreted cautiously, many factors that can affect the outcome directly are still ignored.

It is necessary to consider some critical conceptual issues relating to the measurement of the performance of public enterprises. For simplification, we will look at two categories: (1) profitability and (2) measurement concerning efficiency. Profitability is the most conventional measure of performance of both sectors. However, there is no single criterion by which profitability can be measured. Different types of criteria have been used; for example, operating surplus, return on equity, and so on (Chang and Singh, 1993). Despite the fact that profitability is widely used, the question as to whether profitability is a reliable indicator for measuring performance, even for private enterprises, may arise. The following considerations suggest that the answer is no. Accounting procedures have an important effect on profitability measurement (see Edwards et al. 1987). Bishop and Kay (1988: 5) emphasise this problem: 'calculation of profits over a short period may be substantially influenced by arbitrariness in accounting conventions, changes in accounting conventions, or actions taken to reconstruct company balance sheets'. The second problem is that short-term profitability may not be a useful indicator for long-term performance. For example, share prices cannot be a good indicator for profitability in the long-run, since share prices may be influenced by short-term considerations. To overcome this problem, it might be better to use the average rates of return for a certain number of years dealing with an enterprise's performance (Chang and Singh, 1993).

The question of how profitability relates to public enterprise must be considered, since the main purpose for the establishment of public enterprise has not been making a profit (Millward, 1982). Many public enterprises are created by, as Vernon (1981b: 14) stresses, 'shifting economic power from the leaders of big business in the private sector to leaders elsewhere, such as leaders of government or leaders of labour'. Other reasons for establishing public enterprises might be regional development or helping a certain ethnic group. Achieving macroeconomic objectives, maintaining employment at a certain level, public enterprise investment, and using public enterprise pricing policy as a device against inflation in certain periods, can all be added to this list (see Millward, 1982). Moreover, public enterprises are often used by the government to promote private industries; for example, lower prices of inputs like steel and electricity (Chang and Singh, 1993). As a result, profitability alone cannot be used as an indicator for measuring the performance of public enterprises. Publicly owned enterprises that make no profit or sometimes make a loss are not necessarily performing badly.

Profitability cannot be a reliable indicator for measuring public enterprise performance because many factors that do not contribute to profitability have a great influence on public enterprise performance. Firstly, public enterprises differ across countries – they may perform very efficiently in one country, but not in another. That may be due, for example, to institutional reasons or less skilful managers, and so on. Secondly, external macroeconomic shocks such as severely constrained foreign exchange during a certain period of time can seriously affect public enterprise. Thirdly, some large public enterprises were originally private enterprises, but became nationalised when they faced bankruptcy (clear examples are the German car manufacturer, Volkswagen, and the British lorry manufacturer, Leyland, which were rescued by their governments from bankruptcy). Fourthly, public enterprises may operate in the 'wrong' industries for a particular reason, for example, in the coal industry in western Europe in order to maintain a certain level of employment. Finally, the public enterprise's own characteristic such as size, market power and age may have a great influence on performance (Chang and Singh, 1993).

All of the defects related to profitability as an indicator have been recognised by many economists. For these reasons, they have tried to use other procedures for measuring performance of public or private enterprises. One procedure, which has been used in many empirical studies of public and private enterprises, is called technical efficiency, which involves looking at whether more or less inputs are used for a unit of output for different firms regardless of their ownership. This type of procedure is used at different levels; for example, a country, an industry, a firm size. The most popular methods in this basis are the use of an appropriate production function and total factor productivity measurement. However, technical efficiency is dismissed by many economists as a performance indicator because there is no obvious method of constructing quantity indices for inputs and outputs of multiproduct firms, on the one hand, and there are difficulties related to quality differences between products of different firms, on the other hand. To overcome those difficulties, another indicator measuring cost per unit of output, which is called cost efficiency, is introduced. However, this creates problems of a different sort. Different prices of different inputs for different firms at different times are serious enough to undermine this indicator as much as the quantity indices and quality differences do the former (see Cook and Kirkpatrick, 1988b).

This analysis has revealed that all the performance indicators, which have been used in empirical studies, involve various measurement problems. Furthermore, apart from all the technical defects related to various indicators, it is important to realise that these methods are based on the neo-classical approach which, as mentioned earlier, suffers seriously from some unrealistic assumptions, such as constant returns to scale, perfect market competition and no externalities (see Fine, 1980). Given those technical problems and unrealistic assumptions, I believe that measuring the performance of public versus private enterprises should not rely on the kinds of measurement procedures discussed here.

## Conclusion

The outcome of comparison between public and private sectors in terms of their relative performance is mixed. Bishop and Thompson (1992) in their study on the privatisation impact in the UK dismiss the idea that the result is always positive and improved productivity is the inevitable result. The main consideration is whether indeed privately owned enterprises perform better than publicly owned, and privatisation is a preferable economic policy in all circumstances, while the comparisons of performance of public versus private enterprises are beset with difficulties. Other studies are based on different methodologies and the performance measurements vary substantially. Different procedures have also been used; some compare the performance of public enterprises with private, while some compare the performance before and after privatisation.

Privatisation should be seen as a broader economic and social policy. The claim that privatisation will enhance economic efficiency is a very narrow and defective statement. Parker (1998: 11) emphasises that

> privatisation and related market liberalisation are industrial policies only in a negative sense. Whereas in earlier years in some member states the state was seen as having an instrumental role in industrial development, privatisation and market liberalisation imply essentially that the state's role should be limited to defining and protecting private property rights. Undoubtedly, privatisation involves a shift in property rights and therefore economic power.

As Clarke (1993: 212) claims,

> at British steel this involved a cut in workers from 166,000 to 52,000 a reduction in government external funding from £1,119 million to £24 million achieving a net profit of £178 million instead of a net loss of £1,784 million on a similar £3,000 million turnover.

In terms of defining appropriate measurements of performance of both public and private enterprises, it should be stressed that the criteria that are used mostly favour the private sector. These cause further difficulties since it is known that the public sector may operate subject to other constraints than the private sector. State industries were established across the world, not with the aim of pursuing their own efficiency, but instead looking at wider goals. This priority, which is different from private goals, creates a complication in comparing these two sectors. Associated with that, the impact of privatisation becomes much more complicated when there is no common agreement on what constitutes successful performance (Parker, 1998). Privatisation studies have been concentrating on the issue of productivity efficiency, while the other impacts like income distribution or other social welfare implications are ignored (Parker, 1998).

The comparative performance of public and private sector enterprises do not show that the public sector enterprises are less efficient than the private enterprises. As Chang and Singh (1992: 42) emphasise,

> there exist neither compelling theoretical reasons nor unambiguous empirical evidence. for either developed or developing countries suggesting the pervasive 'inefficiency' of public enterprises. The picture is far more complex than one of 'efficient' private enterprises versus inefficient public enterprises.

Parker (1998: 34) stresses that

> more generally, research cautions against drawing simple conclusions about public versus private ownership. There is a body of theoretical and empirical evidence, which suggest that market for corporate control is likely to be a weak deterrent against inefficiency, especially in large private sector firms.

It is hard to make substantial improvements happen when privatisation takes place. There are many restrictions in practice, which limit chances at least in the short-term period. Parker (1998: 35) emphasises that 'certainly improvement in economic performance following privatisation are less likely the more difficult it is to make substantial changes in the way enterprises are managed and operated'. Chang and Singh (1993: 45) claim that 'The finding is that there is no clear-cut evidence that public ownership necessarily results in inferior performance.' If this claim is the case then privatisation as an economic stratagem to improve the efficiency of public enterprises would be of doubtful value. The available evidence on performance of public versus private enterprises fails to prove that public enterprises are inherently less efficient than private enterprises. If so, the hypothesis brought forward by all those theories can be regarded as rejected.

# 4
# Why Factor Analysis?

## Introduction

The purpose of this chapter is to define why factor analysis has been used for measuring corporate performance in the context of privatisation. Measuring corporate performance is complex and controversial, with different theories suggesting different approaches. The most widely used approach is the neo-classical, present in nearly all university textbooks for several decades (Parker, 1998). This approach relies on some strong assumptions such as perfect competition, no externalities in the market and constant returns to scale, and it has been subject to the Cambridge capital critique.

Apart from its appropriate and immediate dismissal of the neo-classical approach to measuring performance, the critique points to serious issues in measuring and comparing corporate performance. They involve fundamental questions around the understanding of performance in capitalist economies. What are the appropriate methods for determining the processes of production, distribution and accumulation? Prior to empirical investigation, the meaning of price and the source of value need to be considered. Paradoxically, the Cambridge critique had the effect of narrowing down the question to one of whether capital is quantifiable or not. This has been an issue since 1950, but neo-classical theory has continued its dominance regardless of its lack of sound foundations in this respect.

Parallel to these theoretical confrontations about fundamental economic issues, the neo-classical approach suggests the total factor productivity method for measuring corporate performance. I will focus on the total factor productivity method in order to reveal its main advantages and disadvantages regarding the measurement of corporate performance. This will reveal the reason I do not use total factor productivity and I have a preference for using factor analysis instead.

In short, neo-classical theory, especially in its one-sector version as the basis for measuring economic/corporate performance through total factor productivity draws upon a particular and questionable understanding of the capitalist economy and even accepts the (invalid) one-sector model of the economy.

The assessment of performance of private versus public sector and the effects of privatisation are difficult with several heavy methodological problems. The first difficulty concerns the measurement of performance in principle. In practice, performance has mainly been considered in terms of the objectives of private capital. An alternative method is to evaluate private performance in terms of macroeconomic targets. In this regard, one of the main objectives of privatisation is the reduction of the budget deficit through contributing to government revenue through receipts and elimination of public enterprise deficits.

The second frequently used measurements of private versus public sector and privatisation performance are in terms of economic efficiency or financial profitability. In both cases, a range of indicators can be used in assessing performance of privatised enterprises, for instance, profit margins, profit–asset ratios, labour productivity, sales and export performance. Another approach to measuring the consequences of privatisation is to look at outcomes in terms of social impact. Here the main concern is employment, wage levels and associated employment-related benefits. A significant issue is labour redundancy resulting from privatisation and the cost of unemployment and redundancy payments, and related safety-net provisions. Finally, performance can be considered more broadly in terms of the effect on economic welfare. A cost-benefit approach is relevant. This requires the contribution of different effects to be measured in terms of a common unit of measurement and aggregated to give a single, overall impact of privatisation.

Privatisation has inevitably reduced state ownership in many countries and has had an effect on global stock markets. Enthusiasm for it can be summarised as follows: firstly, it is assumed that privately owned firms outperform SOEs, and, secondly, that governments have usually raised significant revenues through the sale of SOEs.

Thus the rationale behind privatisation in many parts of the world is that private ownership improves corporate performance. A study by Megginson et al. (1994) compares the pre- and post-privatisation performance of selected privatised firms. Other studies, which compare the performance of state-owned firms with either private or privatised firms operating under reasonably similar conditions, have shown performance after privatisation to be much more efficient (Boardman and Vining, 1989; Pohl et al., 1997). Djankov et al. (1997) show that privatisations in the west have sometimes had dramatic effects on performance: British Steel, for example, is reported to have reduced its payroll by 40% prior to privatisation without losing any revenues; British Airways reduced its labour force by the same percentage, while actually increasing the number of flights. On the other hand, many other past and current studies in transition economies and developing countries show the reverse. For instance, a study based on a panel of over 200 privatised and state firms in the Czech Republic, Hungary and Poland, casts some doubt on the claims previously advanced in the literature (Frydman et al., 1998a). These mixed results have cast a shadow over theoretical and empirical claims in favour of superiority of private over public sector as well as privatisation.

Privatisation is often justified on grounds of efficiency itself categorised as productive, allocative and dynamic. Allocative efficiency has received less attention than productive efficiency. Neo-classical economics, for instance, is much concerned with productive efficiency and associated with static gains rather than allocative efficiency and dynamic gains (Parker, 1998). Allocative efficiency is tied more to the competitive environment than to issues of ownership. For this reason, when a monopoly firm is privatised, there are potential risks of allocative inefficiency. As a remedy, governments have formed regulatory bodies to restrict monopoly power and protect consumer interests. Whether this remedy has succeeded is highly controversial, and the results are mixed across sectors and countries (Parker, 1998).

This chapter is organised as follows: the second section is devoted to the neo-classical approach including the total factor productivity procedure. Fundamentals of the neo-classical approach as a benchmark for understanding the measurement of total factor productivity will be discussed. It measures the residual through the relation between inputs and outputs over a certain period of time, whether at firm, sector or national level. This procedure has been criticised from different angles. The next section considers various criticisms of the neo-classical approach. It consists of three parts covering internal critiques: the Cambridge critique, limitations of the latter and more fundamental criticisms of the neo-classical approach.

The penultimate section provides an informal description of factor analysis. It is a statistical technique used to identify a relatively small number of factors in place of many interrelated variables. Since measuring corporate performance is highly complex and dependent upon highly correlated indices, factor analysis is a useful tool for identifying patterns of performance. In the final section, the conclusion will briefly summarise, including the rationale for my preferred way of measuring corporate performance.

## The neo-classical approach

Concentrating on neo-classical capital theory demonstrates how this theory treats different variables involved in the production process, and, how the relation between variables is determined. An aggregate production function represents the relationship between the output, $Y$, and inputs. In a one-good world it is supposed that inputs consist only of capital $K$ and labour $L$, with the product, $Y$, being the same as $K$. Represented in mathematical terms, $Y = F\ (K,\ L)$. Consequently, the logic behind an aggregated production is to represent the product economy as a whole by this simple formula.

From this, the validity of the neo-classical approach can be assessed, although many critics from different points of view find disadvantages in the whole approach. The main difficulty arises when the relative proportions of inputs and outputs do not remain constant. For according to the above formula, the measurement of outputs and inputs must be done by single indices. At this stage it can be observed, quite apart from the narrow technical deficiencies of representing an economy in this way, that the approach ignores the broader social content of the processes.

Based on the assumptions of diminishing marginal products, constant returns to scale and perfect competition, the relation between output and capital can be reduced to per capita terms $y = f(k)$ and the profit rate determined by $f'(k)$ and wages by $w = f(k) - kf''(k)$. Increasing capital per worker leads to an increase in output per worker but not in the same proportion, since the slope of the production function declines as capital increases. On the other hand, as the capital per worker increases, the rate of profit decreases. From this technical analysis a significant economic proposition can be reached: technological relations (explicitly the production function $f$ and $k$ in use) alone can determine distribution.

The neo-classical propositions can be summarised as:

1. a negative relation between the rate of profit and capital per worker
2. a negative relation between the rate of profit and the capital – output ratio

3. a negative relation between the rate of profit and sustainable steady-state levels of consumption per head
4. in a competitive environment, the marginal productivity theory is able to determine the distribution of income between wage earners and profit-receivers.

### Total factor productivity

Studies of total factor productivity (TFP) have blossomed since Solow's (1957) classic contribution. From the mid-1970s, studies of the quality of labour and capital inputs attracted great interest. The early 1990s witnessed a renewal of interest in studies of TFP. In the earlier literature, the most commonly used production functions in estimating TFP were the Cobb–Douglas function, CES (constant elasticity of substitution) and occasionally VES (variable elasticity of substitution). But nowadays increasingly popular is the transcendental logarithmic production function or, more simply, the translog production function of Christensen et al. (1973) and Chen (1997). The translog production function is specified as follows:

$$\begin{aligned} Y = \exp[&a_0 + a_L \ln L + a_T T + 1/2\, \beta_{KK} (\ln K)^2 + \beta_{KL} \ln K \ln L \\ &+ \beta_{KK} T \cdot \ln K + 1/2\, \beta_{LL} (\ln L)^2 + \beta_{LT} \ln L \cdot T + \Omega \beta_{TT} T^2] \end{aligned}$$

It shows the relationship between output and an exponential function of the logarithms of inputs. Comparison of the Cobb-Douglas function, the CES production function and the translog production function shows that the latter is more general. The reasons for this are twofold: firstly, it is not constrained by the restriction of constant elasticity of substitution and, secondly, it provides a theoretical justification for the use of average factor shares in the calculation of productivity growth. It uses data at discrete points of time to estimate the production function.

Both supporters and critics of the neo-classical school of thought have critically assessed the credibility and reliability of the TFP procedure for measuring the growth of a single corporation, a particular sector of the economy, or the national economy. I consider both sets of views in order to assess the TFP approach.

## Critiques against the neo-classical total factor productivity approach

### Insider critiques

Despite some favourable technical properties, the translog production function poses serious problems of factor input measurement (Creamer, 1972). Capital input measurement is the first and most serious problem.

It involves the determination of capital deflators, the methods used for determining depreciation, the allocation of capacity adjustments, capital valuation and the content of the capital inputs and the level of aggregation/disaggregation. The choice of the content of capital input should determine the type of price deflators to be used in making quality change adjustments, and factor and prices, which are often estimated on the basis of various assumptions for lack of readily available data, are necessary since value shares must be estimated as weights (Creamer, 1972).

The use of capital is inevitably based on a particular situation and time period, not least over business cycles of different periodicity. The residual or TFP might be thought to be understated if excess capacity is understated. This, in turn, could significantly affect the relative importance of capital as a source of economic growth. With this in mind, various studies have adopted different methods.

Kendrick and Creamer (1961) and Denison (1962) made no specific adjustment for capacity utilisation of capital. Solow (1957, 1963) and Jorgenson and Griliches (1967) used the unemployment rate as a measure of underutilisation of capital and Griliches (1964) used the power utilisation rate as a measure. In making a utilisation adjustment, it is important to determine whether it spreads over all capital sub-inputs or only to some categories, such as non-residential structures and producer goods (Creamer, 1972). A third difficulty involves the choice between gross capital or net of depreciation. Gross capital was used by Denison (1962), Solow (1957, 1963) and (Creamer, 1972). Some stress that the adoption of net measures of capital increases the risk of overstating depreciation. Thirlwall (1972) observes that obsolescence rather than physical deterioration is possible to override feature of depreciation. He stresses that capital turns out to be economically obsolete before it losses its physical usefulness, while obsolete equipment is still capable of contributing to production. This will result in flow of capital service remains in use despite reaching the ended age at the rate frequently suggested by allowances for depreciation. Adjusting capital for physical depreciation rather than obsolescence is usually not possible in practice. If overdepreciation occurs, it will overstate the residual or TFP.

However, these issues reflect deeper problems derived from the limitations of the approach itself. On the one hand, the one-factor model with its battery of supporting assumptions is incapable of incorporating the real processes of the business cycle, economic obsolescence and technologies that might be chosen in the knowledge that excess capacity will prevail from time to time. On the other hand, the very presence of these phenomena indicates that the theoretical assumptions are inconsistent with those used to construct the data set by which TFP is measured in practice. This, then, is not simply a matter of practical difficulties in constructing a data set, but of the underlying understanding of the economy itself.

A third problem is that physical capital cannot be measured directly. Indirect measurement, in turn, involves two possible valuations, namely resource-cost or user-value. The commonly used approach is to value capital at resource-cost because of data availability. Both valuations highlight changes in cost, which may represent quality improvement in the capital input, while the value of capital in the translog production function approach shifts away from 'non-proportionality' and 'embodiment'. As a result, there is always a risk of underestimating the value of capital when 'non-proportional' quality improvements occur. An explicit example of this is the increase in revenue resulting from a technological innovation of a capital good that is greater than an increase in the selling price. Gordon (1990) suggests that the above differences should embody nominal price changes. Another solution provided by Denison (1962) provides that changes in the quality of capital based on non-proportionality are included in the 'residual' TFP rather than in the measurement of the capital output. Thirlwall (1972) argues that valuing capital as resource-cost can be problematical; for example, when items used for producing other items cost twice as much, these in turn represent twice as much capital, which would not be reflected in the price index.

The importance of technological change embodied in the newer capital input, which is part of quality change, was emphasised in the earlier literature on productivity studies by Solow (1957), Phelps (1962) and Bliss (1968). The embodiment hypothesis is one way of viewing heterogeneity in labour input. The growth accounting approach, as used in many studies, has been adjusted according to the age–sex composition of the labour force and the level of education. Unlike the valuation of capital input, in which the resource-cost is a commonly used measure, the user-value approach is adopted when adjustments take place for education. Differences in income earned by different categories of the labour force are treated as a quality adjustment based on different levels of education. A study by Denison (1962) points out that 60% of the difference in income is related to education, while another study by Griliches (1970) assumes that education explains 100% of income differences.

All the points above indicate that TFP, which, however, is a residual restricted in theory to disembodied, exogenous and Hicks-neutral technological change in growth accounting, is in practice an umbrella for deviations from unrealistic assumptions and corresponding adjustments in data set construction (quite apart from errors in data). If capital and labour are measured wrongly, as in a sense they must be, the corresponding quality changes (including embodied technological change) will also turn up in the residual. As a result, the residual is no longer solely disembodied technological change but contains embodied technological change and other quality improvements.

It has long been transparent that the measurement of TFP for any economy is subject to all kinds of theoretical and measurement errors. The methodology used and the ways that factor inputs are aggregated and measured have a substantial impact on the measurement of TFP and its correspondingly chaotic meaning or content. Jorgenson and Griliches (1967) have at an early stage argued that TFP is a consequence of mismeasurement of factor inputs and therefore does not really exist as long as all inputs are fully and correctly measured. They made the following adjustments on the contribution of input growth to output growth:

1. disaggregating the price index for capital to obtain a better measure of capital input
2. correcting capacity utilisation of capital
3. taking flow prices for capital and labour services into account to obtain better measures of quality of capital and labour inputs.

After these corrections, Jorgenson and Griliches (1967) found that very little residual (only 3.3% of it remained). On the other hand, if one does not make any adjustment to the measurement of capital and labour inputs, all the quality improvements and measurement errors will show up in the residual or TFP. But, as already suggested, the problems with TFP fundamentally derive not from measurement problems but from the underlying theory. Even if data could be perfect, TFP measurement would remain invalid.

## The Cambridge critique

The neo-classical model has been subject to the Cambridge critique. This section will establish whether this critique provides a valid alternative to the neo-classical model or not; that is, does it offer anything to replace what it has criticised?

Sraffa (1960) stresses that there is no measure of capital independent of distribution and prices, thereby undermining neo-classical theory in its different aspects such as the production function, and theories of supply, distribution and growth. A very precise question is: how is capital measured? Joan Robinson (1953) posed the challenge of what constitutes 'capital'. This challenge was left unanswered until 1960, when Sraffa reached the conclusion that there is no independent measure of 'capital'. He rejected a physical measure except for a particular sort of capital, which contains a single good or a uniform bundle of goods. He emphasised that a prior set of relative prices causes an aggregate price measure of capital to be unsuccessful. Moreover, aggregate production functions depend on 'capital' as a single factor, whereas capital goods, including fixed capital, are heterogeneous.

Robinson (1975a: vi) clearly recognises that the initial problem is not the measurement of 'capital', but the writer's way of thinking about it – whether he or she is concentrating on institutional frameworks or social relationship nature of capitalism, in other words. These propositions, at least in principle, have long been accepted by neo-classical economists, although the practice is otherwise.

Significantly, Sraffa (1960) has a different viewpoint. He sees the main problem as being that capital is 'concerned exclusively with such properties of an economic system as do not depend on change in the scale of production or in the proportions of "factors"'. This immediately reflects that we are dealing with a level of abstraction that eliminates continuous changes in real economic systems. Changes are introduced to the economic system during one 'year' as a fixed time for producing commodities and distributing them. Economic relationships are examined over this period of time alone. Because of this, Sraffa found the assumption of constant returns totally unnecessary. This elimination of variations in scale in 'factors' is sufficient for the author to rule out marginal productivity of inputs as determining outcomes. But it offers a weak alternative in its place.

Formally, of course, Sraffa's contribution has given rise to models with constant returns to scale and linear, input–output technology. These have, however, played little role in measuring economic performance, certainly by comparison with TFP, and are fully compatible with neo-classical economics as a special case (as in the non-substitution theory).

Significantly, Robinson (1974, 1979, 1980) and Bhaduri and Robinson (1980) dismissed Sraffian 'values' or 'prices of production' and argued that the nature of these terms in his analysis could not be incorporated into a theory set in historical time. At best it is an example of comparative statistics. Robinson (1980: 134) rejects timeless comparative-static analysis and stresses that 'it is a mistake in methodology to compare two technical systems … and then to switch one to the other'.

Thus, whilst the Cambridge critique challenges the neo-classical approach, it remains defective in offering any alternative especially for the measurement of economic performance.

## The main criticisms

The problem with the neo-classical approach and the methodology it uses for TFP measurement, whether at the level of a corporate performance or at a national level, is that its assumptions are or cannot be met. The result is a mish-mash of measurement. For example, Fine (1992: 282) argues that

> since factor shares are, by marginal productivity theory, to measure factor contribution to output, it is necessary to assume that the economy is perfectly competitive, for otherwise TFP will be measuring the monopoly position within particular markets, rather than real contribution to output, and/or TFP will be measuring changes in the level of capacity utilisation in the absence of full employment.

One of the most significant aspects of any corporate performance measurement is the quality of the commodities produced. In the neo-classical procedure for measuring corporate performance, quality has been set aside when adjusted by price changes. However, quality should be part of measuring corporate performance and, on a national level, should be part of the residual and labour inputs (Fine, 1992). This restriction of quality of inputs and outputs will be explored by concentrating on mathematical approaches that are part of any neo-classical framework. The mathematical form does not leave room for qualitative changes. Failure to consider qualitative changes, in any measurement, casts a shadow over the results based on such a framework. The quality itself simply reflects changes in technologies in use in any production. If these were ignored, how could one expect the resulting measurements to take all different aspects of the whole production process into account? One way to avoid this problem, even if we do not agree with any single-good model, is to use value instead of physical quantities, as Fine (1992: 284) suggests:

> within the method already adopted for the measurement of heterogeneous capital stock, there is the obvious solution of measuring output in value rather than physical quantities. This should then take account of quality differences in output.

In terms of capital stock, the value of the output index needs to be deflated according to the level of inflation. Inflation and other adjustments are ignored by the neo-classical procedure and, as a result, the capital stock and its value remain constant through time. Again, even if we do not agree with the one-good model, it may be possible to provide an inflation index as a remedy. However, whether two corporate performances are being compared or the performance at a national level is being measured, this remedy would be effective only if markets were perfectly competitive (Fine, 1992: 283). Fine states:

> It has been shown that, even within the one-good economy, the measurement of output in physical terms without a price evaluation still requires, in principle, perfect competition in the sector concerned. Thus, it is legitimate to examine competition in the production of output as well as in the purchase of factor inputs. (Fine, 1992: 286)

He also acknowledges that 'the laissez-faire model [is] essential to support the use of TFP methods'.

Another point which needs to be considered is the validity of the marginal product of labour, even in a one-good model. Again, the use of TFP or other neo-classical procedure requires a perfectly competitive market for labour in which wages will remain in balance between employees. Otherwise, different wages for different parties undermine the whole process of finding the marginal productivity of labour as the source of the distribution.

For all these reasons, the use of TFP for measuring corporate performance is problematic and misleading. Hence I turn to another approach, factor analysis, which is arguably less problematic.

## Defining different aspects of factor analysis

The purpose of this section is to describe factor analysis performance and why it can contribute to the assessment of corporate performance. Generally, factor analysis is applicable across many different problems and contexts and as such it involves no economic theory. Factor analysis is merely a means of organising data descriptively. In other words, it poses questions rather than starting with preconceived assumptions or hypotheses.

Factor analysis determines which variables are correlated with one another. Thurstone first introduced the term in 1931. He used it for three main purposes:

1. to determine which variables mutually reflect an underlying characteristic

2. to reduce a large number of variables to a smaller set
3. to help thereby to make sense of the complexity of social behaviour by reducing it to a limited number of factors (Thurstone, 1931).

In this light, let us examine the advantages (and disadvantages) of factor analysis in broad principle and in the context of our study. Firstly, as already discussed, measurement of total factor productivity as a technique for assessing economic and corporate performance is invalid in principle, quite apart from the empirical problems that arise in practice in terms of measuring inputs and outputs, especially against the assumptions of a single good, full employment of all factors, and perfectly competitive markets for them. Measuring total factor productivity does not depend upon use of econometric estimation, but regression can be used to estimate a production function in which a trended constant term represents productivity increase. This indicates that TFP measurement does depend upon an underlying economic theory even if it is not always explicitly tested statistically.

Factor analysis does not posit any theory except in the weakest sense of including some variables and excluding others although this is often a matter of pragmatism in terms of data availability. This is an advantage for two reasons. Firstly, economic theories of corporate performance suggest that there is a very wide range of possible outcomes and relationships between variables according to specific circumstances (initial conditions, the 'game' being played and the strategies adopted) so that one theory is not liable to be validated across a wide range of data. Secondly, there is likely to be substantial multicollinearity across the variables characterising and explaining corporate performance. For these reasons, although it does handle a large number of variables simultaneously, multiple regression is likely to be inappropriate. It tests a single theory and is weakened statistically by the presence of multicollinearity. By contrast, factor analysis is a simple device for examining regularities between corporate characteristics, irrespective of how they have been produced. In a sense, it cuts across a range of models and, in the case of our own topic of interest, asks the simple question of whether private or public ownership is associated with differences in corporate outcomes. This is its strength. It investigates what is to be explained. Its weakness is that it does not itself offer an explanation, although it can suggest answers, as is the case for any organised descriptive interrogation of data. Thus, suppose that private firms do perform better than public. This might be because public firms do tend to perform better than private but are always privatised whenever successful (although this might also be examined in factor analysis by including a variable reflecting history of ownership; see below). The point is not whether this hypothesis is correct or not, but merely to demonstrate that the explanation as such is not being tested within factor analysis.

## Practical procedure

### *Correlation matrix*

The first step in factor analysis involves computing the correlation matrix. If there are no significant correlations between variables under investigation, then it will be pointless to continue. The inverse of the correlation matrix indicates if the variables chosen are to be linearly dependent, for which the matrix is singular.

### *Sample size*

The reliability of a factor analysis depends on the size of the sample. But there are no rules by which the size should be determined. However, there must be more observations than variables. Gorsuch (1983) suggests that the size of the sample should not be less than five observations per variable and not less than 100 individual observations per analysis.

### *Principal components*

The two most widely used forms of factor analysis are:

1. the principal components
2. principal–axis factoring (SPSS).

As stated earlier, factor analysis is principally about variance–covariance analysis. Variance that is shared by the scores of each variable is called common variance. Moreover, variance that is unique to a variable and it is not shared with other variables is called specific variance. The variance that refers to mistakes through measurement actions is called error variance. Hence it can be concluded that total variance is comprised of three components:

> Total variance = common variance + specific variance + error variance.

The disaggregation of total variance distinguishes principal–components analysis and principal–axis factoring. In the former analysis all three types of variance are included in order to eliminate any errors. But the latter model deals only with the common variance, which is shared by the test. Dealing merely with the common variance will result in the exclusion of the unique variance from analysis. The principal–components analysis sets the total variance at 1, but for the principal–axis factoring, it varies between 0 and 1.

### *How factors are extracted*

The first component extracted from running factor analysis accounts for the largest variance among all variables. The second factor expresses the next largest amount of variance, which is not related to or expressed by the first one. The number of factors extracted is the same as the number of variables, although the degree of variance expressed by successive factors necessarily decreases.

There are two main criteria by which one can decide which factors can be excluded from subsequent analyses. The first criterion is called Kaiser's criterion. This suggests that those factors should be selected which have an eigenvalue of greater than one. Selecting an eigenvalue of greater than one will result in excluding those factors, which explain less variance than a single variable on average.

The second method is a graphical method called a Scree test, which was suggested by Cattell (1966). In the Scree test, a graph is drawn of variances for those factors that are initially extracted and the plot is broken down into two visible slopes. The steep slope represents the primary factors and the gentle slope represents the secondary factors. So it can be concluded that factors which lie before the point at which the eigenvalues (or explained variance) seem to level off should be retained.

Which criteria should be chosen for factor analysis is affected by the size of average communalities, the number of variables and the number of observations. If the number of variables is less than 30 and the average communality is greater than 0.7, or the number of observations is greater than 250 and the mean communality is greater than or equal to 0.60, then the Kaiser criterion should be chosen (Stevens, 1996).

### *Rotation of factors*

The last step in factor analysis involves rotation of factors. The goal of the rotation is to maximise the variance (variability) of the 'new' variable (factor), while minimising the variance around the new variable. This rotation of factors increases the interpretability of factors and maximises the loadings of some of the items. These items, in turn, are used to identify the meaning of the factor. When there are more than two variables, the same procedure will be applied as for defining a 'space' with just two variables. Thus when there are three variables, one could plot a three-dimensional scatter plot and fit in a plane through the data. However, the logic of rotating the axes so as to maximise the variance of the new factor remains the same.

There are two commonly used methods. The first is the orthogonal rotation method, which provides factors that are independent or unrelated to one another. The second method, the oblique rotation, is based on correlated factors. Selecting one method as the only right method is rather controversial. Both methods have some drawbacks and some strengths. Since the orthogonal rotation is about unrelated factors, using this method will force factors to be uncorrelated, whereas they may not be uncorrelated in reality (Bryman and Cramer, 1999).

## Conclusion

Measuring corporate performance was found to be highly complex and controversial. Even in a world of perfect competition, the neo-classical method for measuring corporate performance through total factor productivity is fundamentally flawed, as revealed in the Cambridge critique. Further, in the absence of perfect competition (and a single good), mainstream industrial economics is a variety of models and techniques, with a multiplicity of outcomes and connections between variables that are mutually inconsistent. Accordingly, empirical study has been pursued here by the simple expedient of examining whether ownership as such is or is not a strong element in association with other variables that are deemed to be significant for corporate performance. This suggested the use of factor analysis, to which I now turn in practice.

# 5
# Results from the Empirical Study: Part I

## Introduction

This and the following chapter present the empirical results found by the use of factor analysis as a technique for measuring comparative corporate performance and subsequent privatisation performance. Throughout, the output results from the use of the Statistical Package for the Social Sciences (SPSS) will be discussed. The output from the package, however, is comprised of many different elements ranging from descriptive statistics to the rotated component matrix. The main focus will be on a table, the principal component matrix. In general, further refinement of the factor analysis – through rotation, for example – has not significantly enhanced or modified the results. Consequently, the principal components alone are reported here, but other output is available upon request.

The main purpose of this exercise is, firstly, to ascertain which variables are highly loaded (that is, highly correlated to a factor) or, in other words, which extracted factors pick up which variables, and, secondly, to determine common characteristics.

Four types of analysis have been conducted using factor analysis. The principal type was designed to compare the performance of three types of companies: private, mixed and state-owned. State-owned companies include companies that are owned by the federal and local governments of each country, as well as those companies that are owned by governments of other countries but which are operating in the country of investigation. Mixed companies are those companies in which the state is one of the shareholders by virtue of holding a certain number of shares. Private companies are comprised of several kinds of private ownership, for instance, private and public through quotes in a stock market, and corporate-owned companies. The second type of analysis looks at privatisation performance by comparing state-owned with privatised company performance. The third test examines the characteristics of ownership, by creating some new variables and finding out how the ownership variable reacts to these new variables. The last investigation looks at the effect of concentration on corporate performance. This chapter will analyse the findings of the first type of analysis. The three remaining types of analysis will be discussed in the next chapter.

From the previous discussion of industrial performance and of privatisation, no general conclusions are liable to be drawn either about the relative merits of public and private sectors or about the decisive factors in performance from one case to the next. For the most important large-scale privatisations, the most appropriate method of analysis is on a case-by-case basis. In any case, sample size is liable to be small once various factors are taken into account.

Most of the arguments in favour of privatisation are independent of scale of enterprise. They apply equally to small and large firms. So it is appropriate to take each firm to be representative of either the private or the public sector (or a mixture of both), irrespective of size. In practice, because of the small sample size of state-owned firms and random sampling of private firms, the latter are liable to be small. But there is an argument that smaller private firms are more likely to be efficient because of the greater immediacy of the profit motive for owners.

From the arguments put forward in the previous chapters, it can be stressed that different elements of corporate behaviour are related to one another in complex ways, suggesting the usefulness of factor analysis. Particular variables representing corporate performance are chosen in order to reflect a judicious combination of theory derived from industrial economies, on the one hand, and the heavy constraints imposed by data availability, on the other.

It is assumed that performance is a function of turnover, profit, total assets, productivity, performance, ownership, concentration, and total number of employees:

> Performance = *f* (turnover, profit, total assets [or tassets], total number of employees, productivity, performance, ownership and concentration).

Data on turnover, profit, total assets and total number of employees for the years 1998 and 2000 have been collected from four different sources: 'Major Companies of Europe', Amadeus, DataStream and Statistics

Sweden for 14 European countries: Austria, Belgium, Bulgaria, Denmark, Finland, France, Germany, Italy, the Netherlands, Norway, Poland, Portugal, Sweden and the UK. All the data have been converted to a same-based currency, the US dollar. A brief discussion of the data sources is provided in the appendix to this chapter.

Productivity is represented by a variable called PROD; another variable, called PROF, represents performance. The PROD variable is created through the turnover divided by the number of employees (essentially a crude measure of gross labour productivity) and PROF through profit divided by the number of employees. Throughout, with PROD and PROF measuring some aspect of performance, we will refer to them together as reflecting 'productivity and performance' even though this is slightly misleading (through this analysis, performance will be represented by 'Perf'). The rate of profit has not been used as a variable, although it could have been, since it is given by PROD/PROF, which means that its constitutive elements are included in the empirical analysis.

Ownership is treated as a categorical/nominal variable. Nominal data relate to qualitative variables or attributes, such as gender or ownership, and are records of category membership. Nominal data are merely labels: they may take the form of numbers, but such numbers are merely arbitrary code numbers.

In type-one factor analysis (which compares the performance of state, mixed and private companies of 14 European countries) state companies are assigned a value of 0, private companies a value of 1, and mixed companies a value between 0 and 1 depending on the percentage of shares owned by the state. Two years, 1998 and 2000, have been chosen for analysis, and annual data for these three types of companies have been collected. The number of companies (state, mixed and private) taken from each country is shown in Table 5.1 below. In addition to country-by-country experiments, two total-country experiments have been conducted for two years (1998 and 2000). These experiments are based on a sample taken from each country using the same variables.

The rest of this chapter is organised as follows. The next section is devoted to type-one factor analysis, in which country-by-country and total-country results for the years 1998 and 2000 are discussed. In this section I try to identify two main elements. The first element considers extracted factors, that is, whether case-by-case experiments and total-country analyses will recognise two or three characteristics by which corporate performance can be distinguished. The second element concentrates on the variable of ownership. Is ownership correlated with other variables or does it stand alone? If it is correlated to a factor with

*Table 5.1* List of companies based on their ownership

| Countries | Years | Number of companies | State-owned companies | Mixed companies | Privately-owned companies |
|---|---|---|---|---|---|
| Austria | 1998 | 70 | 15 | 4 | 51 |
| | 2000 | 60 | 11 | 2 | 47 |
| Belgium | 1998 | 100 | 35 | 5 | 60 |
| | 2000 | 120 | 53 | 2 | 65 |
| Bulgaria | 1998 | 340 | 109 | 60 | 171 |
| | 2000 | 600 | 196 | 104 | 300 |
| Denmark | 1998 | 60 | 17 | 0 | 43 |
| | 2000 | 80 | 30 | 6 | 44 |
| Finland | 1998 | 110 | 48 | 6 | 56 |
| | 2000 | 200 | 75 | 8 | 117 |
| France | 1998 | 500 | 243 | 7 | 250 |
| | 2000 | 600 | 280 | 7 | 313 |
| Germany | 1998 | 500 | 174 | 67 | 259 |
| | 2000 | 460 | 177 | 52 | 231 |
| Italy | 1998 | 70 | 30 | 3 | 37 |
| | 2000 | 90 | 41 | 4 | 45 |
| The Netherlands | 1998 | 90 | 40 | 5 | 45 |
| | 2000 | 120 | 55 | 1 | 64 |
| Norway | 1998 | 120 | 43 | 14 | 63 |
| | 2000 | 200 | 66 | 33 | 101 |
| Poland | 1998 | 340 | 148 | 19 | 173 |
| | 2000 | 420 | 172 | 33 | 215 |
| Portugal | 1998 | 60 | 8 | 5 | 47 |
| | 2000 | 60 | 10 | 4 | 46 |
| Sweden | 1998 | 756 | 344 | 33 | 379 |
| | 2000 | 750 | 338 | 37 | 375 |
| The UK | 1998 | 200 | 90 | 0 | 110 |
| | 2000 | 200 | 100 | 0 | 100 |
| Total countries | 1998 | 3,316 | 1,344 | 228 | 1,744 |
| | 2000 | 3,960 | 1,604 | 293 | 2,063 |

other variables, does it represent a characteristic that suggests difference in performance from state-owned companies? The last section offers a discussion of the overall results by way of conclusion.

## The type-one factor analysis

Theoretical benchmarks for the school of thought supporting the superiority of the private sector and privatisation point to the idea that state-owned enterprises are inefficient and wasteful. In Chapter 1,

I discussed different schools of thought supporting privatisation as a remedy against the inefficiency of state-owned companies. In Chapter 2, I examined different empirical studies. Some comparative studies have found that private companies are more efficient than state-owned companies. Ownership is seen as one of the most important influences on corporate performance. In order to investigate this claim, empirical study was carried out through the use of factor analysis.

For the two years 1998 and 2000, data were collected representing aspects of company performance for 14 European countries across state, mixed and private ownership. Factor analysis was based on the use of four variables: turnover, profit, tassets (total assets) and total number of employees, plus two created variables, which were PROD, PROF and, along with one categorical variable, owners (ownership).

Total-country analysis was done through taking the samples from each country involved. Factor analysis outputs were taken from each experiment and the main elements are summarised in two tables: the component matrix and the rotated component matrix. The former will be the main focus. In general, the many other results computed confirm those presented here and do not warrant what is already a dry and repetitive summary of the empirical investigations.

## Austria

For Austria, data were compiled for 70 companies for 1998 and 60 companies for 2000. Descriptive statistics for the two years are presented in Table 5.2. There are limited numbers of non-private companies to include within the empirical analysis (and these declined slightly between the two years), correspondingly limiting the number of private companies that it was decided to incorporate. Leaving aside the relatively small number of mixed companies, the tables indicate a wide range of

*Table 5.2(a)* Descriptive statistics for 4 mixed companies, Austria 1988

| | Minimum | Maximum | Mean | Std. Deviation |
|---|---|---|---|---|
| Turnover | 2,917 | 1,915,762 | 525,386 | 929,201 |
| Profit | −874,927 | 11,317 | −213,574 | 440,944 |
| Tassets | 70,470 | 7,506,825 | 2,025,362 | 3,655,781 |
| Employees | 22 | 4,162 | 1,291 | 1,927 |
| Owners | 0.5 | 0.99 | 0.63 | 0.24 |
| PROD | 64.02 | 460.3 | 239.64 | 177.8 |
| PROF | −210.22 | 514.42 | 80.59 | 307.32 |

*Table 5.2(b)* Descriptive statistics for 2 mixed companies, Austria 2000

| | **Minimum** | **Maximum** | **Mean** | **Std. Deviation** |
|---|---|---|---|---|
| Turnover | 7,723 | 680,289 | 344,006 | 475,576 |
| Profit | 1,768 | 32,661 | 17,214 | 21,844 |
| Tassets | 29,962 | 1,758,554 | 894,258 | 1,222,299 |
| Employees | 48 | 2,750 | 1,399 | 1,911 |
| Owners | 0.6 | 0.75 | 0.68 | 0.1 |
| PROD | 160.9 | 247.38 | 204.14 | 61.15 |
| PROF | 11.88 | 36.83 | 24.35 | 17.65 |

*Table 5.2(c)* Descriptive statistics for 51 private companies, Austria 1998

| | **Minimum** | **Maximum** | **Mean** | **Std. Deviation** |
|---|---|---|---|---|
| Turnover | 430 | 150,391 | 32,179 | 20,741 |
| Profit | −10,635 | 24,492 | 2310 | 5,800 |
| Tassets | 5,425 | 588,613 | 46,649 | 91,528 |
| Employees | 10 | 610 | 177 | 128 |
| Owners | 1 | 1 | 1 | 0 |
| PROD | 0.7 | 1,969.42 | 312.84 | 332.63 |
| PROF | −53.17 | 603.35 | 34.27 | 108.95 |

*Table 5.2(d)* Descriptive statistics for 47 private companies, Austria 2000

| | **Minimum** | **Maximum** | **Mean** | **Std. Deviation** |
|---|---|---|---|---|
| Turnover | 53,147 | 3,487,039 | 265,744 | 510,262 |
| Profit | −53,039 | 155,884 | 12,462 | 30,419 |
| Tassets | 16,807 | 4,032,791 | 319,355 | 690,794 |
| Employees | 44 | 5,073 | 996 | 1,067 |
| Owners | 1 | 1 | 1 | 0 |
| PROD | 68.5 | 1,543.62 | 343.19 | 336.62 |
| PROF | −36.81 | 96.24 | 15.17 | 24.2 |

*Table 5.2(e)* Descriptive statistics for 15 state companies, Austria 1998

| | **Minimum** | **Maximum** | **Mean** | **Std. Deviation** |
|---|---|---|---|---|
| Turnover | 898 | 1,070,587 | 291,129 | 341,658 |
| Profit | −378 | 245,362 | 36,019 | 66,084 |
| Tassets | 5,869 | 5,654,416 | 943,991 | 1,507,437 |
| Employees | 2 | 2,401 | 872 | 769 |
| Owners | 0 | 0 | 0 | 0 |
| PROD | 52.22 | 1,277.56 | 382.89 | 314.29 |
| PROF | −11.44 | 967.7 | 102.32 | 251.15 |

*Table 5.2(f)* Descriptive statistics for 11 state companies, Austria 2000

| | Minimum | Maximum | Mean | Std. Deviation |
|---|---|---|---|---|
| Turnover | 15,725 | 1,520,625 | 326,491 | 424,990 |
| Profit | −67,336 | 38,709 | 7,794 | 29,055 |
| Tassets | 34,242 | 1,882,217 | 438,520 | 548,818 |
| Employees | 251 | 33,421 | 4,073 | 9,752 |
| Owners | 0 | 0 | 0 | 0 |
| PROD | 12.72 | 336.82 | 167.69 | 105.11 |
| PROF | −39.4 | 29.21 | 4.24 | 18.2 |

*Table 5.3* Company performances: Austria

| | 1998 | | 2000 | |
|---|---|---|---|---|
| **Variables** | **Component 1 (Size)** | **Component 2 (Perf)** | **Component 1 (Size/Perf)** | **Component 2 (Perf/Own)** |
| Turnover | 0.944 | −0.004 | 0.880 | −0.242 |
| Profit | −0.693 | 0.356 | 0.846 | 0.192 |
| Total Assets | 0.862 | 0.242 | 0.626 | −0.439 |
| Number of employees | 0.931 | −0.141 | 0.342 | −0.739 |
| Ownership | −0.505 | −0.374 | 0.061 | 0.635 |
| PROD | 0.082 | 0.676 | 0.555 | 0.404 |
| PROF | −0.081 | 0.867 | 0.581 | 0.543 |
| Variance extracted | 46.417 | 22.204 | 37.815 | 24.223 |

performance, although with a relatively small standard deviation for PROD for both private and state-owned companies.

For both years, only two factors explained more than an average amount of variance. These are indicated in Table 5.3, together with the amount of variance explained by each factor. In each case, the main component can be designated as size (although profit is negative for 1998; probably an artefact of the sample for which overall profit is negative across all companies), with some loading of this towards performance (PROD and PROF) in 2000. For 1998, the second component is attached to performance but with a negative association with private ownership. This result is reversed for 2000. For that year, there is considerable difference between the original and the rotated (not shown) component matrices. Across the results, this is unusual and might be explained by the even smaller number of non-private companies in the later year for Austria.

## Belgium

For Belgium, 100 and 120 companies for the years 1998 and 2000, respectively, have been taken as a sample of the three types (state, mixed, and private). Table 5.4 shows descriptive statistics for the two years. Relatively small standard deviations for Employees and PROD for mixed companies of the year 2000 are recognisable.

*Table 5.4(a)* Descriptive statistics for 5 mixed companies, Belgium 1998

| | Minimum | Maximum | Mean | Std. Deviation |
|---|---|---|---|---|
| Turnover | 2,051 | 2,661,300 | 563,845 | 1,173,760 |
| Profit | −14,201 | 75,837 | 11,483 | 36,507 |
| Tassets | 2,139 | 2,707,969 | 794,676 | 1,151,458 |
| Employees | 2 | 9,411 | 1,967 | 4,164 |
| Owners | 0.5 | 1 | 0.81 | 0.19 |
| PROD | 168.9 | 2,193.83 | 817.44 | 837.45 |
| PROF | −2,950.06 | 545.25 | −488.16 | 1,397.38 |

*Table 5.4(b)* Descriptive statistics for 2 mixed companies, Belgium 2000

| | Minimum | Maximum | Mean | Std. Deviation |
|---|---|---|---|---|
| Turnover | 14,286 | 14,515 | 14,400 | 162 |
| Profit | −26 | 2,358 | 1,166 | 1,686 |
| Tassets | 5,874 | 146,730 | 76,302 | 99,600 |
| Employees | 18 | 94 | 56 | 54 |
| Owners | 0.8 | 0.82 | 0.81 | 0.02 |
| PROD | 151.98 | 806.38 | 479.18 | 462.73 |
| PROF | −0.28 | 130.99 | 65.36 | 92.82 |

*Table 5.4(c)* Descriptive statistics for 59 private companies, Belgium 1998

| | Minimum | Maximum | Mean | Std. Deviation |
|---|---|---|---|---|
| Turnover | 21,023 | 8,750,438 | 774,204 | 1,647,371 |
| Profit | −31,502 | 1,203,336 | 45,033 | 178,622 |
| Tassets | 6,740 | 13,716,241 | 762,278 | 2,181,541 |
| Employees | 22 | 31,321 | 2,320 | 5,655 |
| Owners | 1 | 1 | 1 | 0 |
| PROD | 39.22 | 21,174.18 | 1,049.2 | 2,774.97 |
| PROF | −33.01 | 814.2 | 27.2 | 109.78 |

*Table 5.4(d)* Descriptive statistics for 65 private companies, Belgium 2000

| | Minimum | Maximum | Mean | Std. Deviation |
|---|---|---|---|---|
| Turnover | 146,559 | 8,237,821 | 1,467,247 | 1,536,347 |
| Profit | −77,985 | 432,620 | 54,654 | 102,813 |
| Tassets | 74,583 | 5,709,256 | 940,987 | 1,207,557 |
| Employees | 17 | 46,131 | 4,101 | 7,367 |
| Owners | 1 | 1 | 1 | 0 |
| PROD | 68.88 | 95,550.31 | 4,862.14 | 14,588.92 |
| PROF | −873.69 | 1,564.44 | 50.46 | 242.91 |

*Table 5.4(e)* Descriptive statistics for 36 state companies, Belgium 1998

| | Minimum | Maximum | Mean | Std. Deviation |
|---|---|---|---|---|
| Turnover | 979 | 2,010,620 | 128,564 | 361,931 |
| Profit | −12,728 | 210,040 | 11,083 | 41,633 |
| Tassets | 2,489 | 3,578,501 | 202,042 | 650,365 |
| Employees | 7 | 41,432 | 1,339 | 6,880 |
| Owners | 0 | 0 | 0 | 0 |
| PROD | 48.53 | 8,718.81 | 688.92 | 1,443.87 |
| PROF | −208.18 | 2,302.02 | 75.66 | 396.46 |

*Table 5.4(f)* Descriptive statistics for 53 state companies, Belgium 2000

| | Minimum | Maximum | Mean | Std. Deviation |
|---|---|---|---|---|
| Turnover | 462 | 4,981,551 | 254,590 | 802,472 |
| Profit | −264,379 | 453,441 | 13,721 | 102,873 |
| Tassets | 4,438 | 11,145,163 | 735,606 | 1,967,023 |
| Employees | 2 | 40,324 | 1,621 | 6,359 |
| Owners | 0 | 0 | 0 | 0 |
| PROD | 24.72 | 1,809.08 | 331.96 | 357.47 |
| PROF | −40,895.98 | 6,167.14 | −500.13 | 5,763.27 |

As can be seen in Table 5.5, three factors explain more than average amount of variance for both years. The first component for the year 1998 indicates that the variables turnover, profit, total assets and employees, variables representing size, are significantly correlated to the factor. The second component discloses that PROD and PROF are significantly correlated to it. The third factor shows a higher correlation coefficient (0.881) for only a single variable, ownership. The Belgian case for the year 1998 indicates clearly through Table 5.5 how variables

*Table 5.5* Company performances: Belgium

| Variables | 1998 | | | 2000 | | |
|---|---|---|---|---|---|---|
| | Component 1 (Size) | Component 2 (Perf) | Component 3 (Own) | Component 1 (Size) | Component 2 (Perf) | Component 3 (Own) |
| Turnover | 0.954 | 0.008 | 0.054 | 0.889 | 0.182 | 0.034 |
| Profit | 0.916 | 0.039 | −0.058 | 0.640 | 0.163 | −0.298 |
| Total Assets | 0.958 | 0.051 | −0.048 | 0.711 | −0.582 | 0.109 |
| Number of employees | 0.798 | −0.083 | −0.117 | 0.741 | −0.003 | −0.360 |
| Ownership | 0.208 | −0.136 | 0.855 | 0.463 | 0.442 | 0.354 |
| PROD | −0.049 | 0.713 | 0.479 | 0.182 | 0.247 | 0.835 |
| PROF | 0.047 | 0.795 | −0.290 | −0.114 | 0.875 | −0.295 |
| Variance extracted | 47.862 | 16.699 | 15.231 | 35.939 | 20.299 | 16.304 |

*Table 5.6(a)* Descriptive statistics for 60 mixed companies, Bulgaria 1998

| | Minimum | Maximum | Mean | Std. Deviation |
|---|---|---|---|---|
| Turnover | 433 | 133,947 | 8,321 | 22,115 |
| Profit | −28,212 | 4,966 | −681 | 4,156 |
| Tassets | 399 | 118,771 | 8,248 | 18,668 |
| Employees | 98 | 5,300 | 644 | 950 |
| Owners | 0.25 | 0.94 | 0.5 | 0.18 |
| PROD | 2.15 | 31.43 | 8.53 | 6.22 |
| PROF | −10.2 | 2.71 | −0.26 | 1.75 |

representing size, performance and ownership are correlated to three extracted factors. The three characteristics, size, performance and ownership, have been well established throughout the overall results for the year 1998. Moreover, it can be emphasised that ownership stands alone. So ownership barely figures as the third factor extracted and also has little association with other measures of performance.

For the year 2000 the characteristic of size is established through component 1. The second factor picks out PROF, negatively with total assets, and the third does associate ownership positively, if weakly, with PROD. It is rare if not unique in doing so. In short, there is no obvious intuitive interpretation of the second and third components for 2000.

## Bulgaria

In this instance, data were collected for 340 companies for 1998 and for 600 companies for 2000. Descriptive statistics for the two years are presented in Table 5.6. Relatively small standard deviations for owners and PROD for the year 1998, and for employees, owners and PROD for the year 2000 of mixed companies are observable.

*Table 5.6(b)* Descriptive statistics for 104 mixed companies, Bulgaria 2000

| | Minimum | Maximum | Mean | Std. Deviation |
|---|---|---|---|---|
| Turnover | 212 | 16,917 | 2,058 | 2,619 |
| Profit | −5,311 | 3,745 | −152 | 783 |
| Tassets | 170 | 64,440 | 3,815 | 7,727 |
| Employees | 31 | 1,316 | 393 | 289 |
| Owners | 0.25 | 0.94 | 0.5 | 0.15 |
| PROD | 0.48 | 35.08 | 6.5 | 6.24 |
| PROF | −17.41 | 5.56 | −0.39 | 2.06 |

*Table 5.6(c)* Descriptive statistics for 171 private companies, Bulgaria 1998

| | Minimum | Maximum | Mean | Std. Deviation |
|---|---|---|---|---|
| Turnover | 160 | 894,626 | 28,696 | 77,701 |
| Profit | −19,826 | 82,776 | 1,179 | 7,557 |
| Tassets | 240 | 509,226 | 19,135 | 45,481 |
| Employees | 14 | 10,281 | 782 | 1,285 |
| Owners | 1 | 1 | 1 | 0 |
| PROD | 0.57 | 2,885.62 | 79.63 | 250.25 |
| PROF | −13.18 | 71.57 | 2.78 | 8.82 |

*Table 5.6(d)* Descriptive statistics for 300 private companies, Bulgaria 2000

| | Minimum | Maximum | Mean | Std. Deviation |
|---|---|---|---|---|
| Turnover | 79 | 337,180 | 15,235 | 23,457 |
| Profit | −17,540 | 19,440 | 436 | 2,516 |
| Tassets | 52 | 101,982 | 11,807 | 16,089 |
| Employees | 2 | 6,235 | 534 | 704 |
| Owners | 1 | 1 | 1 | 0 |
| PROD | 2.46 | 10,011.66 | 132.15 | 624.96 |
| PROF | −62.74 | 130.21 | 1.73 | 10.51 |

*Table 5.6(e)* Descriptive statistics for 109 state companies, Bulgaria 1998

| | Minimum | Maximum | Mean | Std. Deviation |
|---|---|---|---|---|
| Turnover | 121 | 1,155,996 | 28,224 | 126,545 |
| Profit | −4,064 | 180,628 | 2,750 | 18,852 |
| Tassets | 28 | 1,730,854 | 38,486 | 184,344 |
| Employees | 17 | 32,785 | 1,363 | 4,628 |
| Owners | 0 | 0 | 0 | 0 |
| PROD | 0.66 | 342.91 | 15.9 | 36.05 |
| PROF | −12.48 | 14.44 | 0.19 | 2.59 |

*Table 5.6(f)* Descriptive statistics for 196 state companies, Bulgaria 2000

| | Minimum | Maximum | Mean | Std. Deviation |
|---|---|---|---|---|
| Turnover | 47 | 929,996 | 18,473 | 83,193 |
| Profit | −21,928 | 149,216 | 1,112 | 13,353 |
| Tassets | 41 | 865,374 | 20,240 | 82,180 |
| Employees | 17 | 25,477 | 764 | 2,419 |
| Owners | 0 | 0 | 0 | 0 |
| PROD | 0.68 | 4,474.88 | 67.42 | 429.53 |
| PROF | −42.29 | 106.45 | −0.53 | 9.96 |

*Table 5.7* Company performances: Bulgaria

| | 1998 | | 2000 | |
|---|---|---|---|---|
| **Variables** | **Component 1 (Size)** | **Component 2 (Perf/Own)** | **Component 1 (Size)** | **Component 2 (Perf)** |
| Turnover | 0.937 | 0.068 | 0.932 | 0.032 |
| Profit | 0.928 | 0.008 | 0.894 | 0.035 |
| Total Assets | 0.953 | −0.068 | 0.929 | −0.068 |
| Number of employees | 0.859 | −0.173 | 0.784 | −0.131 |
| Ownership | −0.050 | 0.629 | −0.066 | 0.372 |
| PROD | 0.089 | 0.698 | 0.044 | 0.776 |
| PROF | 0.160 | 0.698 | 0.120 | 0.796 |
| Variance extracted | 48.881 | 20.130 | 45.255 | 19.974 |

From Table 5.7 for the years 1998 and 2000, two factors have been extracted. From factor 1 for 1998, it can be ascertained that the first characteristic, size, is well established. Variables turnover, profit, total assets and employees are highly loaded with that component. But factor 2 shows that performance variables PROD and PROF, and ownership are significantly correlated to the factor. It can be confirmed that the ownership variable is retained with performance variables to build up a common factor, which does not confirm with other results in general.

For the year 2000 the first characteristic, size, is established by virtue of turnover, profit, total assets and employees. The second characteristic, performance, is well established in the second factor by virtue of the PROD and PROF variables. It means that the two elements of size and performance for the year 2000 occupy large proportions of the total variance. The ownership variable is not picked up by either of the factors.

## Denmark

The sample size for Denmark for the year 1998 and 2000 consists of 60 and 80 companies, respectively (no mixed companies for the year 1998). The descriptive statistics for the different types of companies are shown in Table 5.8, with nothing remarkable on which to comment except the absence of mixed companies for 1998.

*Table 5.8(a)* Descriptive statistics for 6 mixed companies, Denmark 2000

| | Minimum | Maximum | Mean | Std. Deviation |
|---|---|---|---|---|
| Turnover | 63,142 | 662,851 | 406,176 | 282,774 |
| Profit | −13,889 | 167,256 | 43,630 | 67,443 |
| Tassets | 73,645 | 3,156,803 | 838,040 | 1,200,642 |
| Employees | 177 | 3,422 | 1,245 | 1,344 |
| Owners | 0.44 | 0.95 | 0.68 | 0.2 |
| PROD | 169.74 | 2,761.88 | 719.84 | 1,010.84 |
| PROF | −78.47 | 696.9 | 119.42 | 287.41 |

*Table 5.8(b)* Descriptive statistics for 43 private companies, Denmark 1998

| | Minimum | Maximum | Mean | Std. Deviation |
|---|---|---|---|---|
| Turnover | 41,197 | 2,293,033 | 259,452 | 405,303 |
| Profit | −51,828 | 212,623 | 13,265 | 37,831 |
| Tassets | 14,666 | 1,290,765 | 174,796 | 261,930 |
| Employees | 27 | 6,037 | 960 | 1,261 |
| Owners | 1 | 1 | 1 | 0 |
| PROD | 66.33 | 2,727.53 | 496.5 | 678.51 |
| PROF | −219.61 | 483.21 | 17.89 | 82.74 |

*Table 5.8(c)* Descriptive statistics for 44 private companies, Denmark 2000

| | Minimum | Maximum | Mean | Std. Deviation |
|---|---|---|---|---|
| Turnover | 13,591 | 312,737 | 103,408 | 45,945 |
| Profit | −8,049 | 22,794 | 2,773 | 6,513 |
| Tassets | 6,581 | 161,319 | 65,313 | 37,308 |
| Employees | 62 | 1,331 | 540 | 372 |
| Owners | 1 | 1 | 1 | 0 |
| PROD | 71.32 | 1,278.24 | 295.62 | 263.61 |
| PROF | −30.27 | 76.36 | 7.49 | 18.95 |

*Table 5.8(d)* Descriptive statistics for 17 state companies, Denmark 1998

| | Minimum | Maximum | Mean | Std. Deviation |
|---|---|---|---|---|
| Turnover | 10,460 | 1,365,048 | 239,162 | 403,442 |
| Profit | −25,213 | 174,767 | 8,142 | 44,167 |
| Tassets | 2,983 | 1,912,505 | 347,893 | 545,431 |
| Employees | 7 | 2,889 | 437 | 702 |
| Owners | 0 | 0 | 0 | 0 |
| PROD | 98.38 | 10,859.83 | 1,228.06 | 2,682.56 |
| PROF | −990.54 | 865.18 | 9.18 | 349.5 |

*Table 5.8(e)* Descriptive statistics for 30 state companies, Denmark 2000

| | Minimum | Maximum | Mean | Std. Deviation |
|---|---|---|---|---|
| Turnover | 5,294 | 3,494,961 | 481,968 | 850,339 |
| Profit | −116,100 | 433,258 | 39,440 | 103,165 |
| Tassets | 2,823 | 3,706,780 | 590,605 | 1,089,113 |
| Employees | 23 | 9,523 | 984 | 1,951 |
| Owners | 0 | 0 | 0 | 0 |
| PROD | 46.4 | 7,532.04 | 953.93 | 1,488.82 |
| PROF | −114.5 | 2,957.06 | 190.99 | 572.53 |

*Table 5.9* Company performances: Denmark

| | 1998 | | | 2000 | |
|---|---|---|---|---|---|
| Variables | Component 1 (Size) | Component 2 (Perf) | Component 3 (Own) | Component 1 (Size/Perf) | Component 2 (Perf/Employee) |
| Turnover | 0.949 | −0.098 | −0.081 | 0.753 | 0.476 |
| Profit | 0.815 | 0.202 | 0.238 | 0.819 | −0.028 |
| Total Assets | 0.833 | −0.048 | −0.398 | 0.8 | 0.38 |
| Number of employees | 0.842 | −0.377 | 0.085 | 0.364 | 0.699 |
| Ownership | 0.025 | −0.375 | 0.857 | −0.513 | 0.003 |
| PROD | 0.093 | 0.839 | −0.059 | 0.69 | −0.667 |
| PROF | 0.289 | 0.746 | 0.439 | 0.61 | −0.707 |
| Variance extracted | 43.72 | 22.798 | 16.558 | 44.591 | 25.797 |

As shown by the factor analysis output summarised in the Table 5.9, three factors have been extracted for the year 1998, and two factors for the year 2000. For the year 1998, in the first factor, turnover, profit, total assets and employees are most weighted in the factor significantly occupying the highest score variance. The results underscore the first characteristic, size. The second factor establishes the second characteristic, performance, with PROD and PROF having the highest weights. Ownership is the only highly loaded item in the third extracted factor. This result demonstrates that ownership and other corporate performance activities are separate from one another. The results as a whole parallel other results found for other countries in the study. For the year 2000 only two factors explained more than an average amount of variance. The first component reveals higher correlations among some variables representing size like turnover, profit and total assets with variables representing the performance, PROD and PROF, but also with some negative amount with ownership. Factor 2 indicates that number of employees positively, and PROD and PROF negatively, are highly loaded compared with the other variables. As a result, one characteristic, size and performance, can be ascertained through component 1, which is not generally the case in study results. Through component 2, unusually, employment is loaded heavily alongside performance but negatively so. Among all of the variables, only ownership is not significantly correlated to any factors for 2000.

## Finland

Sample sizes of 110 and 200 companies have been used for Finland, for the years 1998 and 2000, respectively. Descriptive statistics for the samples of mixed, private and state companies for the years 1998 and 2000 are presented in Table 5.10. As far as the table is concerned, there is nothing remarkable on which to comment.

For 1998 and 2000, two factors have been retained which explain more than an average amount of variance, as indicated in Table 5.11. For

*Table 5.10(a)* Descriptive statistics for 6 mixed companies, Finland 1998

| | Minimum | Maximum | Mean | Std. Deviation |
|---|---|---|---|---|
| Turnover | 82,259 | 10,063,608 | 3,324,792 | 3,491,841 |
| Profit | −4,906 | 440,142 | 179,039 | 192,792 |
| Tassets | 715,320 | 13,040,599 | 4,112,434 | 4,509,247 |
| Employees | 29 | 19,003 | 10,620 | 6,301 |
| Owners | 0.4 | 0.71 | 0.54 | 0.1 |
| PROD | 145.02 | 2,836.52 | 706.87 | 1,051.47 |
| PROF | −0.35 | 1,468.88 | 259.36 | 592.77 |

Table 5.10(b) Descriptive statistics for 8 mixed companies, Finland 2000

| | Minimum | Maximum | Mean | Std. Deviation |
|---|---|---|---|---|
| Turnover | 80,132 | 10,482,093 | 2,998,287 | 3,286,576 |
| Profit | −10,599 | 1,730,732 | 379,857 | 579,463 |
| Tassets | 430,000 | 13,797,467 | 4,180,187 | 4,724,421 |
| Employees | 49 | 16,220 | 9,553 | 5,108 |
| Owners | 0.4 | 1 | 0.58 | 0.2 |
| PROD | 75.56 | 1,635.35 | 443.44 | 512.22 |
| PROF | −2.31 | 699.2 | 120.34 | 240.17 |

Table 5.10(c) Descriptive statistics for 56 private companies, Finland 1998

| | Minimum | Maximum | Mean | Std. Deviation |
|---|---|---|---|---|
| Turnover | 22,307 | 7,329,901 | 290,417 | 991,687 |
| Profit | −12,526 | 155,158 | 9,397 | 25,404 |
| Tassets | 6,499 | 2,968,691 | 187,123 | 460,998 |
| Employees | 12 | 11,172 | 1,001 | 2,151 |
| Owners | 1 | 1 | 1 | 0 |
| PROD | 59.81 | 3,631.45 | 474.43 | 712.44 |
| PROF | −22.3 | 499.01 | 20.79 | 67.11 |

Table 5.10(d) Descriptive statistics for 117 private companies, Finland 2000

| | Minimum | Maximum | Mean | Std. Deviation |
|---|---|---|---|---|
| Turnover | 3,219 | 3,123,878 | 213,734 | 442,139 |
| Profit | −43,307 | 162,170 | 9,464 | 28,949 |
| Tassets | 3,823 | 3,407,494 | 182,271 | 443,929 |
| Employees | 28 | 23,480 | 1,139 | 2,811 |
| Owners | 1 | 1 | 1 | 0 |
| PROD | 42.63 | 7,295.81 | 316.86 | 695.55 |
| PROF | −176.83 | 423.22 | 8.94 | 45.92 |

Table 5.10(e) Descriptive statistics for 48 state companies, Finland 1998

| | Minimum | Maximum | Mean | Std. Deviation |
|---|---|---|---|---|
| Turnover | 3,633 | 2,716,595 | 182,538 | 423,631 |
| Profit | −18,086 | 318,480 | 14,306 | 47,264 |
| Tassets | 773 | 7,938,643 | 330,998 | 1,163,037 |
| Employees | 11 | 9,994 | 608 | 1,504 |
| Owners | 0 | 0 | 0 | 0 |
| PROD | 52.08 | 12,104.34 | 812.4 | 2,159.67 |
| PROF | −283.43 | 606.48 | 28.74 | 116.49 |

*Table 5.10(f)* Descriptive statistics for 75 state companies, Finland 2000

| | Minimum | Maximum | Mean | Std. Deviation |
|---|---|---|---|---|
| Turnover | 1,594 | 4,798,003 | 220,825 | 631,886 |
| Profit | −52,999 | 224,171 | 14,103 | 44,722 |
| Tassets | 1,367 | 9,405,995 | 316,826 | 1,157,086 |
| Employees | 10 | 9,373 | 555 | 1,190 |
| Owners | 0 | 0 | 0 | 0 |
| PROD | 7.62 | 15,327.61 | 712.94 | 1,896.39 |
| PROF | −274.61 | 587.42 | 28.64 | 104.96 |

*Table 5.11* Company performances: Finland

| | 1998 | | 2000 | |
|---|---|---|---|---|
| **Variables** | **Component 1 (Size)** | **Component 2 (Perf)** | **Component 1 (Size)** | **Component 2 (Perf)** |
| Turnover | 0.942 | −0.008 | 0.934 | −0.041 |
| Profit | 0.908 | 0.084 | 0.780 | 0.080 |
| Total Assets | 0.959 | 0.082 | 0.942 | −0.004 |
| Number of employees | 0.930 | −0.072 | 0.835 | −0.169 |
| Ownership | 0.038 | −0.521 | −0.013 | −0.441 |
| PROD | −0.079 | 0.715 | 0.007 | 0.811 |
| PROF | −0.007 | 0.637 | 0.137 | 0.797 |
| Variance extracted | 50.060 | 17.264 | 44.062 | 21.766 |

both years the main component can be designated as size. The second component is attached to performance for both years with a negative association with ownership. From these results it is clear that two characteristics can be established for both years: size and performance. This outcome is similar to other cases. The variable ownership does not occupy a relatively significant share of common variance; hence it is not highly loaded with either of the two extracted factors for both years.

## France

The data on 500 companies were used for factor analysis for the year 1998 and 600 companies for the year 2000. Descriptive statistics for the samples are summarised in Table 5.12, which shows that the standard deviations for the variables Owners and PROD mixed companies for both years are relatively small.

*Table 5.12(a)* Descriptive statistics for 7 mixed companies, France 1998

| | Minimum | Maximum | Mean | Std. Deviation |
|---|---|---|---|---|
| Turnover | 6,691 | 28,757,032 | 4,857,182 | 10,649,770 |
| Profit | 2,032 | 3,150,187 | 518,386 | 1,165,902 |
| Tassets | 8,457 | 53,853,759 | 8,755,345 | 19,948,860 |
| Employees | 28 | 169,099 | 26,494 | 63,080 |
| Owners | 0.51 | 0.99 | 0.7 | 0.2 |
| PROD | 67.46 | 646.4 | 294.88 | 181.64 |
| PROF | 2.89 | 627.53 | 128.31 | 229.06 |

*Table 5.12(b)* Descriptive statistics for 7 mixed companies, France 2000

| | Minimum | Maximum | Mean | Std. Deviation |
|---|---|---|---|---|
| Turnover | 49,791 | 31,333,687 | 8,286,603 | 11,922,596 |
| Profit | −12,909 | 2,520,727 | 473,313 | 929,212 |
| Tassets | 305,589 | 120,578,958 | 25,463,172 | 44,471,034 |
| Employees | 190 | 302,221 | 79,707 | 120,226 |
| Owners | 0.5 | 0.95 | 0.61 | 0.15 |
| PROD | 50.42 | 293.1 | 195.17 | 79.55 |
| PROF | −67.94 | 15.06 | −9.58 | 30.04 |

*Table 5.12(c)* Descriptive statistics for 250 private companies, France 1998

| | Minimum | Maximum | Mean | Std. Deviation |
|---|---|---|---|---|
| Turnover | 9,070 | 24,803,407 | 412,274 | 2,096,641 |
| Profit | −236,501 | 1,158,558 | 15,755 | 95,286 |
| Tassets | 3,155 | 34,581,729 | 477,848 | 3,220,790 |
| Employees | 14 | 118,272 | 1,971 | 11,310 |
| Owners | 1 | 1 | 1 | 0 |
| PROD | 33.91 | 117,163.94 | 1,032.59 | 7,791.89 |
| PROF | −674.66 | 190.79 | 10.06 | 58.34 |

*Table 5.12(d)* Descriptive statistics for 313 private companies, France 2000

| | Minimum | Maximum | Mean | Std. Deviation |
|---|---|---|---|---|
| Turnover | 14,327 | 29,225,172 | 322,018 | 2,366,381 |
| Profit | [illegible]0,053 | 1,556,728 | 9,632 | 96,809 |
| Tassets | [illegible]966 | 39,991,067 | 408,655 | 3,523,120 |
| Employees | 10 | 143,014 | 1,632 | 11,757 |
| Owners | 2 | 1 | 1 | 0 |
| PROD | −213 | 5,347.96 | 307.5 | 441.2 |
| PROF | | 416.49 | 10.93 | 37.29 |

*Table 5.12(e)* Descriptive statistics for 243 state companies, France 1998

| | Minimum | Maximum | Mean | Std. Deviation |
|---|---|---|---|---|
| Turnover | 2,578 | 43,432,051 | 529,063 | 3,254,234 |
| Profit | −115,258 | 1,997,970 | 14,310 | 133,669 |
| Tassets | 1,455 | 52,204,585 | 704,560 | 4,525,115 |
| Employees | 4 | 210,437 | 2,881 | 17,414 |
| Owners | 0 | 0 | 0 | 0 |
| PROD | 16.96 | 21,711.38 | 567.71 | 2,049.87 |
| PROF | −520.61 | 312.52 | 5.15 | 67.31 |

*Table 5.12(f)* Descriptive statistics for 280 state companies, France 2000

| | Minimum | Maximum | Mean | Std. Deviation |
|---|---|---|---|---|
| Turnover | 501 | 33,187,156 | 453,227 | 2,503,097 |
| Profit | −141,989 | 1,070,004 | 20,292 | 110,182 |
| Tassets | 1,065 | 113,696,647 | 919,632 | 7,300,393 |
| Employees | 6 | 216,605 | 2,560 | 16,207 |
| Owners | 0 | 0 | 0 | 0 |
| PROD | 0.36 | 8,109.09 | 393.95 | 759.76 |
| PROF | −893.01 | 5,567.28 | 29.29 | 344.16 |

*Table 5.13* Company performances: France

| | 1998 | | | 2000 | |
|---|---|---|---|---|---|
| Variables | Component 1 (Size) | Component 2 (Perf) | Component 3 (Own) | Component 1 (Size) | Component 2 (Perf) |
| Turnover | 0.976 | 0.03 | 0.005 | 0.973 | −0.008 |
| Profit | 0.887 | −0.035 | 0.046 | 0.87 | 0.052 |
| Total Assets | 0.982 | 0.01 | −0.01 | 0.956 | −0.001 |
| Number of employees | 0.957 | 0.013 | −0.022 | 0.88 | −0.037 |
| Ownership | −0.02 | −0.003 | 0.911 | −0.043 | −0.343 |
| PROD | −0.01 | 0.734 | 0.317 | −0.033 | 0.759 |
| PROF | 0.018 | −0.742 | 0.307 | 0.009 | 0.737 |
| Variance extracted | 51.733 | 15.591 | 14.686 | 48.495 | 17.743 |

Table 5.13 shows that three factors explain more than an average amount of variance for the year 1998. The variables with higher weight in component 1 are turnover, profit, total assets and employees. The second component shows that PROD and PROF are highly loaded, one positively and one negatively. The last component shows that the only variable that is highly loaded is ownership, with the correlation coefficient of (0.911). Again we can conclude that three characteristics (size, performance, and ownership) can be extracted from the analysis. Also,

*Table 5.14(a)* Descriptive statistics for 67 mixed companies, Germany 1998

| | Minimum | Maximum | Mean | Std. Deviation |
|---|---|---|---|---|
| Turnover | [illegible],903 | 18,293,431 | 375,579 | 2,225,013 |
| Profit | −6,4[illegible]7 | 761,171 | 16,235 | 92,708 |
| Tassets | 7,508 | 14,762,455 | 443,311 | 1,799,788 |
| Employees | 12 | 252 491 | 4,243 | 31,537 |
| Owners | 0.03 | 1 | 0.65 | 0.22 |
| PROD | 52.47 | 2,[illegible]07.09 | 452.46 | 436.74 |
| PROF | −16.93 | 311.[illegible]3 | 28.22 | 43.12 |

*Table 5.14(b)* Descriptive statistics for 52 mixed companies, Germany 2000

| | Minimum | Maximum | Mean | Std. Deviation |
|---|---|---|---|---|
| Turnover | 20,378 | 31,559,799 | 697,227 | [illegible],365,256 |
| Profit | −23,263 | 1,896,361 | 41,227 | 262,615 |
| Tassets | 14,753 | 139,835,674 | 2,899,992 | [illegible]9,363,[illegible]93 |
| Employees | 12 | 319,998 | 6,536 | 44,32[illegible] |
| Owners | 0.03 | 1 | 0.59 | 0.23 |
| PROD | 41.91 | 2,419.3 | 422.25 | 380.[illegible]7 |
| PROF | −254.78 | 187.6 | 24.19 | 69.8 |

*Table 5.14(c)* Descriptive statistics for 259 private companies, Germany 1998

| | Minimum | Maximum | Mean | Std. Deviation |
|---|---|---|---|---|
| Turnover | 933 | 70,777,272 | 867,631 | 4,998,466 |
| Profit | −76,420 | 3,151,441 | 56,709 | 309,067 |
| Tassets | 4,131 | 66,826,508 | 690,085 | 4,451,137 |
| Employees | 13 | 401,000 | 3,674 | 26,342 |
| Owners | 1 | 1 | 1 | 0 |
| PROD | 32.6 | 173,130.15 | 1,216.81 | 10,817.99 |
| PROF | −2,053.44 | 6,909.04 | 38.36 | 454.67 |

*Table 5.14(d)* Descriptive statistics for 231 private companies, Germany 2000

| | Minimum | Maximum | Mean | Std. Deviation |
|---|---|---|---|---|
| Turnover | 48,107 | 45,491,258 | 999,605 | 3,825,942 |
| Profit | −157,813 | 1,051,163 | 35,200 | 130,053 |
| Tassets | 11,073 | 20,780,876 | 643,511 | 2,226,661 |
| Employees | 78 | 234,351 | 4,612 | 19,060 |
| Owners | 1 | 1 | 1 | 0 |
| PROD | 13.65 | 15,829.85 | 298.6 | 1,049.94 |
| PROF | −62.11 | 1,133.11 | 16.99 | 81.51 |

*Table 5.14(e)* Descriptive statistics for 174 state companies, Germany 1998

| | Minimum | Maximum | Mean | Std. Deviation |
|---|---|---|---|---|
| Turnover | 19,251 | 22,125,656 | 538,645 | 2,401,814 |
| Profit | −72,337 | 986,583 | 15,774 | 90,044 |
| Tassets | 12,099 | 40,789,406 | 753,597 | 3,315,585 |
| Employees | 9 | 198,989 | 2,566 | 15,899 |
| Owners | 0 | 0 | 0 | 0 |
| PROD | 26.1 | 17,950.9 | 645.81 | 1,727.83 |
| PROF | −248.6 | 420.02 | 14.33 | 65.07 |

*Table 5.14(f)* Descriptive statistics for 177 state companies, Germany 2000

| | Minimum | Maximum | Mean | Std. Deviation |
|---|---|---|---|---|
| Turnover | 651 | 21,453,908 | 347,245 | 1,713,730 |
| Profit | −183,309 | 536,341 | 8,495 | 53,100 |
| Tassets | 11,439 | 17,223,106 | 510,315 | 1,794,625 |
| Employees | 11 | 76,392 | 1,449 | 6,319 |
| Owners | 0 | 0 | 0 | 0 |
| PROD | 0.68 | 19,370.84 | 560.05 | 1,585.75 |
| PROF | −608.93 | 394.09 | 9.59 | 92.84 |

with respect to corporate performance, ownership is not associated with other elements such as turnover and profit.

The result for 2000 indicates that two factors have been retained. Factor 1 shows that turnover, profit, total assets and employees are highly loaded with it. Factor 2 identifies that the two highly loaded variables are PROD and PROF. Two characteristics can be identified: size and performance. The ownership variable remains insignificant, as in many other cases.

## Germany

For this country data on 500 companies for the year 1998 and 460 companies for the year 2000 have been used. The descriptive statistics table, Table 5.14, shows relatively small standard deviations for variables Owners and PROD of mixed companies for both years.

From Table 5.15 it can be seen that three factors explained more than an average amount of variance for the year 1998. The variables that are again loaded more heavily than others with factor 1 are turnover, profit, total assets and employees. PROD and PROF are highly loaded with factor 2. In the last factor the only variable that has a significant correlation coefficient is ownership (0.993). This demonstrates again that it is possible to establish three characteristics: size, performance and some sort of ownership. Ownership again remains unlinked to other characteristics.

Table 5.15 also indicates that three factors have been extracted for the year 2000. Factor 1 tells the same story as the preceding case. The variables turnover, profit, total assets and employees are weighted heavily with the component 1. The second component gives information about two highly loaded variables, PROD and PROF. The last factor indicates that only one variable, ownership, with the associated value of (0.888), is highly loaded.

It is possible to establish three characteristics: size, performance and some type of ownership. Variables that are normally used as corporate performance indicators are not associated with ownership through any particular factor.

## Italy

This case uses data on 70 and 90 companies for the years 1998 and 2000, respectively. Descriptive statistics of the samples are summerised in Table 5.16. It can be emphasised that there is nothing remarkable in the table which to comment on.

*Table 5.15* Company performances: Germany

| | 1998 | | | 2000 | | |
|---|---|---|---|---|---|---|
| Variables | Component 1 (Size) | Component 2 (Perf) | Component 3 (Own) | Component 1 (Size) | Component 2 (Perf) | Component 3 (Own) |
| Turnover | 0.967 | −0.031 | −0.019 | 0.907 | 0.020 | −0.015 |
| Profit | 0.712 | 0.010 | 0.122 | 0.920 | 0.062 | 0.060 |
| Total Assets | 0.946 | −0.131 | 0.068 | 0.891 | −0.035 | −0.108 |
| Number of employees | 0.939 | −0.173 | −0.037 | 0.963 | −0.067 | −0.049 |
| Ownership | 0.044 | 0.066 | 0.991 | 0.095 | −0.228 | 0.888 |
| PROD | 0.153 | 0.972 | −0.045 | 0.013 | 0.783 | −0.166 |
| PROF | 0.161 | 0.971 | −0.040 | 0.044 | 0.714 | 0.451 |
| Variance extracted | 46.688 | 27.718 | 14.373 | 48.605 | 16.932 | 14.831 |

*Table 5.16(a)* Descriptive statistics for 3 mixed companies, Italy 1998

| | Minimum | Maximum | Mean | Std. Deviation |
|---|---|---|---|---|
| Turnover | 60,028 | 52,952,981 | 26,049,041 | 26,458,343 |
| Profit | 63 | 4,894,620 | 3,251,364 | 2,815,765 |
| Tassets | 108,488 | 56,198,657 | 34,993,915 | 30,444,994 |
| Employees | 907 | 100,212 | 58,748 | 51,638 |
| Owners | 0.3 | 0.95 | 0.65 | 0.33 |
| PROD | 66.18 | 704.87 | 340.62 | 328.68 |
| PROF | 0.07 | 64.69 | 37.87 | 33.68 |

*Table 5.16(b)* Descriptive statistics for 4 mixed companies, Italy 2000

| | Minimum | Maximum | Mean | Std. Deviation |
|---|---|---|---|---|
| Turnover | 180,530 | 62,012,301 | 22,929,949 | 28,039,907 |
| Profit | −232,132 | 10,113,614 | 3,320,092 | 4,822,215 |
| Tassets | 381,324 | 53,358,643 | 26,582,288 | 28,075,597 |
| Employees | 2,762 | 85,377 | 47,912 | 37,902 |
| Owners | 0.3 | 0.68 | 0.55 | 0.17 |
| PROD | 65.36 | 858.62 | 344.12 | 354.45 |
| PROF | −7.42 | 140.03 | 43.6 | 67.44 |

*Table 5.16(c)* Descriptive statistics for 37 private companies, Italy 1998

| | Minimum | Maximum | Mean | Std. Deviation |
|---|---|---|---|---|
| Turnover | 530,159 | 11,624,046 | 2,257,270 | 2,358,631 |
| Profit | −898,316 | 2,772,996 | 136,194 | 492,169 |
| Tassets | 206,396 | 28,148,330 | 3,055,696 | 5,289,132 |
| Employees | 263 | 45,457 | 6,883 | 9,996 |
| Owners | 1 | 1 | 1 | 0 |
| PROD | 132.84 | 9,785.11 | 1,194.22 | 2,238.2 |
| PROF | −24.88 | 266.36 | 38.65 | 64.62 |

*Table 5.16(d)* Descriptive statistics for 45 private companies, Italy 2000

| | Minimum | Maximum | Mean | Std. Deviation |
|---|---|---|---|---|
| Turnover | 62,934 | 10,042,627 | 1,256,921 | 2,058,257 |
| Profit | −563,992 | 1,867,768 | 64,843 | 301,793 |
| Tassets | 36,227 | 18,719,288 | 1,360,199 | 3,141,189 |
| Employees | 55 | 40,208 | 3,761 | 7,675 |
| Owners | 1 | 1 | 1 | 0 |
| PROD | 128.7 | 3,237.35 | 690.9 | 829.74 |
| PROF | −27.96 | 188.51 | 17.41 | 36.02 |

*Table 5.16(e)* Descriptive statistics for 30 state companies, Italy 1998

| | Minimum | Maximum | Mean | Std. Deviation |
|---|---|---|---|---|
| Turnover | 3,188 | 13,485,967 | 739,350 | 2,563,343 |
| Profit | −127,744 | 623,653 | 19,396 | 116,750 |
| Tassets | 3,690 | 9,402,395 | 632,180 | 1,930,255 |
| Employees | 8 | 18,405 | 1,518 | 4,211 |
| Owners | 0 | 0 | 0 | 0 |
| PROD | 17.33 | 5,283.69 | 612.02 | 980.54 |
| PROF | −116.93 | 213.88 | 11.99 | 51.99 |

*Table 5.16(f)* Descriptive statistics for 41 state companies, Italy 2000

| | Minimum | Maximum | Mean | Std. Deviation |
|---|---|---|---|---|
| Turnover | 2,216 | 12,476,428 | 941,226 | 2,333,531 |
| Profit | −738,516 | 1,444,363 | 63,958 | 323,565 |
| Tassets | 3,961 | 16,797,354 | 1,244,243 | 3,278,134 |
| Employees | 18 | 45,865 | 3,001 | 8,302 |
| Owners | 0 | 0 | 0 | 0 |
| PROD | 44.3 | 14,737.52 | 1,286.89 | 3,173.76 |
| PROF | −163.71 | 538.43 | 35.39 | 124.75 |

*Table 5.17* Company performances: Italy

| | 1998 | | 2000 | |
|---|---|---|---|---|
| Variables | Component 1 (Size) | Component 2 (Perf) | Component 1 (Size) | Component 2 (Perf) |
| Turnover | 0.944 | −0.008 | 0.975 | −0.004 |
| Profit | 0.931 | 0.006 | 0.935 | 0.031 |
| Total Assets | 0.972 | −0.075 | 0.977 | −0.067 |
| Number of employees | 0.948 | −0.122 | 0.909 | −0.127 |
| Ownership | 0.140 | 0.367 | −0.014 | −0.296 |
| PROD | −0.028 | 0.921 | −0.014 | 0.916 |
| PROF | 0.181 | 0.914 | 0.186 | 0.893 |
| Variance extracted | 52.221 | 26.262 | 52.000 | 24.946 |

The results of factor analysis are indicated in Table 5.17. They show that two factors have been extracted for the year 1998. The first factor demonstrates that turnover, profit, total assets and employee numbers are heavily weighted. The second factor indicates that PROD and PROF are highly loaded. Two characteristics are well established: size and performance. The type of ownership in this case is unimportant with respect to corporate performance.

The result for the year 2000 demonstrates that two factors have been extracted. Like the year 1998, size and performance as two main characteristics are well established. Similarly to many other cases, the type of ownership does not occupy a significant part of the common variance; therefore, it is not strongly correlated to either of the two factors.

## The Netherlands

Data of 90 companies for the year 1998 and 200 companies for the year 2000 were taken and factor analysis was subsequently carried out. The descriptive statistics in Table 5.18 demonstrate that the standard deviations of variables Owners, PROD and PROF for mixed companies of both years are relatively small.

*Table 5.18(a)* Descriptive statistics for 5 mixed companies, the Netherlands 1998

| | Minimum | Maximum | Mean | Std. Deviation |
|---|---|---|---|---|
| Turnover | 48,351 | 9,450,434 | 3,871,809 | 4,766,100 |
| Profit | 9,854 | 1,650,721 | 517,980 | 697,194 |
| Tassets | 126,587 | 15,947,021 | 4,928,545 | 6,615,133 |
| Employees | 122 | 101,582 | 28,916 | 43,206 |
| Owners | 0.25 | 0.76 | 0.45 | 0.21 |
| PROD | 85.72 | 396.32 | 236.87 | 138.66 |
| PROF | 7.19 | 82.68 | 44.89 | 37.06 |

*Table 5.18(b)* Descriptive statistics for 5 mixed companies, the Netherlands 2000

| | Minimum | Maximum | Mean | Std. Deviation |
|---|---|---|---|---|
| Turnover | 37,423 | 12,571,998 | 4,612,216 | 5,871,537 |
| Profit | 9,612 | 1,916,832 | 582,786 | 807,817 |
| Tassets | 101,410 | 49,749,230 | 11,875,797 | 21,350,588 |
| Employees | 138 | 129,675 | 37,417 | 55,119 |
| Owners | 0.25 | 0.76 | 0.45 | 0.21 |
| PROD | 71.3 | 322.75 | 201.43 | 117.84 |
| PROF | 6.01 | 81.26 | 40.88 | 34.65 |

*Table 5.18(c)* Descriptive statistics for 45 private companies, the Netherlands 1998

| | Minimum | Maximum | Mean | Std. Deviation |
|---|---|---|---|---|
| Turnover | 69,354 | 31,128,203 | 2,567,097 | 4,679,778 |
| Profit | −2,275 | 920,737 | 136,731 | 213,493 |
| Tassets | 19,303 | 13,667,415 | 1,711,665 | 2,819,660 |
| Employees | 69 | 214,000 | 15,299 | 39,117 |
| Owners | 1 | 1 | 1 | 0 |
| PROD | 12.36 | 8,677.1 | 907.83 | 1,516.87 |
| PROF | −32.97 | 1,438.83 | 71.57 | 245.74 |

*Table 5.18(d)* Descriptive statistics for 64 private companies, the Netherlands 2000

| | Minimum | Maximum | Mean | Std. Deviation |
|---|---|---|---|---|
| Turnover | 8[illegible],536 | 7,643,699 | 1,374,920 | 1,566,807 |
| Profit | −318,730 | 1,550,926 | 105,272 | 260,092 |
| Tassets | 38,218 | 8,250,715 | 1,375,272 | 1,983,846 |
| Employees | 25 | 53,800 | 6,301 | 10,478 |
| Owners | 1 | 1 | 1 | 0 |
| PROD | 74.97 | 13,472.54 | 1,040.92 | 2,158.88 |
| PROF | −189.72 | 1,475.67 | 63.51 | 219.34 |

*Table 5.18(e)* Descriptive statistics for 40 state companies, the Netherlands 1998

| | Minimum | Maximum | Mean | Std. deviation |
|---|---|---|---|---|
| Turnover | 3,609 | 9,231,654 | 556,697 | 1,5[illegible]3,141 |
| Profit | −86,361 | 148,271 | 12,725 | 34,071 |
| Tassets | 5,641 | 8,792,478 | 665,326 | 1,645,742 |
| Employees | 13 | 23,794 | 1,931 | 4,555 |
| Owners | 0 | 0 | 0 | 0 |
| PROD | 48.12 | 24,507.96 | 1,148.57 | 3,912.76 |
| PROF | −1,151.48 | 787.45 | 43.16 | 278.55 |

*Table 5.18(f)* Descriptive statistics for 51 state companies, the Netherlands 2000

| | Minimum | Maximum | Mean | Std. Deviation |
|---|---|---|---|---|
| Turnover | 6,245 | 7,408,581 | 632,635 | 1,393,620 |
| Profit | −1,359,876 | 3,953,731 | 66,425 | 615,087 |
| Tassets | 4,984 | 33,272,026 | 1,550,091 | 5,047,508 |
| Employees | 14 | 22,853 | 2,095 | 4,806 |
| Owners | 0 | 0 | 0 | 0 |
| PROD | 52.29 | 385,107 | 8,550.39 | 53,913.51 |
| PROF | −679.94 | 3,604.49 | 163.95 | 750.04 |

The story here is the same as in the case of Italy. Table 5.19 illustrates that two factors have been retained for the year 1998. Through the first factor, it can be observed that turnover, profit, total assets and employees are heavily weighted within the associated component. The second factor reveals that two variables, PROD and PROF, are highly loaded. From these results it is possible to establish two characteristics, size and performance. The ownership characteristic has little correlation with

*Table 5.19* Company performances: the Netherlands

| | 1998 | | 2000 | | |
|---|---|---|---|---|---|
| **Variables** | **Component 1 (Size)** | **Component 2 (Perf)** | **Component 1 (Size)** | **Component 2 (Perf)** | **Component 3 (Own)** |
| Turnover | 0.897 | −0.015 | 0.964 | −0.119 | 0.043 |
| Profit | 0.853 | 0.137 | 0.721 | 0.112 | 0.035 |
| Total Assets | 0.858 | 0.024 | 0.699 | −0.287 | −0.323 |
| Number of employees | 0.756 | −0.135 | 0.681 | −0.386 | 0.028 |
| Ownership | 0.345 | 0.047 | 0.076 | −0.277 | 0.935 |
| PROD | −0.084 | 0.811 | 0.238 | 0.813 | 0.084 |
| PROF | 0.034 | 0.848 | 0.382 | 0.851 | 0.13 |
| Variance extracted | 42.379 | 20.229 | 37.287 | 24.556 | 14.37 |

the two factors and it is unimportant when considering corporate performance.

For the year 2000 three factors are extracted. The first factor, as usual, demonstrates that turnover, profit, total assets and employees are highly loaded within the associated factor. The variables PROD and PROF are highly loaded in the second factor. The third factor shows that only the ownership variable has a significant correlation coefficient, with a value of (0.935). From these three factors, three characteristics of corporate performance can be recognised: size, performance and the kind of ownership. This is consistent with most of the preceding cases.

## Norway

The data on 120 and 200 Norwegian companies for the years 1998 and 2000, respectively, have been collected to complete the factor analysis for this country. Descriptive statistics of our samples for two years 1998 and 2000 are presented in Table 5.20, with nothing on which to comment.

The output, which is shown in the Table 5.21, shows that three factors have been extracted for the year 1998. The variables of turnover, profit, total assets and employees are heavily weighted in the first factor. Items PROD and PROF are highly loaded in the second factor, while the other variables are insignificant. The last factor has just one highly loaded variable, the ownership, with associated value of (0.973). From this analysis, once again, it is found that three characteristics of corporate performance are well established, namely size, performance and the kind of ownership.

*Table 5.20(a)* Descriptive statistics for 14 mixed companies, Norway 1998

| | **Minimum** | **Maximum** | **Mean** | **Std. Deviation** |
|---|---|---|---|---|
| Turnover | 3,923 | 12,824,737 | 988,828 | 3,410,396 |
| Profit | −244 | 767,237 | 59,384 | 203,948 |
| Tassets | 2,985 | 14,960,658 | 1,163,070 | 3,974,785 |
| Employees | 18 | 9,329 | 808 | 2,456 |
| Owners | 0.25 | 0.9 | 0.5 | 0.17 |
| PROD | 26.13 | 34,203.22 | 2,889.1 | 9,059.38 |
| PROF | −1.21 | 1,812.87 | 157.66 | 479.94 |

*Table 5.20(b)* Descriptive statistics for 33 mixed companies, Norway 2000

| | **Minimum** | **Maximum** | **Mean** | **Std. Deviation** |
|---|---|---|---|---|
| Turnover | 2,935 | 23,524,439 | 1,305,084 | 5,037,340 |
| Profit | −20,324 | 4,302,537 | 238,876 | 939,441 |
| Tassets | 1,713 | 22,190,654 | 1,415,935 | 5,200,076 |
| Employees | 16 | 10,293 | 704 | 2,336 |
| Owners | 0.25 | 0.9 | 0.5 | 0.19 |
| PROD | 25.21 | 22,167.39 | 1,385.27 | 3,897.76 |
| PROF | −307.93 | 1,993.66 | 124.7 | 387.52 |

*Table 5.20(c)* Descriptive statistics for 63 private companies, Norway 1998

| | **Minimum** | **Maximum** | **Mean** | **Std. Deviation** |
|---|---|---|---|---|
| Turnover | 377 | 10,941,711 | 389,465 | 1,386,022 |
| Profit | −176,974 | 307,830 | 8,392 | 47,211 |
| Tassets | 9,044 | 7,153,158 | 254,509 | 917,755 |
| Employees | 32 | 4,912 | 491 | 670 |
| Owners | 1 | 1 | 1 | 0 |
| PROD | 3.77 | 113,976.15 | 2,813.08 | 14,438.02 |
| PROF | −1,843.48 | 2,033.02 | 47.79 | 366.62 |

*Table 5.20(d)* Descriptive statistics for 101 private companies, Norway 2000

| | **Minimum** | **Maximum** | **Mean** | **Std. Deviation** |
|---|---|---|---|---|
| Turnover | 190 | 4,218,986 | 273,771 | 619,934 |
| Profit | −11,682 | 907,313 | 19,966 | 92,703 |
| Tassets | 193 | 17,714,200 | 385,278 | 1,800,323 |
| Employees | 14 | 7,400 | 534 | 877 |
| Owners | 1 | 1 | 1 | 0 |
| PROD | 0.33 | 29,096.46 | 1,846.62 | 4,178.51 |
| PROF | −118.46 | 10,681.11 | 233.43 | 1,181.54 |

*Table 5.20(e)* Descriptive statistics for 43 state companies, Norway 1998

| | Minimum | Maximum | Mean | Std. Deviation |
|---|---|---|---|---|
| Turnover | 1,215 | 3,734,211 | 268,653 | 664,624 |
| Profit | −51,711 | 512,895 | 21,171 | 90,638 |
| Tassets | 840 | 5,234,211 | 376,280 | 880,291 |
| Employees | 12 | 3,978 | 448 | 918 |
| Owners | 0 | 0 | 0 | 0 |
| PROD | 11.72 | 5,042.44 | 805.91 | 1,272.64 |
| PROF | −1,017.04 | 767.95 | 37.52 | 243.44 |

*Table 5.20(f)* Descriptive statistics for 66 state companies, Norway 2000

| | Minimum | Maximum | Mean | Std. Deviation |
|---|---|---|---|---|
| Turnover | 74 | 3,374,131 | 178,819 | 484,230 |
| Profit | −35,260 | 541,094 | 21,583 | 82,115 |
| Tassets | 264 | 3,531,107 | 248,700 | 575,595 |
| Employees | 10 | 4,064 | 349 | 806 |
| Owners | 0 | 0 | 0 | 0 |
| PROD | 0.26 | 9,216.57 | 776 | 1,707.34 |
| PROF | −770.67 | 6,680.18 | 173.33 | 864.53 |

*Table 5.21* Company performances: Norway

| | 1998 | | | 2000 | |
|---|---|---|---|---|---|
| Variables | Component 1 (Size) | Component 2 (Perf) | Component 3 (Own) | Component 1 (Size) | Component 2 (Perf) |
| Turnover | 0.953 | −0.267 | 0.014 | 0.982 | −0.074 |
| Profit | 0.747 | 0.574 | 0.026 | 0.959 | −0.07 |
| Total Assets | 0.981 | −0.02 | −0.032 | 0.925 | 0.085 |
| Number of employees | 0.779 | 0.313 | 0.055 | 0.844 | −0.25 |
| Ownership | −0.026 | −0.166 | 0.973 | 0.074 | 0.244 |
| PROD | 0.38 | −0.782 | 0.04 | 0.195 | 0.849 |
| PROF | −0.147 | 0.715 | 0.229 | 0.113 | 0.792 |
| Variance extracted | 45.765 | 23.553 | 14.363 | 50.111 | 21.239 |

Table 5.21 above demonstrates that two factors have been extracted for the year 2000. The variables of turnover, profit, total assets and employees are highly loaded within the first extracted factor that a common characteristic, size, can be established. The second component demonstrates that two variables, PROD and PROF, are highly loaded.

From the above result, like many other cases, it is again possible to establish two characteristics of corporate performance; that is, size and performance.

## Poland

A total of 340 companies of different types (state, mixed and private) have been chosen for the year 1998 and a larger sample of 420 companies has been selected for the year 2000. Table 5.22 introduces the

*Table 5.22(a)* Descriptive statistics for 19 mixed companies, Poland 1998

| | Minimum | Maximum | Mean | Std. Deviation |
|---|---|---|---|---|
| Turnover | 1,617 | 576,727 | 53,288 | 134,438 |
| Profit | −21,910 | 3,096 | −798 | 5,231 |
| Tassets | 1,756 | 496,029 | 59,625 | 135,698 |
| Employees | 34 | 4,199 | 678 | 994 |
| Owners | 0.16 | 1 | 0.51 | 0.21 |
| PROD | 6.8 | 285.26 | 63.99 | 73.53 |
| PROF | −29.69 | 78.93 | 3.14 | 19.79 |

*Table 5.22(b)* Descriptive statistics for 33 mixed companies, Poland 2000

| | Minimum | Maximum | Mean | Std. Deviation |
|---|---|---|---|---|
| Turnover | 574 | 1,377,894 | 131,441 | 292,892 |
| Profit | −17,856 | 182,400 | 6,629 | 32,080 |
| Tassets | 457 | 1,804,279 | 141,113 | 329,255 |
| Employees | 44 | 18,562 | 1,310 | 3,271 |
| Owners | 0.16 | 1 | 0.53 | 0.22 |
| PROD | 1.31 | 4,746.63 | 237.95 | 819.43 |
| PROF | −55.2 | 261.1 | 8.77 | 48.02 |

*Table 5.22(c)* Descriptive statistics for 173 private companies, Poland 1998

| | Minimum | Maximum | Mean | Std. Deviation |
|---|---|---|---|---|
| Turnover | 192 | 2,680,347 | 185,420 | 349,224 |
| Profit | −377,199 | 102,665 | −469 | 33,276 |
| Tassets | 1,276 | 6,592,793 | 138,982 | 522,266 |
| Employees | 10 | 214,135 | 2,914 | 17,955 |
| Owners | 1 | 1 | 1 | 0 |
| PROD | 0.64 | 35,728.55 | 652.77 | 3,008.75 |
| PROF | −240.76 | 792.54 | 3.91 | 70.63 |

*Table 5.22(d)* Descriptive statistics for 215 private companies, Poland 2000

| | Minimum | Maximum | Mean | Std. Deviation |
|---|---|---|---|---|
| Turnover | 6,084 | 3,903,277 | 237,027 | 385,026 |
| Profit | −195,310 | 478,874 | 3,506 | 38,962 |
| Tassets | 2,680 | 7,964,693 | 182,722 | 622,054 |
| Employees | 11 | 101,255 | 2,052 | 8,436 |
| Owners | 1 | 1 | 1 | 0 |
| PROD | 6.33 | 14,990.84 | 679.79 | 1,430.01 |
| PROF | −1,128.96 | 385.1 | −1.12 | 96.37 |

*Table 5.22(e)* Descriptive statistics for 148 state companies, Poland 1998

| | Minimum | Maximum | Mean | Std. Deviation |
|---|---|---|---|---|
| Turnover | 1,736 | 3,829,119 | 122,158 | 360,037 |
| Profit | −192,053 | 68,787 | 33 | 21,860 |
| Tassets | 840 | 3,917,758 | 141,376 | 460,369 |
| Employees | 41 | 47,350 | 1,957 | 5,428 |
| Owners | 0 | 0 | 0 | 0 |
| PROD | 6.91 | 7,960.75 | 139.32 | 667.3 |
| PROF | −298.86 | 116.79 | 1.37 | 28.35 |

*Table 5.22(f)* Descriptive statistics for 172 state companies, Poland 2000

| | Minimum | Maximum | Mean | Std. Deviation |
|---|---|---|---|---|
| Turnover | 1,325 | 3,314,315 | 123,906 | 313,334 |
| Profit | −94,524 | 110,168 | 1,762 | 16,281 |
| Tassets | 953 | 3,692,635 | 119,066 | 347,714 |
| Employees | 16 | 32,500 | 1,609 | 3,842 |
| Owners | 0 | 0 | 0 | 0 |
| PROD | 7.5 | 6,628.63 | 178.24 | 625.36 |
| PROF | −159.08 | 289.92 | 5.18 | 30.22 |

descriptive statistics for our samples for both the years 1998 and 2000, with nothing on which to comment.

Factor analysis results are shown in Table 5.23. Two factors for the year 1998 have been extracted. It can be seen that turnover, total assets and employees are highly loaded within factor 1, but profit is also negatively loaded. Looking at the second factor, it can be seen that two items, PROD and PROF, are highly loaded. From the first factor it can be recognised that size is a characteristic of corporate performance. The second

*Table 5.23* Company performances: Poland

| | 1998 | | 2000 | | |
|---|---|---|---|---|---|
| **Variables** | **Component 1 (Size)** | **Component 2 (Perf)** | **Component 1 (Size)** | **Component 2 (Perf)** | **Component 3 (Own)** |
| Turnover | 0.717 | 0.244 | 0.892 | −0.167 | 0.021 |
| Profit | −0.715 | 0.216 | 0.625 | 0.581 | 0.222 |
| Total Assets | 0.921 | 0.029 | 0.909 | −0.122 | −0.184 |
| Number of employees | 0.914 | −0.024 | 0.738 | 0.201 | −0.193 |
| Ownership | 0.061 | 0.189 | 0.166 | −0.319 | 0.75 |
| PROD | 0.031 | 0.905 | 0.193 | −0.665 | 0.372 |
| PROF | −0.071 | 0.9 | −0.092 | 0.764 | 0.495 |
| Variance extracted | 38.834 | 25.32 | 37.578 | 22.112 | 15.25 |

factor emphasises the role of a second characteristic, performance. Ownership is not an influential variable in either factor.

According to Table 5.23, three factors have been extracted for the year 2000. The result shows that turnover, profit, total assets and employees are heavily weighted within the first factor. The first characteristic, size, is well established. PROD (negatively), profit and PROF are highly loaded with the second factor. The third factor demonstrates that ownership is the only highly loaded variable. This emphasises the third characteristic, the kind of ownership, but with little correlation with other variables. The results here are mixed and not open to immediate interpretation, although they do not seem to support a strong relationship between private ownership and performance. This may be a consequence of an economy still in transition or restating its effects, a matter beyond the scope of this study.

## Portugal

This exercise uses the data on 60 Portuguese companies of different kinds of ownership for the year 1998, and the same number for the year 2000. Descriptive statistics for those companies are introduced in Table 5.24. According to the table relatively small standard deviations of variables Owners and PROD for mixed companies and PROD for state companies for the year 1998 as well as Owners of mixed companies and PROD of private and state companies for the year 2000 are observable. But it is the small number of mixed and state-owned companies that is apparent, inevitably questioning the usefulness of including this country.

*Table 5.24(a)* Descriptive statistics for 5 mixed companies, Portugal 1998

| | Minimum | Maximum | Mean | Std. Deviation |
|---|---|---|---|---|
| Turnover | 34,569 | 1,256,955 | 356,881 | 509,250 |
| Profit | −67,823 | 17,180 | −22,089 | 35,446 |
| Tassets | 197,755 | 1,857,196 | 836,622 | 795,921 |
| Employees | 1,651 | 8,603 | 4,015 | 2,772 |
| Owners | 0.49 | 1 | 0.77 | 0.23 |
| PROD | 20.94 | 146.11 | 66.51 | 52.38 |
| PROF | −28.91 | 2 | −9.38 | 12.94 |

*Table 5.24(b)* Descriptive statistics for 5 mixed companies, Portugal 2000

| | Minimum | Maximum | Mean | Std. Deviation |
|---|---|---|---|---|
| Turnover | 23 | 1,932,701 | 452,194 | 832,154 |
| Profit | −73,242 | 81,215 | −15,717 | 63,232 |
| Tassets | 85,179 | 2,012,418 | 813,216 | 962,736 |
| Employees | 6 | 4,189 | 1,683 | 1,629 |
| Owners | 0.4 | 1 | 0.63 | 0.26 |
| PROD | 3.87 | 3,158.01 | 659.9 | 1,397.01 |
| PROF | −52.69 | 132.7 | 19.2 | 71.57 |

*Table 5.24(c)* Descriptive statistics for 47 private companies, Portugal 1998

| | Minimum | Maximum | Mean | Std. Deviation |
|---|---|---|---|---|
| Turnover | 31,077 | 1,545,100 | 179,097 | 327,857 |
| Profit | −145,063 | 220,508 | 5,665 | 40,153 |
| Tassets | 12,935 | 2,104,603 | 193,865 | 431,286 |
| Employees | 83 | 11,644 | 1,085 | 1,901 |
| Owners | 1 | 1 | 1 | 0 |
| PROD | 11.93 | 1,531.2 | 254.47 | 267.74 |
| PROF | −65.73 | 43.9 | 4.08 | 14.54 |

*Table 5.24(d)* Descriptive statistics for 46 private companies, Portugal 2000

| | Minimum | Maximum | Mean | Std. Deviation |
|---|---|---|---|---|
| Turnover | 26,785 | 1,753,844 | 167,847 | 270,818 |
| Profit | −12,441 | 125,973 | 6,748 | 19,327 |
| Tassets | 8,160 | 1,205,537 | 157,535 | 245,902 |
| Employees | 108 | 14,847 | 1,057 | 2,184 |
| Owners | 1 | 1 | 1 | 0 |
| PROD | 27.87 | 1,092.96 | 263.19 | 221.94 |
| PROF | −21.19 | 72.32 | 9.33 | 15.07 |

*Table 5.24(e)* Descriptive statistics for 8 state companies, Portugal 1998

| | Minimum | Maximum | Mean | Std. Deviation |
|---|---|---|---|---|
| Turnover | 560 | 587,698 | 167,249 | 213,622 |
| Profit | −23,207 | 32,968 | 2,233 | 16,875 |
| Tassets | 10,374 | 1,819,718 | 446,503 | 628,148 |
| Employees | 19 | 3,061 | 1,103 | 1,212 |
| Owners | 0 | 0 | 0 | 0 |
| PROD | 23.78 | 429.5 | 179.84 | 145.02 |
| PROF | −36.45 | 27.7 | 1.61 | 19.37 |

*Table 5.24(f)* Descriptive statistics for 9 state companies, Portugal 2000

| | Minimum | Maximum | Mean | Std. Deviation |
|---|---|---|---|---|
| Turnover | 1,906 | 775,745 | 289,233 | 286,074 |
| Profit | −160,329 | 151,695 | 14,591 | 87,452 |
| Tassets | 66,520 | 2,571,036 | 954,089 | 968,373 |
| Employees | 25 | 17,844 | 2,771 | 5,692 |
| Owners | 0 | 0 | 0 | 0 |
| PROD | 19.98 | 793.07 | 268.78 | 266 |
| PROF | −79.41 | 110.48 | 13.17 | 58.98 |

Nonetheless, the results for these two years are shown in Table 5.25. Three factors have been retained for the year 1998. According to the first factor, the variables turnover, total assets and employees are heavily weighted. The second factor demonstrates that PROD and PROF are highly loaded, although other variables enter also. The last factor picks up PROD as the only highly loaded variable. Through components 1 and 2 the characteristic of size and performance will be well established. Through the last component it is possible to establish a characteristic of productivity again with other variables present. However, it is anomalous with respect to other findings, and not open to natural interpretation.

For the year 2000, Table 5.25 shows that two factors have been extracted. The variables of turnover, profit, total assets, PROD and PROF are highly loaded in the first factor. Through component 2 it can be seen that variables profit, ownership and PROF have higher correlation coefficients (not significantly) than the other variables. Common characteristics relevant to preceding findings cannot be extracted through components 1 and 2. Ownership again has no strong relationship with the extracted factors.

*Table 5.25* Company performances: Portugal

| | 1998 | | | 2000 | |
|---|---|---|---|---|---|
| **Variables** | **Component 1 (Size)** | **Component 2 (Perf)** | **Component 3 (Prod)** | **Component 1 (Size/Perf)** | **Component 2 (Profit/Own/Prof)** |
| Turnover | 0.869 | −0.103 | 0.429 | 0.881 | −0.166 |
| Profit | 0.727 | 0.479 | −0.345 | 0.725 | 0.445 |
| Total Assets | 0.815 | −0.305 | −0.07 | 0.582 | −0.682 |
| Number of employees | 0.729 | −0.524 | 0.115 | 0.306 | −0.745 |
| Ownership | −0.131 | 0.363 | 0.42 | −0.399 | 0.487 |
| PROD | 0.134 | 0.553 | 0.68 | 0.7 | 0.343 |
| PROF | 0.476 | 0.725 | −0.386 | 0.809 | 0.498 |
| Variance extracted | 39.159 | 22.44 | 15.839 | 43.395 | 26.402 |

### Sweden

The data on 756 companies are used to investigate corporate performance through factor analysis for the year 1998 as well as a similarly large sample size of 750 companies for the year 2000. Descriptive statistics presented in Table 5.26 indicate relatively small standard deviations for Owners of mixed companies for both years and for PROD of mixed companies for the year 1998.

Factor analysis results are given in Table 5.27 for the year 1998 and 2000. It demonstrates that two factors have been extracted for the year 1998. Variables turnover, profit, total assets and employees are heavily loaded in the first component. In the second factor, the performance variables, PROD and PROF, are highly loaded. The same result is retained for the year 2000.

This investigation demonstrates that two characteristics can be established: size through the first component and performance through the second component for both years. In other words, corporate performance is characterised by size of the corporation, on the one hand, and the performance for both years, on the other. In this case, ownership cannot be included as a possible characteristic.

### The UK

The data of 200 companies each for the years 1998 and 2000 were researched to complete the factor analysis. No mixed companies are included in this investigation. Descriptive statistics for both years are introduced in Table 5.28, with nothing on which to comment.

*Table 5.26(a)* Descriptive statistics for 33 mixed companies, Sweden 1998

| | Minimum | Maximum | Mean | Std. Deviation |
|---|---|---|---|---|
| Turnover | 5,753 | 7,119,836 | 439,244 | 1,343,146 |
| Profit | −145,904 | 843,320 | 27,131 | 151,138 |
| Tassets | 2,460 | 8,231,485 | 664,638 | 1,608,261 |
| Employees | 10 | 31,320 | 1,524 | 5,520 |
| Owners | 0.5 | 0.99 | 0.76 | 0.16 |
| PROD | 58.37 | 1,368.96 | 373.14 | 277.26 |
| PROF | −241.61 | 119.11 | 13.79 | 59.71 |

*Table 5.26(b)* Descriptive statistics for 37 mixed companies, Sweden 2000

| | Minimum | Maximum | Mean | Std. Deviation |
|---|---|---|---|---|
| Turnover | 6,543 | 6,629,749 | 321,562 | 1,156,097 |
| Profit | −83,464 | 1,241,800 | 52,986 | 212,492 |
| Tassets | 2,607 | 13,005,670 | 631,663 | 2,215,779 |
| Employees | 10 | 30,307 | 1,471 | 5,421 |
| Owners | 0.5 | 0.99 | 0.73 | 0.17 |
| PROD | 55.44 | 5,175.69 | 455.74 | 876.26 |
| PROF | −619.45 | 290.91 | 13.92 | 128.75 |

*Table 5.26(c)* Descriptive statistics for 379 private companies, Sweden 1998

| | Minimum | Maximum | Mean | Std. Deviation |
|---|---|---|---|---|
| Turnover | 4 | 10,370,798 | 145,840 | 663,508 |
| Profit | −78,007 | 760,203 | 9,961 | 52,544 |
| Tassets | 555 | 12,572,634 | 192,847 | 799,610 |
| Employees | 2 | 53,493 | 598 | 3,239 |
| Owners | 1 | 1 | 1 | 0 |
| PROD | 0.04 | 16,150.2 | 618.72 | 1,270.11 |
| PROF | −2,785.96 | 15,281.85 | 76.5 | 821.4 |

*Table 5.26(d)* Descriptive statistics for 375 private companies, Sweden 2000

| | Minimum | Maximum | Mean | Std. Deviation |
|---|---|---|---|---|
| Turnover | 2,237 | 8,095,914 | 123,963 | 533,422 |
| Profit | −42,154 | 573,473 | 10,709 | 48,105 |
| Tassets | 502 | 11,706,322 | 191,462 | 799,231 |
| Employees | 3 | 46,025 | 555 | 2,896 |
| Owners | 1 | 1 | 1 | 0 |
| PROD | 33.05 | 6,623.64 | 612.2 | 925.15 |
| PROF | −1,277.38 | 2,467.56 | 46.73 | 210.76 |

*Table 5.26(e)* Descriptive statistics for 344 state companies, Sweden 1998

| | Minimum | Maximum | Mean | Std. Deviation |
|---|---|---|---|---|
| Turnover | 485 | 3,554,398 | 126,053 | 383,262 |
| Profit | −352,190 | 867,696 | 10,740 | 67,109 |
| Tassets | 888 | 10,340,653 | 285,021 | 964,158 |
| Employees | 6 | 42,108 | 617 | 3,289 |
| Owners | 0 | 0 | 0 | 0 |
| PROD | 23.07 | 3,931.6 | 492.23 | 540.48 |
| PROF | −182 | 1,383.04 | 49.76 | 146.08 |

*Table 5.26(f)* Descriptive statistics for 338 state companies, Sweden 2000

| | Minimum | Maximum | Mean | Std. Deviation |
|---|---|---|---|---|
| Turnover | 380 | 3,845,689 | 132,696 | 393,405 |
| Profit | −293,042 | 549,944 | 7,904 | 51,944 |
| Tassets | 1,628 | 12,188,543 | 278,808 | 1,003,940 |
| Employees | 10 | 41,522 | 698 | 3,375 |
| Owners | 0 | 0 | 0 | 0 |
| PROD | 32.78 | 4,831.88 | 462.32 | 481.85 |
| PROF | −357.64 | 992.23 | 39.53 | 116.05 |

*Table 5.27* Company performances: Sweden

| | 1998 | | 2000 | |
|---|---|---|---|---|
| **Variables** | **Component 1 (Size)** | **Component 2 (Perf)** | **Component 1 (Size)** | **Component 2 (Perf)** |
| Turnover | 0.951 | −0.023 | 0.966 | −0.030 |
| Profit | 0.854 | 0.081 | 0.851 | 0.160 |
| Total Assets | 0.914 | 0.002 | 0.925 | −0.005 |
| Number of employees | 0.869 | −0.068 | 0.856 | −0.136 |
| Ownership | −0.002 | 0.115 | −0.004 | 0.323 |
| PROD | −0.014 | 0.893 | −0.047 | 0.758 |
| PROF | 0.026 | 0.890 | 0.068 | 0.746 |
| Variance extracted | 46.093 | 23.050 | 46.468 | 18.296 |

Factor analysis results are reported in Table 5.29 for the year 1998 and 2000. The results for the years 1998 and 2000 highlight the extraction of two components. The first component shows that the variables turnover, profit, total assets, employees and ownership are highly loaded. The second component indicates that PROD and PROF are

*Table 5.28(a)* Descriptive statistics for 110 private companies, the UK 1998

| | Minimum | Maximum | Mean | Std. Deviation |
|---|---|---|---|---|
| Turnover | 9,404 | 13,309,100 | 2,273,237 | 2,962,621 |
| Profit | −495,092 | 2,934,923 | 211,972 | 492,575 |
| Tassets | 14,881 | 35,314,111 | 2,725,210 | 5,971,282 |
| Employees | 24 | 87,384 | 9,335 | 16,158 |
| Owners | 1 | 1 | 1 | 0 |
| PROD | 38.42 | 11,417.36 | 848.72 | 1,803.05 |
| PROF | −116.33 | 1,442.25 | 61.16 | 184.82 |

*Table 5.28(b)* Descriptive statistics for 100 private companies, the UK 2000

| | Minimum | Maximum | Mean | Std. Deviation |
|---|---|---|---|---|
| Turnover | 10,043 | 17,454,491 | 3,743,685 | 3,870,097 |
| Profit | −4,930,862 | 4,836,778 | 241,639 | 900,756 |
| Tassets | 14,875 | 81,214,563 | 5,704,809 | 10,540,423 |
| Employees | 70 | 93,519 | 15,432 | 22,580 |
| Owners | 1 | 1 | 1 | 0 |
| PROD | 34.17 | 14,435.66 | 996.02 | 2,409.45 |
| PROF | −1,689.56 | 1,763.83 | 51.45 | 295.28 |

*Table 5.28(c)* Descriptive statistics for 90 state companies, the UK 1998

| | Minimum | Maximum | Mean | Std. Deviation |
|---|---|---|---|---|
| Turnover | 2,030 | 2,096,157 | 194,914 | 407,563 |
| Profit | −265,754 | 284,146 | 433 | 57,930 |
| Tassets | 1,543 | 3,768,425 | 245,987 | 614,248 |
| Employees | 11 | 14,235 | 924 | 2,002 |
| Owners | 0 | 0 | 0 | 0 |
| PROD | 36.88 | 4,187.61 | 381.97 | 633.27 |
| PROF | −1,276.86 | 302.84 | −34.72 | 230.86 |

*Table 5.28(d)* Descriptive statistics for 100 state companies, the UK 2000

| | Minimum | Maximum | Mean | Std. Deviation |
|---|---|---|---|---|
| Turnover | 715 | 3,827,962 | 260,775 | 694,308 |
| Profit | −244,108 | 294,027 | 3,687 | 53,414 |
| Tassets | 1,261 | 10,487,281 | 446,384 | 1,592,839 |
| Employees | 10 | 11,514 | 923 | 1,956 |
| Owners | 0 | 0 | 0 | 0 |
| PROD | 27.49 | 9,434.17 | 567.46 | 1,267.29 |
| PROF | −1,251.83 | 1,301.01 | 23.3 | 239.86 |

*Table 5.29* Company performances: the UK

| | 1998 | | 2000 | |
|---|---|---|---|---|
| **Variables** | **Component 1 (Size/Own)** | **Component 2 (Perf)** | **Component 1 (Size/Own)** | **Component 2 (Perf)** |
| Turnover | 0.883 | −0.115 | 0.894 | −0.041 |
| Profit | 0.824 | 0.016 | 0.481 | 0.339 |
| Total Assets | 0.801 | −0.113 | 0.688 | −0.115 |
| Number of employees | 0.761 | −0.344 | 0.807 | −0.270 |
| Ownership | 0.553 | 0.276 | 0.690 | 0.038 |
| PROD | 0.086 | 0.796 | 0.053 | 0.734 |
| PROF | 0.299 | 0.735 | 0.133 | 0.795 |
| Variance extracted | 44.012 | 19.914 | 37.886 | 19.631 |

highly loaded. The first component of both years demonstrates that variables representing size of companies are correlated within a factor including ownership, which is unusual according to our preceding findings. The second component for both years again establishes performance as a common characteristic.

## Total-country analysis

The investigation continues by combining sample data from all countries together. As a result, two sample sizes of 3,316 companies for the year 1998 and 3,960 companies for the year 2000 are obtained. Descriptive statistics are summarised in Table 5.30, with nothing on which to comment.

From Table 5.31 it can be seen that two components are extracted for the year 1998. The first component proves that turnover, profit, total assets and employees are highly loaded, with higher respective correlation coefficients. The second component demonstrates that the two variables, PROD and PROF, are heavily weighted. These results confirm that it is possible to establish two characteristics: size and performance. Ownership remains unestablished as a characteristic with lower correlation coefficients for both components.

For the year 2000, the SPSS analysis extracts two components. The first component reveals that turnover, profit, total assets and employees are highly loaded. The second component demonstrates that the PROD and PROF variables are heavily weighted. Two characteristics can be found from this analysis; size from the first factor, and performance

*Table 5.30(a)* Descriptive statistics for 228 mixed companies, total countries 1998

| | Minimum | Maximum | Mean | Std. Deviation |
|---|---|---|---|---|
| Turnover | 433 | 52,952,981 | 934,976 | 4,671,242 |
| Profit | −874,927 | 4,894,620 | 82,886 | 524,370 |
| Tassets | 399 | 56,198,657 | 1,321,886 | 6,356,906 |
| Employees | 2 | 258,491 | 4,397 | 23,078 |
| Owners | 0.03 | 1 | 0.61 | 0.22 |
| PROD | 2.15 | 34,203.22 | 432.87 | 2,290.93 |
| PROF | −2,950.06 | 1,812.87 | 22.91 | 260.9 |

*Table 5.30(b)* Descriptive statistics for 298 mixed companies, total countries 2000

| | Minimum | Maximum | Mean | Std. Deviation |
|---|---|---|---|---|
| Turnover | 23 | 62,012,301 | 999,872 | 5,129,795 |
| Profit | −232,132 | 10,113,614 | 116,364 | 733,225 |
| Tassets | 170 | 139,835,674 | 2,061,670 | 12,152,641 |
| Employees | 6 | 319,998 | 5,146 | 29,650 |
| Owners | 0.03 | 1 | 0.56 | 0.2 |
| PROD | 0.48 | 22,167.39 | 366.93 | 1,431.36 |
| PROF | −619.45 | 1,993.66 | 28.2 | 155.06 |

*Table 5.30(c)* Descriptive statistics for 1,743 private companies, total countries 1998

| | Minimum | Maximum | Mean | Std. Deviation |
|---|---|---|---|---|
| Turnover | 4 | 70,777,272 | 560,430 | 2,513,325 |
| Profit | −898,316 | 3,151,441 | 35,397 | 204,484 |
| Tassets | 240 | 66,826,508 | 561,648 | 2,891,526 |
| Employees | 2 | 401,000 | 2,642 | 14,937 |
| Owners | 1 | 1 | 1 | 0 |
| PROD | 0.04 | 173,130.15 | 819.1 | 5,966.61 |
| PROF | −2,785.96 | 15,281.85 | 35.84 | 434.03 |

*Table 5.30(d)* Descriptive statistics for 2,063 private companies, total countries 2000

| | Minimum | Maximum | Mean | Std. Deviation |
|---|---|---|---|---|
| Turnover | 79 | 45,491,258 | 545,532 | 2,056,698 |
| Profit | −4,930,862 | 4,836,778 | 27,901 | 224,626 |
| Tassets | 52 | 81,214,563 | 609,513 | 3,147,266 |
| Employees | 2 | 234,351 | 2,460 | 10,622 |
| Owners | 1 | 1 | 1 | 0 |
| PROD | 0.33 | 95,550.31 | 658.64 | 3,036.9 |
| PROF | −1,689.56 | 10,681.11 | 31.27 | 296.38 |

*Table 5.30(e)* Descriptive statistics for 1,345 state companies, total countries 1998

| | Minimum | Maximum | Mean | Std. Deviation |
|---|---|---|---|---|
| Turnover | 121 | 43,432,051 | 285,136 | 1,730,674 |
| Profit | −352,190 | 1,997,970 | 10,441 | 80,839 |
| Tassets | 28 | 52,204,585 | 413,548 | 2,392,611 |
| Employees | 2 | 210,437 | 1,583 | 9,913 |
| Owners | 0 | 0 | 0 | 0 |
| PROD | 0.66 | 24,507.96 | 496.06 | 1,475.18 |
| PROF | −1,276.86 | 2,302.02 | 20.42 | 148.33 |

*Table 5.30(f)* Descriptive statistics for 1,599 state companies, total countries 2000

| | Minimum | Maximum | Mean | Std. Deviation |
|---|---|---|---|---|
| Turnover | 47 | 33,187,156 | 261,159 | 1,337,740 |
| Profit | −1,359,876 | 3,953,731 | 13,362 | 137,331 |
| Tassets | 41 | 113,696,647 | 469,984 | 3,388,221 |
| Employees | 2 | 216,605 | 1,381 | 7,779 |
| Owners | 0 | 0 | 0 | 0 |
| PROD | 0.26 | 385,107 | 694.38 | 9,706.4 |
| PROF | −40,895.98 | 6,680.18 | 18.24 | 1,084.07 |

*Table 5.31* Company performances: total countries

| | 1998 | | 2000 | |
|---|---|---|---|---|
| **Variables** | **Component 1 (Size)** | **Component 2 (Perf)** | **Component 1 (Size)** | **Component 2 (Perf)** |
| Turnover | 0.948 | 0.012 | 0.940 | 0.024 |
| Profit | 0.800 | 0.020 | 0.691 | 0.093 |
| Total Assets | 0.937 | −0.044 | 0.877 | −0.067 |
| Number of employees | 0.846 | −0.101 | 0.850 | −0.080 |
| Ownership | 0.065 | 0.136 | 0.060 | 0.037 |
| PROD | 0.064 | 0.798 | 0.032 | 0.728 |
| PROF | 0.051 | 0.794 | 0.019 | 0.752 |
| Variance extracted | 44.907 | 18.528 | 40.849 | 15.962 |

from the second. Among the variables, ownership demonstrates a less influential role in both factors.

## Conclusion

This chapter investigated the performance of private and state-owned enterprises together and sought to find out whether or not one is superior to the other.

Type-one factor analysis compared the performance of state, mixed and private companies, using data from the years 1998 and 2000. Fourteen European countries were chosen for this investigation: Austria, Belgium, Bulgaria, Denmark, Finland, France, German, Italy, the Netherlands, Norway, Poland, Portugal, Sweden and the UK. Data on turnover, profit, total assets, the number of employees, ownership, productivity (PROD) and profitability (PROF) were collected and factor analysis was used for the years 1998 and 2000. The size of the sample taken for each country was restricted by the availability of the data on state-owned companies; the more data available on state-owned companies, the larger the size of the sample. The last part of the type-one factor analysis was devoted to total-country analysis, in which the sample data from each country were combined for the years 1998 and 2000.

Thirty factor analyses of two years (1998 and 2000), including the total-country approach, show that in ten cases, three factors are extracted, and in 20 cases, two factors are extracted. In most cases of three extracted factors, the characteristics of size, performance and some type of ownership are well established. In most cases of two extracted factors, the characteristics of size and performance are recognised. The first findings (the cases of three factors) demonstrate that corporate performance is a function of three separate characteristics; variables representing size, performance and ownership are correlated in separate factors. The latter findings (the cases of two factors) demonstrate a similar outcome, but here the type of ownership is not a separate characteristic of corporate performance.

What can be concluded explicitly is that, in the three-characteristic cases, ownership is a unique characteristic and does not share common traits with either size or performance. Moreover, in the two-characteristic cases, ownership is not even a characteristic of corporate performance. These findings undermine theories which argue that ownership is an influential aspect of corporate performance.

The findings in many cases confirm that size and performance are two characteristics of corporate performance, while in some other cases the characteristics are increased to size, performance and some sorts of ownership. As a result, it can be concluded that ownership is not correlated to any other variable such as size and performance. Moreover, it is not an influential aspect of corporate performance, since in most cases it takes up a smaller area of common variance shared by all involved variables.

## Appendix: notes on the data sources

In general, in undertaking an empirical exercise of the sort included in this thesis, considerable attention has to be devoted to searching out data sources and ensuring they are suitable and compatible. In short, it is desirable to address the following issues.

1. What sources have been used?
2. What alternative data sources were available but not used?
3. In what way did the sources meet the specific requirements of the study?
4. In particular, what data were used from each of the sources?
5. How and why are the data from different sources comparable? In particular, are there any measurement considerations that have to be made in pooling data?

To a large extent, these issues are addressed directly in the account of the data that follows that is in large part, drawn from the data sources themselves. But, as a preliminary, it is worth highlighting a number of more general points, specific to the study. Firstly, I would ideally have liked to have deployed a very wide range of variables reflecting enterprise characteristics and performance. In practice, the ready and cheap availability of such data is a serious problem. Very little choice is open, especially when considering the necessity of availability of data on state-owned companies. In short, in effect, there has been very little choice in what data to use, both in terms of sampling and the variables attached to the samples.

Secondly, even on this limited basis, it would be desirable in principle to confirm consistency across the data, especially for the purposes to hand. There is no reason to believe that the data collected discriminate one way or the other in examining the impact of ownership on firm characteristics and performance. But, as in the construction of data itself, the toil and trouble of testing this (rather than constructing a data set of one's own), would be extremely arduous.

Thirdly, it is only to a limited extent that such interrogation, and possibly amendment, of the data set can be undertaken without prior preconceptions about performance and the impact of ownership upon it. Put another way, and a point to be taken up in the concluding remarks in this volume, careful scrutiny of the data would itself be tantamount to undertaking a whole series of case studies. If so, it might be preferable to do this directly rather than indirectly through data modification. In other words, if, for example, one wishes to modify measurement of capital assets in order to take account of excess capacity, it makes more sense to do this in the context of sectoral studies and other considerations than through what is liable to be some more or less arbitrary adjustment of the data.

Fourthly, and more specifically, in the broader analytical and ideological context of this study, the thrust is to demonstrate that the case in favour of privatisation as improving performance is far from borne out by a 'first cut' consideration of the data. Marginal returns in terms of research results through taking a 'second cut' by the arduous task of refining the data are liable to be less than those gained through concerted case study analysis (which is, in effect, what data refinement is in a narrow sense).

Of course, this can be interpreted as, and in essence is, making a virtue out of necessity. The data sources are limited; interrogating and improving them is liable to be less rewarding than more rounded research. This is the light in which to locate the following discussion of the data themselves.

The sources that have been used for collecting data are: DataStream, Amadeus, 'Major Companies of Europe' and Statistics Sweden. There are many different data sources available nowadays. Most of them are useful for collecting data of non-state companies.

DataStream is a well-known expensive data source, which gives nearly all information about company accounts of non-state companies. It has been available to SAOS (School of African and Oriental Studies) students through a share agreement with Birkbeck. As can be seen below, Amadeus collects data from 30 different sources, with corresponding advantage over consulting those sources individually. But, collecting data on state-owned enterprises is more difficult. This is because fewer sources contain such information, and the number of state-owned companies has shrunk since the 1980s when an extensive privatisation programme began to be carried out by many governments from European countries. For our purposes, DataStream is useful for collecting data of private and mixed companies. Amadeus and 'Major Companies of Europe' are useful for data on state-owned enterprises. Statistics Sweden is used in order to find data regarding concentration for measuring competitiveness in a sector.

DataStream supplies current as well as historical data for international equity, bond, commodities, and foreign exchange and futures markets.

A wider range of information from company accounts to macroeconomic statistics is available from this source. Due to availability of company accounts, information is provided for a maximum of ten years. Company accounts data are based on the currency of the country in which the company is registered.

Amadeus provides data on 5 million public and private companies. Data are collected from 30 sources and from 26 European countries. It is claimed that additional criteria have been employed in order to prevent any bias in coverage towards countries where information is more readily available. A total of 3 million ownership links are also provided. 'Major Companies of Europe' (western Europe companies serials), a hard printed source, published by Graham & Trotman from 1983 onwards, is also useful for data on state-owned and mixed enterprises since mix of ownership is given in percentages.

Statistics Sweden is a central government authority for official statistics and other government statistics and in this capacity also has the responsibility for coordinating and supporting the Swedish system for official statistics.

DataStream provides company accounts data as consolidated accounts; parent accounts are only used when consolidated accounts are not available. The profit and loss accounts are presented in published and adjusted form. The latter will vary from country to country. As is mentioned in the main body of the text, I have used four of their variables for the research: turnover, profit, total assets and number of employees. DataStream has composed those variables as follows:

*Turnover* is presented as total sales net of sales-related taxes excluding additional incomes, rental incomes and other operating incomes when the goods and services are being sold to third parties. Furthermore, any revenues from non-industrial activities like insurance, property, investment and loan financing are not taken into account.

Operating *profit* is calculated based on operational activities excluding initial financial income/expense (capital grants and investment credits), financial and extraordinary provisions and extraordinary profits/losses. Adjustments to the published figure in this regard made by DataStream are where capital grants and investment credits, if treated as operating incomes by the company, are excluded from operating profit. Furthermore, operating profit is also adjusted for any special non-recurring items.

Total *number of employees* is presented as the average number of employees as published by the company. If the average number is not available then the year-end number is presented.

A standard method is being used to disclose aggregate values (*total assets*): for each company in the list the latest value available is used for calculating aggregate values for the latest year. Annualised data is always used to calculate aggregate values. Data of those companies which do not have a financial period of 12 months are converted to a 12-month base (see the DataStream package for details).

With the use of enterprise data from different sources, there is the possibility of inconsistency – either in the 'row' data themselves or in how they have been constructed. Some checking indicates that this is not the case and, for example, similar methods around exchange rates have been used.

### Exchange rates

Amadeus uses a monthly electronic feed of exchange rates from the International Monetary Fund. The data supplied list the monthly exchange rates of each currency to the US dollar. The package uses the nearest exchange rate to the period-end data of the financial accounts based on the US dollar as a cross-referencing base for any financial accounts presented in a local currency. For those countries which have been using national currency fixed to the euro, the package uses the appropriate fixed conventional rate to convert all available years of data. The 1999 rate is used as the base year. For countries not having national currency fixed to the euro, the package uses the variable exchange rate from 1999 onwards for converting all available years of data (see the Amadeus package).

# 6
# Results from the Empirical Study: Part II

## Introduction

This chapter presents research findings relating to the effects of privatisation on companies' performance. I will focus in particular on the question of whether the characteristics of ownership and concentration have substantial effects on corporate performance.

Type-two factor analysis is devoted to the investigation of privatisation performance. Data on European privatised (as opposed to private) and state-owned companies were collected for two years, 1998 and 2000. This exercise was repeated with the same variables as those used in the type-one factor analysis, that is, turnover, PROD and PROF, total assets, total number of employees and ownership. For this experiment ownership is divided into two categories, with values of 0 and 1 assigned to state and privatised companies, respectively. The number of state-owned and privatised companies of the type-two experiments is listed in Table 6.1.

Type-three factor analysis was carried out to investigate further characteristics of the ownership variable using four methods. The first method used the same variables as those used in the privatisation performance analysis along with a new variable, Sale Year. This new

*Table 6.1* Samples for type-two factor analysis: comparison between state-owned and privatised companies

| | | | **1998** | **2000** |
|---|---|---|---|---|
| Privatisation performance | In the ownership variable (0) for state and (1) for privatised companies | State-owned | 58 | 54 |
| | | Privatised | 52 | 56 |
| | | Total | 110 | 110 |

*Table 6.2* Samples for type-three factor analysis

| Characteristic of ownership variable | | 1998 | 2000 |
|---|---|---|---|
| *Method 1* | | | |
| State and privatised company comparison with a new variable (0) for state companies and number of years since privatisation for privatised companies | State-owned | 58 | 54 |
| | Privatised | 52 | 56 |
| | Total | 110 | 110 |
| *Method 2* | | | |
| Cross-country analysis with a new variable (0) for state and private companies and (1) for privatised companies | State-owned companies | 1,344 | 1,601 |
| | Private companies | 1,962 | 2,347 |
| | Privatised companies | 52 | 56 |
| | Total companies | 3,358 | 4,004 |
| *Method 3* | | | |
| Cross-country analysis with a new variable (0) for state and private companies and number of years since Privatisation for privatised companies | State-owned companies | 1,344 | 1,601 |
| | Private companies | 1,962 | 2,347 |
| | Privatised companies | 52 | 56 |
| | Total companies | 3,358 | 4,004 |
| *Method 4* | | | |
| Cross-country analysis with a new variable (0) for state, number of years for privatised companies since privatisation and maximum of years since the first privatisation for private companies | State-owned companies | 1,344 | 1,601 |
| | Private companies | 1,962 | 2,347 |
| | Privatised companies | 52 | 56 |
| | Total companies | 3,358 | 4,004 |

variable designates the number of years for which a company has been privatised; a value of 0 is used to identify state-owned companies. This is to assess whether length of time since privatisation has any significance.

In the second, third and fourth methods, the total-country sample, which consists of the whole sample taken from the sample of each country plus the privatised companies, is used for the years 1998 and 2000.

The numbers of state-owned, private and privatised companies of this type of experiment are listed in Table 6.2. The second method uses the same variables as those in the type-one experiment, plus a new variable called Newone in which a value of 0 is assigned to state and private companies and a value of 1 is assigned to privatised companies. The purpose is to test whether privatisation as such makes a difference as opposed to remaining in state or private ownership.

The third method uses the same procedure with the exception that the new variable, called Newtwo, is designed so that 0 is assigned to both state and always-private companies, and the number of years a company has been privatised is assigned to privatised companies. The same purpose as in the previous method applies. This experiment was also conducted for the two years of 1998 and 2000.

The fourth method was conducted with the same variables as before for the years of 1998 and 2000; but the new variable was set differently. In this new variable, which is called Newthree, 0 is assigned to state companies, the number of years since privatisation is assigned to privatised companies, and the maximum number of years since the first privatisation among all privatised companies is assigned to private companies. The purpose once again is the same as that in the two preceding methods.

Type-four factor analysis is designed to assess the effect of concentration on corporate performance. It measures the degree of monopoly/competition in a sector, and can give some indication of how competitive a market is. The simplest measure of industrial concentration involves adding together the market share of the largest so many firms: for instance, the largest four. This would give what is known as the 'four-firm concentration ratio'. The Swedish samples for the years 1998 and 2000 are used, including a new variable, Concentration. Ideally, the same exercise would be carried out for other countries, but this would prove too costly in time and funding. The same applies to the thwarted intention of including sectoral import and export ratios as factors representing competitiveness, not least because of the non-traded character of many of the enterprises covered.

This chapter is organised as follows. The second section looks at the results taken from the type-two factor analysis. In this section the performance of state and privatised companies for the two years 1998 and 2000 will be considered. Again, two major elements, extracted factors and character of ownership, will be discussed to ascertain the main characteristics of corporate performance and ownership. The third section is dedicated to a discussion of the third experiment (the type-three factor analysis), which concerns the characteristics of the ownership variable. This is done by creating a new variable based on different types of ownership and examining how this new variable performs in the factor analysis. The fourth section looks at the effect of concentration on corporate performance by using the Swedish samples. The last section offers some concluding remarks.

## The type-two factor analysis

The type-two factor analysis investigates the effects of privatisation on corporate performance by comparing the performance of state and privatised companies for two years, 1998 and 2000. The aim is to discover which and how many characteristics can be established to explain the performance of state and privatised companies. For these reasons, data of state and privatised companies are collected using the same variables as type-one factor analysis. Table 6.1 shows the number of companies of both types that are used for the analysis. The SPSS outputs for two years, 1998 and 2000, are reported in Table 6.3

### Privatisation performance

A total of 110 companies were used to carry out the factor analysis. Of these, for the year 1998, 58 were state-owned and 52 were privatised; for the year 2000, 54 were state-owned and 56 were privatised. Descriptive statistics of the samples for the two years are presented in Table 6.3, with nothing on which to comment.

The variable ownership, as usual, is treated as a categorical variable. State-owned companies are designated 0 and privatised companies 1. The SPSS result presented in Table 6.4 shows that three components have been extracted for the year 1998. The first component indicates that the variables turnover, profit, total assets and employees are highly loaded. The second component indicates two loaded variables, PROF and ownership. The third component indicates that two variables, PROD and PROF, are heavily weighted. These results establish size as the first characteristic. From the second component, a characteristic of ownership and profitability is indicated. The interesting point that is notable about this finding is that the most data for privatised companies are for companies that were privatised in 1997 and 1998. This indicates that the year before and the years of privatisation are critical for governments. Their intentions are to help companies that are ready for sale to be more profitable and productive than before in order to realise more money at the point of sale. This claim is confirmed by the experiment

*Table 6.3(a)* Type-two factor analysis for 52 privatised companies, 1998

| | Minimum | Maximum | Mean | Std. Deviation |
|---|---|---|---|---|
| Turnover | 12,199 | 68,296,456 | 6,570,717 | 13,546,400 |
| Profit | −51,569 | 6,918,492 | 647,665 | 1,399,835 |
| Total Assets | 14,358 | 84,490,101 | 9,154,841 | 16,878,473 |
| Employees | 19 | 169,099 | 20,168 | 34,926 |
| Owners | 1 | 1 | 1 | 0 |
| PROD | 16.14 | 2,836.52 | 335.46 | 430.57 |
| PROF | −44.93 | 1,468.88 | 55.2 | 203.88 |

*Table 6.3(b)* Type-two factor analysis for 56 privatised companies, 2000

| | Minimum | Maximum | Mean | Std. Deviation |
|---|---|---|---|---|
| Turnover | 11,065 | 146,305,580 | 8,689,896 | 23,589,882 |
| Profit | −1,469,708 | 16,733,811 | 966,826 | 2,972,349 |
| Total Assets | 10,279 | 144,140,555 | 12,175,954 | 28,079,073 |
| Employees | 21 | 188,866 | 19,930 | 36,217 |
| Owners | 1 | 1 | 1 | 0 |
| PROD | 25.79 | 5,085.68 | 537.94 | 960.41 |
| PROF | −81.78 | 2,643.1 | 93.79 | 364.62 |

*Table 6.3(c)* Type-two factor analysis for 58 state companies, 1998

| | Minimum | Maximum | Mean | Std. Deviation |
|---|---|---|---|---|
| Turnover | 21,532 | 21,614,464 | 2,097,349 | 4,204,912 |
| Profit | −265,754 | 986,583 | 61,727 | 168,390 |
| Total Assets | 7,450 | 52,204,585 | 3,056,352 | 8,756,680 |
| Employees | 12 | 210,437 | 13,935 | 38,523 |
| Owners | 0 | 0 | 0 | 0 |
| PROD | 20.67 | 12,104.34 | 1,051.81 | 2,448.54 |
| PROF | −1,219.06 | 213.88 | −12.93 | 206.03 |

*Table 6.3(d)* Type-two factor analysis for 54 state companies, 2000

| | Minimum | Maximum | Mean | Std. Deviation |
|---|---|---|---|---|
| Turnover | 21,499 | 8,461,975 | 1,434,489 | 1,859,649 |
| Profit | −397,094 | 1,007,453 | 77,850 | 196,226 |
| Total Assets | 3,324 | 16,105,575 | 1,789,536 | 2,834,465 |
| Employees | 14 | 61,184 | 6,615 | 12,327 |
| Owners | 0 | 0 | 0 | 0 |
| PROD | 15.41 | 26,554.3 | 1,458.82 | 3,899.47 |
| PROF | −323.89 | 1,525.09 | 64.11 | 232.52 |

*Table 6.4* Type-two factor analysis: company performances

| | 1998 | | | 2000 | |
|---|---|---|---|---|---|
| **Variables** | **Component 1 (Size)** | **Component 2 (Own/Prof)** | **Component 3 (Perf)** | **Component 1 (Size)** | **Component 2 (Perf)** |
| Turnover | 0.947 | −0.105 | 0.044 | 0.948 | 0.07 |
| Profit | 0.863 | 0.038 | 0.078 | 0.879 | 0.129 |
| Total Assets | 0.977 | −0.115 | 0.016 | 0.959 | 0.007 |
| Number of employees | 0.838 | −0.201 | −0.053 | 0.82 | −0.109 |
| Ownership | 0.327 | 0.759 | −0.051 | 0.348 | −0.141 |
| PROD | −0.14 | −0.464 | 0.76 | −0.074 | 0.888 |
| PROF | 0.062 | 0.557 | 0.69 | 0.019 | 0.872 |
| Variance extracted | 48.995 | 16.687 | 15.246 | 48.432 | 22.907 |

for the year 2000, in which there is no sign of a characteristic of ownership and performance. The third component confirms a characteristic of some sort of performance for the year 1998.

The analysis for the year 2000 finds that two components are extracted. The first component shows that turnover, profit, total assets and employees are heavily weighted. PROD and PROF are highly loaded in the second factor. According to Table 6.4, the first extracted factor is a characteristic of size. The second factor demonstrates a characteristic of performance. The results clearly show that ownership is not a strong element of corporate performance. It seems as if the privatisation effect erodes relatively quickly, questioning a cause–effect relationship between the weak evidence found for 1998.

## The type-three factor analysis

The type-three factor analysis specifically explores the variable ownership and is primarily a supplement to the two preceding approaches. This type of analysis is done using four methods.

### Method one

Factor analysis is carried out for the years 1998 and 2000 using the data found for privatisation performance, including a new variable (Sale Year) in which 0 is given to state companies and the number of years since privatisation has taken place for each privatised company is given to that company. Descriptive statistics are given for the new variable Sale Year for privatised companies in Table 6.5; for all other descriptive statistics, see Table 6.3.

*Table 6.5(a)* Type-three factor analysis for 52 privatised companies, 1998, method 1

| | Minimum | Maximum | Mean | Std. Deviation |
|---|---|---|---|---|
| Sale Year | 1 | 22 | 6.02 | 6.16 |

*Table 6.5(b)* Type-three factor analysis for 56 privatised companies, 2000, method 1

| | Minimum | Maximum | Mean | Std. Deviation |
|---|---|---|---|---|
| Sale Year | 3 | 24 | 7.79 | 6.07 |

Table 6.6 shows that for the year 1998 three components are extracted. The first component indicates that the variables turnover, profit, total assets, employees and Sale Year are highly loaded. The second component reveals that owners and the new variable (Sale Year) are heavily weighted. The third component shows that the performance variables, PROD and PROF, are highly loaded. As a result, two characteristics can be established, ownership and performance from components 2 and 3. From the first component, a common characteristic of size can be discerned. From the results, it appears as if early privatisation may have been in large companies but without impact on performance.

For the year 2000, factor analysis extracted three factors. The first component shows that the variables turnover, profit, total assets, employees and Sale Year are highly loaded. The second component illustrates how the performance variables, PROD and PROF, are heavily weighted. The last component shows that the variables owners and the new variable (Sale Year) are highly loaded than others. Two characteristics are established: performance and some type of ownership, corresponding to components 2 and 3 in that order. Results are similar to 1998, except the second and third components have switched places.

## Method two

Data that were collected for total-country analysis, plus the data on privatised companies, are used for this new approach. Descriptive statistics of the samples are presented in Table 6.7. There is nothing remarkable on which to comment.

A new variable (Newone) is introduced and set such that 0 is given to state and private and 1 to privatised companies. The SPSS results for the

*Table 6.6* Type-three factor analysis, method 1: company performances

| | 1998 | | | 2000 | | |
|---|---|---|---|---|---|---|
| **Variables** | **Component 1 (Size/Sale year)** | **Component 2 (Own)** | **Component 3 (Perf)** | **Component 1 (Size/Sale year)** | **Component 2 (Perf)** | **Component 3 (Own)** |
| Turnover | 0.929 | −0.208 | 0.038 | 0.922 | 0.069 | −0.256 |
| Profit | 0.863 | −0.044 | 0.082 | 0.857 | 0.128 | −0.219 |
| Total Assets | 0.957 | −0.231 | 0.011 | 0.933 | 0.006 | −0.234 |
| Number of employees | 0.795 | −0.362 | −0.060 | 0.795 | −0.110 | −0.197 |
| Ownership | 0.416 | 0.791 | 0.004 | 0.458 | −0.138 | 0.794 |
| PROD | −0.153 | −0.311 | 0.704 | −0.085 | 0.888 | −0.078 |
| PROF | 0.069 | 0.299 | 0.748 | 0.052 | 0.873 | 0.231 |
| **Sale year** | 0.568 | 0.602 | −0.025 | 0.636 | 0.004 | 0.655 |
| Variance extracted | 45.997 | 17.542 | 13.351 | 46.380 | 20.044 | 16.577 |

*Table 6.7(a)* Type-three factor analysis for 228 mixed companies, 1998, method 2

| | **Minimum** | **Maximum** | **Mean** | **Std. Deviation** |
|---|---|---|---|---|
| Turnover | 433 | 52,952,981 | 934,976 | 4,671,242 |
| Profit | −874,927 | 4,894,620 | 82,886 | 524,370 |
| Total Assets | 399 | 56,198,657 | 1,321,886 | 6,356,906 |
| Employees | 2 | 258,491 | 4,397 | 23,078 |
| Owners | 0.03 | 1 | 0.61 | 0.22 |
| PROD | 2.15 | 34,203.22 | 432.87 | 2,290.93 |
| PROF | −2,950.06 | 1,812.87 | 22.91 | 260.9 |
| **Newone** | 0 | 1 | 0.02 | 0.15 |

*Table 6.7(b)* Type-three factor analysis for 298 mixed companies, 2000, method 2

| | **Minimum** | **Maximum** | **Mean** | **Std. Deviation** |
|---|---|---|---|---|
| Turnover | 23 | 62,012,301 | 999,872 | 5,129,795 |
| Profit | −232,132 | 10,113,614 | 116,364 | 733,225 |
| Total Assets | 170 | 139,835,674 | 2,061,670 | 12,152,641 |
| Employees | 6 | 319,998 | 5,146 | 29,650 |
| Owners | 0.03 | 1 | 0.56 | 0.2 |
| PROD | 0.48 | 22,167.39 | 366.93 | 1,431.36 |
| PROF | −619.45 | 1,993.66 | 28.2 | 155.06 |
| **Newone** | 0 | 1 | 0.02 | 0.15 |

*Table 6.7(c)* Type-three factor analysis for 785 private companies, 1998, method 2

| | Minimum | Maximum | Mean | Std. Deviation |
|---|---|---|---|---|
| Turnover | 160 | 70,777,272 | 497,579 | 3,158,165 |
| Profit | −236,501 | 2,308,015 | 21,120 | 131,714 |
| Total Assets | 240 | 66,826,508 | 449,173 | 3,201,651 |
| Employees | 10 | 401,000 | 2,199 | 16,494 |
| Owners | 1 | 1 | 1 | 0 |
| PROD | 0.57 | 173,130.15 | 862.69 | 7,656.28 |
| PROF | −674.66 | 6,909.04 | 23.37 | 256.76 |
| **Newone** | 0 | 1 | 0 | 0.04 |

*Table 6.7(d)* Type-three factor analysis for 2,107 private companies, 2000, method 2

| | Minimum | Maximum | Mean | Std. Deviation |
|---|---|---|---|---|
| Turnover | 79 | 146,305,580 | 701,494 | 4,245,537 |
| Profit | −4,930,862 | 16,733,811 | 43,362 | 489,435 |
| Total Assets | 52 | 144,140,555 | 802,726 | 4,996,168 |
| Employees | 2 | 234,351 | 2,744 | 11,483 |
| Owners | 1 | 1 | 1 | 0 |
| PROD | 0.33 | 95,550.31 | 656.82 | 3,008.84 |
| PROF | −1,689.56 | 10,681.11 | 32.54 | 298.92 |
| **Newone** | 0 | 1 | 0.02 | 0.15 |

*Table 6.7(e)* Type-three factor analysis for 1,345 state companies, 1998, method 2

| | Minimum | Maximum | Mean | Std. Deviation |
|---|---|---|---|---|
| Turnover | 121 | 43,432,051 | 285,136 | 1,730,674 |
| Profit | −352,190 | 1,997,970 | 10,441 | 80,839 |
| Total Assets | 28 | 52,204,585 | 413,548 | 2,392,611 |
| Employees | 2 | 210,437 | 1,583 | 9,913 |
| Owners | 0 | 0 | 0 | 0 |
| PROD | 0.66 | 24,507.96 | 496.06 | 1,475.18 |
| PROF | −1,276.86 | 2,302.02 | 20.42 | 148.33 |
| **Newone** | 0 | 0 | 0 | 0 |

*Table 6.7(f)* Type-three factor analysis for 1,599 state companies, 2000, method 2

| | Minimum | Maximum | Mean | Std. Deviation |
|---|---|---|---|---|
| Turnover | 47 | 33,187,156 | 261,159 | 1,337,740 |
| Profit | −1,359,876 | 3,953,731 | 13,362 | 137,331 |
| Total Assets | 41 | 113,696,647 | 469,984 | 3,388,221 |
| Employees | 2 | 216,605 | 1,381 | 7,779 |
| Owners | 0 | 0 | 0 | 0 |
| PROD | 0.26 | 385,107 | 694.38 | 9,706.4 |
| PROF | −40,895.98 | 6,680.18 | 18.24 | 1,084.07 |
| Newone | 0 | 0 | 0 | 0 |

*Table 6.8* Type-three factor analysis, method 2: company performances

| | 1998 | | | 2000 | | |
|---|---|---|---|---|---|---|
| **Variables** | **Component 1 (Size)** | **Component 2 (Perf)** | **Component 3 (Own)** | **Component 1 (Size)** | **Component 2 (Perf)** | **Component 3 (Own)** |
| Turnover | 0.945 | 0.014 | −0.090 | 0.944 | 0.020 | −0.059 |
| Profit | 0.830 | 0.011 | 0.010 | 0.803 | 0.061 | −0.027 |
| Total Assets | 0.945 | −0.034 | −0.079 | 0.897 | −0.057 | −0.107 |
| Number of employees | 0.816 | −0.085 | −0.150 | 0.748 | −0.089 | −0.107 |
| Ownership | 0.097 | 0.127 | 0.860 | 0.085 | 0.056 | 0.891 |
| PROD | 0.047 | 0.800 | −0.079 | 0.020 | 0.732 | −0.121 |
| PROF | 0.042 | 0.795 | −0.070 | 0.018 | 0.748 | 0.011 |
| Newone | 0.395 | −0.010 | 0.498 | 0.403 | 0.041 | 0.445 |
| Variance extracted | 41.361 | 16.201 | 12.948 | 38.362 | 13.940 | 12.913 |

years 1998 and 2000 are given in Table 6.8. From the table, it can be seen that three components are extracted for the year 1998. The first component shows that the variables turnover, profit, total assets and employees are highly loaded. The second component shows that the variables PROD and PROF are highly loaded. The third component demonstrates that Owners and the new variable (Newone) are more highly loaded than the others. Three characteristics are established: size, performance and some type of ownership, corresponding to the components that found them. The same method as the preceding case was used for the year 2000. The analysis extracts three components. Turnover, profit, total assets and employees are highly loaded within the first factor. PROD and PROF are highly loaded within the second component. The third component shows that the variable Owners and the new variable (Newone) are heavily weighted than the others. According to these results, a characteristic of size can be established from the first component. The second component establishes the characteristic of performance as in most previous cases. The last component is characteristic of some type of ownership as the ownership goes with the new variable in a factor. Together these results do not suggest that privatised companies are distinctive in performance.

### Method three

Method three uses total-country data plus privatised company data with a new variable (Newtwo) in which 0 is assigned to both state and private companies and the number of years since privatisation has taken place is assigned to each privatised company. Descriptive statistics are introduced in Table 6.9, with nothing on which to comment.

Three factors have been extracted for the year 1998. As can be seen in Table 6.10, the variables turnover, profit, total assets and employees are heavily loaded within the first factor. PROD and PROF are highly loaded

*Table 6.9(a)* Type-three factor analysis for 228 mixed companies, 1998, method 3

| | **Minimum** | **Maximum** | **Mean** | **Std. Deviation** |
|---|---|---|---|---|
| Turnover | 433 | 52,952,981 | 934,976 | 4,671,242 |
| Profit | −874,927 | 4,894,620 | 82,886 | 524,370 |
| Total Assets | 399 | 56,198,657 | 1,321,886 | 6,356,906 |
| Employees | 2 | 258,491 | 4,397 | 23,078 |
| Owners | 0.03 | 1 | 0.61 | 0.22 |
| PROD | 2.15 | 34,203.22 | 432.87 | 2,290.93 |
| PROF | −2,950.06 | 1,812.87 | 22.91 | 260.9 |
| **Newtwo** | 0 | 2 | 0.03 | 0.22 |

*Table 6.9(b)* Type-three factor analysis for 298 mixed companies, 2000, method 3

| | **Minimum** | **Maximum** | **Mean** | **Std. Deviation** |
|---|---|---|---|---|
| Turnover | 23 | 62,012,301 | 999,872 | 5,129,795 |
| Profit | −232,132 | 10,113,614 | 116,364 | 733,225 |
| Total Assets | 170 | 139,835,674 | 2,061,670 | 12,152,641 |
| Employees | 6 | 319,998 | 5,146 | 29,650 |
| Owners | 0.03 | 1 | 0.56 | 0.2 |
| PROD | 0.48 | 22,167.39 | 366.93 | 1,431.36 |
| PROF | −619.45 | 1,993.66 | 28.2 | 155.06 |
| **Newtwo** | 0 | 4 | 0.08 | 0.55 |

*Table 6.9(c)* Type-three factor analysis for 1,785 private companies, 1998, method 3

| | Minimum | Maximum | Mean | Std. Deviation |
|---|---|---|---|---|
| Turnover | 4 | 70,777,272 | 676,641 | 3,214,280 |
| Profit | −898,316 | 6,918,492 | 46,597 | 290,274 |
| Total Assets | 240 | 84,490,101 | 729,453 | 3,875,761 |
| Employees | 2 | 401,000 | 2,976 | 15,545 |
| Owners | 1 | 1 | 1 | 0 |
| PROD | 0.04 | 173,130.15 | 806.49 | 5,896.64 |
| PROF | −2,785.96 | 15,281.85 | 35.61 | 428.95 |
| **Newtwo** | 0 | 22 | 0.17 | 1.45 |

*Table 6.9(d)* Type-three factor analysis for 2,107 private companies, 2000, method 3

| | Minimum | Maximum | Mean | Std. Deviation |
|---|---|---|---|---|
| Turnover | 79 | 146,305,580 | 701,494 | 4,245,537 |
| Profit | −4,930,862 | 16,733,811 | 43,362 | 489,435 |
| Total Assets | 52 | 144,140,555 | 802,726 | 4,996,168 |
| Employees | 2 | 234,351 | 2,744 | 11,483 |
| Owners | 1 | 1 | 1 | 0 |
| PROD | 0.33 | 95,550.31 | 656.82 | 3,008.84 |
| PROF | −1,689.56 | 10,681.11 | 32.54 | 298.92 |
| **Newtwo** | 0 | 24 | 0.2 | 1.58 |

*Table 6.9(e)* Type-three factor analysis for 1,345 state companies, 1998, method 3

| | Minimum | Maximum | Mean | Std. Deviation |
|---|---|---|---|---|
| Turnover | 121 | 43,432,051 | 285,136 | 1,730,674 |
| Profit | −352,190 | 1,997,970 | 10,441 | 80,839 |
| Total Assets | 28 | 52,204,585 | 413,548 | 2,392,611 |
| Employees | 2 | 210,437 | 1,583 | 9,913 |
| Owners | 0 | 0 | 0 | 0 |
| PROD | 0.66 | 24,507.96 | 496.06 | 1,475.18 |
| PROF | −1,276.86 | 2,302.02 | 20.42 | 148.33 |
| **Newtwo** | 0 | 0 | 0 | 0 |

within the second factor. The variable Owners is highly loaded within the third component with correlation coefficients of (0.926). As a result, three characteristics can be established. The first component establishes the characteristic of size. The second one confirms the establishment of performance as another characteristic. The last one

*Table 6.9(f)* Type-three factor analysis for 1,599 state companies, 2000, method 3

| | Minimum | Maximum | Mean | Std. Deviation |
|---|---|---|---|---|
| Turnover | 47 | 33,187,156 | 261,159 | 1,337,740 |
| Profit | −1,359,876 | 3,953,731 | 13,362 | 137,331 |
| Total Assets | 41 | 113,696,647 | 469,984 | 3,388,221 |
| Employees | 2 | 216,605 | 1,381 | 7,779 |
| Owners | 0 | 0 | 0 | 0 |
| PROD | 0.26 | 385,107 | 694.38 | 9,706.4 |
| PROF | −40,895.98 | 6,680.18 | 18.24 | 1,084.07 |
| Newtwo | 0 | 0 | 0 | 0 |

*Table 6.10* Type-three factor analysis, method 3: company performances

| | 1998 | | | 2000 | | |
|---|---|---|---|---|---|---|
| Variables | Component 1 (Size) | Component 2 (Perf) | Component 3 (Own) | Component 1 (Size/Newtwo) | Component 2 (Perf) | Component 3 (Own) |
| Turnover | 0.943 | 0.017 | −0.075 | 0.946 | 0.017 | −0.036 |
| Profit | 0.833 | 0.012 | 0.018 | 0.811 | 0.065 | 0.004 |
| Total Assets | 0.945 | −0.031 | −0.071 | 0.889 | −0.065 | −0.108 |
| Number of employees | 0.807 | −0.078 | −0.141 | 0.730 | −0.105 | −0.124 |
| Ownership | 0.093 | 0.125 | 0.926 | 0.084 | 0.055 | 0.945 |
| PROD | 0.046 | 0.800 | −0.065 | 0.019 | 0.728 | −0.137 |
| PROF | 0.039 | 0.795 | −0.083 | 0.020 | 0.748 | 0.016 |
| Newtwo | 0.466 | −0.029 | 0.334 | 0.529 | 0.060 | 0.266 |
| Variance extracted | 41.968 | 16.205 | 12.623 | 39.530 | 13.948 | 12.644 |

establishes ownership as a characteristic. The new variable (Newtwo) is not highly correlated to any factors. For the year 2000, three components are extracted. In the first component, turnover, profit, total assets, employees and the variable Newtwo are highly loaded. PROD and PROF are highly loaded within the second component. The only variable which has a higher correlation coefficient in factor 3 is the Owners, with a correlation coefficient of (0.945). From the first component, a common characteristic cannot be established. The second component demonstrates another characteristic of performance. The last component displays the last characteristic, some sort of ownership. It is possible that longer established privatised companies are larger, more so in 2000 than 1998, but otherwise are not distinctive.

### Method four

The last investigation on type-three factor analysis uses data from the total-country analysis and privatised companies to investigate the characteristics of the ownership variable. Descriptive statistics of the samples are presented in Table 6.11, with nothing on which to comment.

*Table 6.11(a)* Type-three factor analysis for 228 mixed companies, 1998, method 4

| | Minimum | Maximum | Mean | Std.Deviation |
|---|---|---|---|---|
| Turnover | 433 | 52,952,981 | 934,976 | 4,671,242 |
| Profit | −874,927 | 4,894,620 | 82,886 | 524,370 |
| Total Assets | 399 | 56,198,657 | 1,321,886 | 6,356,906 |
| Employees | 2 | 258,491 | 4,397 | 23,078 |
| Owners | 0.03 | 1 | 0.61 | 0.22 |
| PROD | 2.15 | 34,203.22 | 432.87 | 2,290.93 |
| PROF | −2,950.06 | 1,812.87 | 22.91 | 260.9 |
| **Newthree** | 0 | 2 | 0.03 | 0.22 |

*Table 6.11(b)* Type-three factor analysis for 298 mixed companies, 2000, method 4

| | Minimum | Maximum | Mean | Std. Deviation |
|---|---|---|---|---|
| Turnover | 23 | 62,012,301 | 999,872 | 5,129,795 |
| Profit | −232,132 | 10,113,614 | 116,364 | 733,225 |
| Total Assets | 170 | 139,835,674 | 2,061,670 | 12,152,641 |
| Employees | 6 | 319,998 | 5,146 | 29,650 |
| Owners | 0.03 | 1 | 0.56 | 0.2 |
| PROD | 0.48 | 22,167.39 | 366.93 | 1,431.36 |
| PROF | −619.45 | 1,993.66 | 28.2 | 155.06 |
| **Newthree** | 0 | 4 | 0.08 | 0.55 |

*Table 6.11(c)* Type-three factor analysis for 1,785 private companies, 1998, method 4

| | Minimum | Maximum | Mean | Std. Deviation |
|---|---|---|---|---|
| Turnover | 4 | 70,777,272 | 676,641 | 3,214,280 |
| Profit | −898,316 | 6,918,492 | 46,597 | 290,274 |
| Total Assets | 240 | 84,490,101 | 729,453 | 3,875,761 |
| Employees | 2 | 401,000 | 2,976 | 15,545 |
| Owners | 1 | 1 | 1 | 0 |
| PROD | 0.04 | 173,130.15 | 806.49 | 5,896.64 |
| PROF | −2,785.96 | 15,281.85 | 35.61 | 428.95 |
| **Newthree** | 1 | 22 | 21.59 | 2.68 |

*Table 6.11(d)* Type-three factor analysis for 2,107 private companies, 2000, method 4

| | Minimum | Maximum | Mean | Std. Deviation |
|---|---|---|---|---|
| Turnover | 79 | 146,305,580 | 701,494 | 4,245,537 |
| Profit | −4,930,862 | 16,733,811 | 43,362 | 489,435 |
| Total Assets | 52 | 144,140,555 | 802,726 | 4,996,168 |
| Employees | 2 | 234,351 | 2,744 | 11,483 |
| Owners | 1 | 1 | 1 | 0 |
| PROD | 0.33 | 95,550.31 | 656.82 | 3,008.84 |
| PROF | −1,689.56 | 10,681.11 | 32.54 | 298.92 |
| **Newthree** | 3 | 24 | 23.64 | 2.54 |

*Table 6.11(e)* Type-three factor analysis for 1,345 state companies, 1998, method 4

| | Minimum | Maximum | Mean | Std. Deviation |
|---|---|---|---|---|
| Turnover | 121 | 43,432,051 | 285,136 | 1,730,674 |
| Profit | −352,190 | 1,997,970 | 10,441 | 80,839 |
| Total Assets | 28 | 52,204,585 | 413,548 | 2,392,611 |
| Employees | 2 | 210,437 | 1,583 | 9,913 |
| Owners | 0 | 0 | 0 | 0 |
| PROD | 0.66 | 24,507.96 | 496.06 | 1,475.18 |
| PROF | −1,276.86 | 2,302.02 | 20.42 | 148.33 |
| **Newthree** | 0 | 0 | 0 | 0 |

*Table 6.11(f)* Type-three factor analysis for 1,599 state companies, 2000, method 4

| | Minimum | Maximum | Mean | Std. Deviation |
|---|---|---|---|---|
| Turnover | 47 | 33,187,156 | 261,159 | 1,337,740 |
| Profit | −1,359,876 | 3,953,731 | 13,362 | 137,331 |
| Total Assets | 41 | 113,696,647 | 469,984 | 3,388,221 |
| Employees | 2 | 216,605 | 1,381 | 7,779 |
| Owners | 0 | 0 | 0 | 0 |
| PROD | 0.26 | 385,107 | 694.38 | 9,706.4 |
| PROF | −40,895.98 | 6,680.18 | 18.24 | 1,084.07 |
| **Newthree** | 0 | 0 | 0 | 0 |

*Table 6.12* Type-three factor analysis, method 4: company performances

| | 1998 | | | 2000 | | |
|---|---|---|---|---|---|---|
| **Variables** | **Component 1 (Size)** | **Component 2 (Own)** | **Component 3 (Perf)** | **Component 1 (Size)** | **Component 2 (Own)** | **Component 3 (Perf)** |
| Turnover | 0.951 | −0.054 | 0.017 | 0.949 | −0.046 | 0.025 |
| Profit | 0.825 | −0.041 | 0.013 | 0.801 | −0.059 | 0.064 |
| Total Assets | 0.946 | −0.085 | −0.025 | 0.903 | −0.078 | −0.047 |
| Number of employees | 0.831 | −0.065 | −0.080 | 0.761 | −0.038 | −0.079 |
| Ownership | 0.124 | 0.972 | −0.071 | 0.111 | 0.978 | −0.008 |
| PROD | 0.053 | 0.090 | 0.797 | 0.021 | −0.002 | 0.737 |
| PROF | 0.044 | 0.068 | 0.798 | 0.018 | 0.017 | 0.747 |
| **Newthree** | 0.093 | 0.976 | −0.064 | 0.083 | 0.981 | −0.005 |
| Variance extracted | 39.999 | 24.077 | 16.095 | 36.963 | 24.159 | 13.935 |

A new variable (Newthree) is added to the conventional variables in which 0 is assigned to state-owned companies, the number of years since the sale year of that company is assigned to each privatised company, and private companies are assigned a value equal to the maximum number of years since the first privatisation among all privatised companies used for the experiment.

Table 6.12 shows three components have been extracted for the year 1998. Turnover, profit, total assets and employees are heavily weighted within the first component. Owners and Newthree are highly loaded in the second component. In the third component, PROD and PROF hold the higher correlation coefficients. The same results have been retained for the year 2000.

From these findings, the three characteristics of size, ownership and performance are well established for both years. It can be concluded that the new variable, which is in fact another aspect of the ownership variable, has a commonality only with the ownership variable (as expected) and not with any other characteristics.

## Type-four factor analysis

Type-four factor analysis has been carried out in order to ascertain the effect of concentration on corporate performance. Swedish samples for the year 1998 and 2000 have been used with an additional variable called Concentration. As mentioned earlier in the introduction to this chapter, concentration gives the degree of monopoly/competitiveness in a sector. Concentration is measured by taking the turnover of the four biggest companies of a sector divided by the total turnover of that sector, which can be called the 'concentration ratio'. With the addition of this variable the total number of variables for carrying out factor analysis increases to eight.

**Sweden (Concentration)**

The Swedish sample, which is comprised of 756 companies for the year 1998 and 750 companies for the year 2000 with the new variable, Concentration, has been used for carrying out factor analysis. Descriptive statistics presented in Table 6.13 indicate relatively small standard deviations for Owners of mixed companies for both years and for PROD of mixed companies for the year 1998.

From Table 6.14 for the year 1998, it can be seen that five variables, representing the size of companies, turnover, profit, total assets and the number of employees, are highly loaded. Factor 2 shows that two

*Table 6.13(a)* Type-four factor analysis for 33 mixed companies, 1998 Sweden (Concentration)

| | Minimum | Maximum | Mean | Std. Deviation |
|---|---|---|---|---|
| Turnover | 5,753 | 7,119,836 | 439,244 | 1,343,146 |
| Profit | −145,904 | 843,320 | 27,131 | 151,138 |
| Total Assets | 2,460 | 8,231,485 | 664,638 | 1,608,261 |
| Employees | 10 | 31,320 | 1,524 | 5,520 |
| **Concentration** | 0.15 | 1 | 0.52 | 0.29 |
| Owners | 0.5 | 0.99 | 0.76 | 0.16 |
| PROD | 58.37 | 1,368.96 | 373.14 | 277.26 |
| PROF | −241.61 | 119.11 | 13.79 | 59.71 |

*Table 6.13(b)* Type-four factor analysis for 39 mixed companies, 2000 Sweden (Concentration)

| | Minimum | Maximum | Mean | Std. Deviation |
|---|---|---|---|---|
| Turnover | 6,543 | 6,629,749 | 286,568 | 1,079,648 |
| Profit | −83,464 | 1,241,800 | 47,460 | 202,871 |
| Total Assets | 2,607 | 13,005,670 | 562,748 | 2,083,506 |
| Employees | 10 | 30,307 | 1,193 | 4,905 |
| **Concentration** | 0.14 | 1 | 0.54 | 0.27 |
| Owners | 0.5 | 0.99 | 0.74 | 0.17 |
| PROD | 55.44 | 5,175.69 | 480.04 | 860.63 |
| PROF | −619.45 | 393.06 | 21.3 | 139.72 |

*Table 6.13(c)* Type-four factor analysis for 379 private companies, 1998 Sweden (Concentration)

| | Minimum | Maximum | Mean | Std. Deviation |
|---|---|---|---|---|
| Turnover | 4 | 10,370,798 | 145,840 | 663,508 |
| Profit | −78,007 | 760,203 | 9,961 | 52,544 |
| Total Assets | 555 | 12,572,634 | 192,847 | 799,610 |
| Employees | 2 | 53,493 | 598 | 3,239 |
| **Concentration** | 0.15 | 1 | 0.39 | 0.24 |
| Owners | 1 | 1 | 1 | 0 |
| PROD | 0.04 | 16,150.2 | 618.72 | 1,270.11 |
| PROF | −2,785.96 | 15,281.85 | 76.5 | 821.4 |

*Table 6.13(d)* Type-four factor analysis for 368 private companies, 2000 Sweden (Concentration)

| | Minimum | Maximum | Mean | Std. Deviation |
|---|---|---|---|---|
| Turnover | 2,237 | 8,095,914 | 124,768 | 538,162 |
| Profit | −42,154 | 573,473 | 10,706 | 48,449 |
| Total Assets | 502 | 11,706,322 | 194,025 | 806,489 |
| Employees | 3 | 46,025 | 559 | 2,922 |
| **Concentration** | 0.08 | 1 | 0.38 | 0.25 |
| Owners | 1 | 1 | 1 | 0 |
| PROD | 33.05 | 6,623.64 | 624.2 | 936.62 |
| PROF | −1,277.38 | 2,467.56 | 47.21 | 212.6 |

*Table 6.13(e)* Type-four factor analysis for 344 state companies, 1998 Sweden (Concentration)

| | Minimum | Maximum | Mean | Std. Deviation |
|---|---|---|---|---|
| Turnover | 485 | 3,554,398 | 126,053 | 383,262 |
| Profit | −352,190 | 867,696 | 10,740 | 67,109 |
| Total Assets | 888 | 10,340,653 | 285,021 | 964,158 |
| Employees | 6 | 42,108 | 617 | 3,289 |
| **Concentration** | 0.15 | 1 | 0.44 | 0.3 |
| Owners | 0 | 0 | 0 | 0 |
| PROD | 23.07 | 3,931.6 | 492.23 | 540.48 |
| PROF | −182 | 1,383.04 | 49.76 | 146.08 |

variables, which represent performance, PROD and PROF, are highly loaded. Factor 3 shows that two variables are highly loaded within that factor, Concentration and Owners, one positively and one negatively. From these results three characteristics can be established, size from factor 1, performance from factor 2 and Concentration and Owners from factor 3. It can be emphasised that Concentration, which represents the

*Table 6.13(f)* Type-four factor analysis for 343 state companies, 2000 Sweden (Concentration)

| | Minimum | Maximum | Mean | Std. Deviation |
|---|---|---|---|---|
| Turnover | 380 | 3,845,689 | 134,539 | 406,475 |
| Profit | −293,042 | 549,944 | 8,328 | 53,777 |
| Total Assets | 1,628 | 12,188,543 | 280,054 | 1,016,420 |
| Employees | 10 | 41,522 | 718 | 3,418 |
| **Concentration** | 0.08 | 1 | 0.46 | 0.29 |
| Owners | 0 | 0 | 0 | 0 |
| PROD | 32.78 | 4,831.88 | 454.87 | 478.01 |
| PROF | −357.64 | 992.23 | 38.45 | 113.8 |

*Table 6.14* Type-four factor analysis: company performances, Sweden

| | 1998 | | | 2000 | | |
|---|---|---|---|---|---|---|
| **Variables** | **Component 1 (Size)** | **Component 2 (Perf)** | **Component 3 (Own/Concen)** | **Component 1 (Size)** | **Component 2 (Perf)** | **Component 3 (Own/Concen)** |
| Turnover | 0.951 | −0.025 | 0.032 | 0.966 | −0.016 | −0.029 |
| Profit | 0.853 | 0.078 | 0.041 | 0.849 | 0.176 | 0.017 |
| Total Assets | 0.913 | −0.001 | 0.022 | 0.923 | 0.033 | −0.034 |
| Number of employees | 0.870 | −0.068 | −0.012 | 0.859 | −0.126 | −0.045 |
| **Concentration** | 0.096 | 0.056 | −0.735 | 0.124 | −0.470 | 0.562 |
| Ownership | −0.006 | 0.107 | 0.739 | −0.018 | 0.433 | −0.630 |
| PROD | −0.013 | 0.893 | −0.015 | −0.051 | 0.640 | 0.408 |
| PROF | 0.028 | 0.889 | −0.032 | 0.060 | 0.697 | 0.385 |
| Variance extracted | 40.411 | 20.183 | 13.630 | 40.794 | 16.910 | 12.907 |

degree of competitiveness of a sector, is not correlated to those variables representing size and performance in a factor. The same results are maintained for the year 2000.

From these two analyses it can be emphasised that Concentration has the same destiny as ownership in many previous analyses, since it is not correlated to a factor including other variables representing size and performance. As a result, it can be established that it is not a permanent characteristic of corporate performance, as size and performance are. However, it appears that privately owned firms are more concentrated in less concentrated sectors given the inverse relationship between ownership and Concentration for the third factor in each year (albeit with reversed signs).

## Conclusion

The second type of factor analysis (type-two) was designed to investigate privatisation performance by comparing the performance of state-owned and privatised companies for two years: 1998 and 2000. Data on state-owned and privatised companies were used with the above-mentioned variables. The result for the year 1998 shows that three characteristics (size, ownership and profitability, and performance) have been established. The second characteristic, ownership and profitability, has been seen as a clear sign of government intentions to enhance the performance of the company for sale in order to earn more money from the sale. This result was different from the result for the year 2000, which showed that only two characteristics are established: size and performance. Once more it can be emphasised that size and performance are the two main characteristics of privatisation performance, while ownership does not occupy a similarly prominent position.

The type-three factor analysis is used to investigate the characteristics of ownership more precisely. Four methods or techniques have been used, through the creation of a new ownership variable that has slightly different interpretations in different experiments. In most cases, the ownership variable and the new ownership variable are correlated to the same component, but not with other components representing other characteristics. This clearly highlights that ownership, which is a characteristic of corporate performance, remains unique; it does not have the potential to build a separate characteristic with variables representing either size or performance.

The last factor analysis was carried out to find out about the effect of concentration on corporate performance. The Swedish samples were used including a new variable, Concentration. The results showed the same characteristic as the ownership variable, indicating that concentration is not a prominent feature in corporate performance.

# 7
# Summary and General Conclusions

The question of whether the private sector, including privatised companies, has outperformed the public sector has been the main concern of this volume. Economic theories have suggested that ownership and the competitive environment have major impacts on economic efficiency, creating potential incentives for management to reduce costs and maximise productive efficiency in order to survive in a competitive environment. The aim of this volume was to put such theories to the test, asking which sector, public or private, has performed better, and to what extent ownership and competitive environment are influential aspects of corporate performance.

Public sector and government economic activities in western European countries resulted in the first instance from recognition of the inadequacies of the private sector and market provision. As Clarke describes it (1993: 207), in the early nineteenth century, local commissions were established to provide street lighting, cleaning, road-building, sewers, water supply and public health services. Later, local authorities began to build low-cost public housing to get the urban population out of the slums, and local education authorities were set up to provide mass education to those neglected by the private schools. Finally, to ensure a low-cost, reliable service, public utilities were established by local councils providing public transport, water, gas and electricity supply. Building on this, the aim of nationalisation and the welfare state in the European countries following the Second World War was the establishment of a sustainable economic infrastructure, reliable social provision and, by cross-subsidy, a comprehensive service which would be available to all ordinary people.

In this light, privatisation and its various implementations should be viewed from a number of different aspects, ranging from the motives for the policy through to its social and political effects. Copying privatisation techniques from other countries without regard for the conditions that each particular country has in terms of its economic, political and social structure may lead to completely different outcomes. Fine (1997b: 391–92) emphasises that it is almost impossible to ignore the wider economic, political and ideological conditions as well as the sectorally specific details attached to particular privatisations. Conditions that are not only taken for granted in developed countries but are also presumed to be neutral in their effects, cannot be overlooked elsewhere except in the market-led pan-globalisation view in which appropriate social economic mechanisms are miraculously conjured forth merely by virtue of the need for them.

It can thus be concluded that privatisation, from a theoretical point of view, does not have a general theory or explanation. Because a given sector differs from others in so many respects (such as its finance, technological prospects, political context, market structure, market position, and so on), privatisation will be different across sectors and countries and any generalisation is likely to be erroneous.

The privatisation process involves some perverse effects. Breaking down the natural monopoly of the public sector and creating a competitive environment through the denationalisation of state enterprise is the main presumed goal. If the aim were to obtain an immediate political gain or immediate revenues, then the effect is to introduce another monopoly, this time with private ownership. As Vickers and Yarrow (1988) demonstrate, the privatisation of telecommunications and gas has led to a situation in which taking on the problem of the new monopoly is presumed to be an easy task for the British government.

The claim that privatisation will lead to a higher level of consumer democracy is also problematic. The position of the consumer in relation to the privatised industry is often one of considerable anxiety. As Clarke explains (1993: 221),

> The fear of consumer bodies is that privatisation of vital utilities of water, gas, electricity and telephone will seriously threaten the most vulnerable sections of society as directors demand higher profits and shareholders higher dividends, both taking precedence over service, with falling standards, higher prices, and greater number of disconnections.

The motives for privatisation vary considerably, from a politically driven conviction that privatisation is best to a simple wish to avoid failure in the face of poor performance in nationalised industries. The range of different motives might include the ideological, which seeks to limit state economic activities in order to stimulate individual and private sector initiatives; the wish to undermine trade union power in order to reduce public sector borrowing; the aim of enhancing efficiency (profitability) in production in order to create a competitive environment in which consumers are better off; or the creation of a laissez-faire economy, relaxing every possible restriction in order to spread capitalism among people through offering share ownership (Wiltshire, 1987).

Privatisation as an economic programme should be seen as a segment of a broader plan to regulate the structure of the economy by the use of macroeconomic monetarist policy complemented by microeconomics, as manifested in the Conservative industrial policy programme in 1979. Additionally, privatisation should be seen as a political strategy, aiming to shift the balance of power in favour of the free market. It has been argued that one of the supposed principles of laissez-faire is to reduce the economic activity of the state. This is also one of the main characteristics of Thatcherism. However, what happened was that intervention by the government continued, but in other forms and under different agencies. Consequently, two unsurprising outcomes appeared: economic power has become concentrated in the hands of fewer people, and political control over that power has weakened (Fine, 1992).

In order to provide adequate answers to the questions mentioned earlier, the issue of how corporate performance should be measured came under consideration. Measuring corporate performance has been found to be highly complex and controversial, as different economic theories have suggested different methods. Most importantly, these economic theories seem to be one-sided in their assumption of the superiority of the private sector and privatisation, and therefore they have not given enough attention to the issue of measurement. Economic theories such as those of the property rights school, the principal–agent theory, the public choice school, the Austrian school of economics and the 'new synthesis', including the new political economy, new institutional economics and neo-Austrian economics, have been found to be ignoring the issue of how to measure corporate performance, while the conventional method of measuring corporate performance suggested by neoclassical theorists, using total factor productivity, has been found to be problematic.

Empirical studies looking at the comparative performance of public and private sectors and privatisation performance next came under consideration. There are numerous studies, looking at different aspects of the relationship between public and private sector, and using different methods with different criteria. The results of those studies showed a mixed picture; some indicating the superiority of the private sector over the public, and some the reverse. Most of these studies used the conventional way of measuring corporate performance, as suggested by the neo-classical approach. I found these results unsatisfactory, particularly because the method makes a number of initial assumptions which may not be justified in all cases. As a result, the procedure measures something other than total factor productivity, which is assumed to be the residual in the relation between inputs and outputs.

In order to examine whether empirical evidence supports the theoretical claims in favour of private sector performance superiority and privatisation performance compared to the public sector, while avoiding the problems associated with these conventional methods of assessing corporate performance, I decided instead to adopt a different method, factor analysis.

Four types of factor analysis experiments were carried out. The type-one factor analysis compared the performance of state, mixed and private companies through the use of variables such as turnover, profit, total assets, number of employees, profitability (represented by a variable, PROF), productivity (represented by a variable, PROD) and ownership, for the two years of 1998 and 2000. Fourteen European countries were chosen and data for each of the three types of companies – state, mixed and private – were collected. This type of experiment was ended by carrying out a total-country analysis comprised of all samples used for each country experiment, again for two different years, 1998 and 2000.

The results show that in two-thirds of the cases two characteristics were well established: the size and the performance of enterprises, and in most of the rest at least three characteristics emerged: the size and the performance before, and some sort of ownership, as well as a third factor. From the two-factor cases, ownership does not figure as a significant factor between firms. From the three-factor cases, ownership does emerge as a difference between firms, but not in a way that connects it with other aspects of performance. In short, ownership is not an important distinguishing factor in performance.

The type-two factor analysis looked at the privatisation performance by comparing the performance of state-owned and privatised companies in European countries for the two years of 1998 and 2000. The 1998 experiment showed that again two of the preceding characteristics found in the previous type of experiment, the size and the performance, were established. The third characteristic was a case of correlation between variables ownership and one of the performance representatives, PROF with that factor. The interesting point about this finding was that since the data collected on privatised companies related mostly to the years 1997 and 1998, it indicated that governments from different countries were attempting to improve the performance of those companies before selling them on, or selecting the more profitable companies for sale. Significantly, the results from the year 2000 did not support the above result concerning profitability and ownership, and confirmed the same result found where two characteristics were extracted, as in the previous type of experiment.

The next type of factor analysis was carried out to find out more about the characteristic of the variable ownership. This was done by using four different methods, adding a new variable of ownership reflecting duration of private ownership or the impact of privatisation (in relation to state and private firms). Again, no evidence was found of privatisation impacting separately upon performance.

The last type of factor analysis was carried out to determine whether competitiveness is a significant part of better corporate performance, as some theories have claimed. For Sweden, 'concentration' (measuring competitiveness of a company) was added for the years 1998 and 2000. Once again, this had little effect on the impact of ownership as a distinguishing feature of corporate performance, although private companies seem more likely to seek shelter from competition.

The overall conclusion is that corporate performance is characterised by two characteristics, such as size and performance, in most cases. Also, in some cases it is characterised by differences of ownership. But ownership has remained insulated without having high correlation with other variables forming other characteristics, such as size and performance. This finding contradicts most theoretical claims made by different schools in favour of the superiority of the private sector and privatisation. Finally, on the limited case study considered, it can be concluded that competitiveness is not a significant characteristic of corporate performance.

There are two major reservations concerning this analysis. Firstly, although the empirical results are extremely powerful, it should be emphasised, as discussed in Chapter 4, that factor analysis is not theory-based, and its results, as such, do not test theories or hypotheses within them. Put purely and simply, I have shown in a limited way and on a limited data set (in scope across firms, countries and time) and in variables (measuring firm characteristics) that there is no immediate association between firm performance and form of ownership (private or public). The most immediate conclusion to draw is that ownership as such is not a major factor in firm performance. But alternative hypotheses can be put forward that suggest otherwise, and it is not too difficult to play devil's advocate on behalf of the privatisation lobby. For example, it might be argued that the privatisation threat has imposed a discipline on the public sector, through demonstration effect and encouraging restructuring or closure of those state-owned firms that do not perform well. Otherwise, for example, it might be expected that profitability would be consistently higher in the private sector given its need to make profits to survive and the greater dispensation to pursue profitability in being free of state 'interference'. The results detailed here cannot be used to reject such hypotheses out of hand.

But they can offer a response. As suggested in Chapters 2 and 3, the theories in favour of privatisation have rarely, if ever, carried through their arguments to direct empirical investigation to the mechanisms on which they are supposedly founded – whether it be the freedom to innovate of the neo-Austrian school or the rent-seeking of the neo-liberals. Rather, these arguments are presumed to lead to empirical outcomes reflecting superior private firm performance by measurement of profitability, productivity, or whatever. And like the theory, the evidence is often presumed to be supportive. This volume has shown this not to be the case to an extent that arguably goes beyond most of what has been done before. Interpreting this evidence is another matter. But the onus has been shifted onto those who favour privatisation. They must show that the apparent uniformity of performance across forms of ownership is, paradoxically, a consequence of the superiority of private ownership. Our suspicion is that this cannot and will not be done, not least because corporate performance (and the role of ownership) is extremely variable according to circumstances, and any general theory will founder on the diversity of the specific.

Secondly, this empirical work is based necessarily upon limited data sets, particularly for the numbers of firms that are of state or mixed ownership. In addition, the number of variables that can be used to assess firm characteristics in general, and performance in particular, is also extremely limited. Further, even with these limitations, there is the problem of standardisation in definition of the variables and their appropriateness in view of the distortions that arise out of differences in accounting practices and the vagaries of exchange rate movements, and so on. Almost indefinite effort could be spent in constructing a more satisfactory data set for the purposes of my analysis.

But it is my suspicion, and this is the lesson to be drawn for future research, that this would not be the best way to proceed in assessing the impact of privatisation. One major conclusion to be drawn from this and other theoretical and empirical research is that there can be no general theory of privatisation and its consequences. Outcomes are bound to depend upon too wide a range of factors and how they interact with one another in specific country, sector and corporate contexts (including political and other factors). Accordingly, the way forward is to accept that privatisation needs to be assessed in a case study methodology in order to be able to accommodate such differences. This seems to be the appropriate response to those who would take, in light of the first reservation expressed above, the view that the general results indicate that even performance across ownership is indicative of the virtues of privatisation in view of their impact on the non-private. This would have to be demonstrated rather than posited as a speculative hypothesis. And, in view of the second reservation, detailed cases studies also seem to be appropriate. Indeed, in order to address the problems of comparability of data, and so on, across companies to make a fair assessment of performance, it is almost inevitable that case study-type considerations will need to be incorporated in any case. Why not make a virtue out of necessity and proceed from an original goal of general empirical comparisons to what they will allow for, case study analysis?

In short, with reservations, this volume indicates that there is no empirical case for supporting the hypothesis that privatisation is a major, general source of enhanced performance or, indeed, a means of distinguishing between firms in other respects. However, rather than taking this as a conclusion with 'closure', I prefer to see it as the basis for more situated analyses of privatisation, and of industrial policy more generally. Industrial performance does need to be assessed, and policy made, in terms of a wide range of variables. One of these is ownership, whose impact should be assessed in relation to other factors, and not otherwise unduly exaggerated.

# Bibliography


Aharoni, Y. (1986) *The Evaluation of Management of state-owned Enterprises*. Cambridge, MA; Melrose, MA: Pitman.

Alchian, A.A. (1977) *Economic Forces at Work*. Indianapolis: Liberty Press.

Alchian, A.A. and H. Demsetz (1972) 'Production Information Cost and Economic Organization'. *American Economic Review* 62(2): 777–95.

Amadeus: www.amaseus.bvdep.com

Anders, C. (1992) 'The "Barbarians" in the Boardroom'. *Harvard Business Review* 70(4): 79.

Anderson, S., A. de Palma and J-F. Thisse (1997) 'Privatization and Efficiency in a Differentiated Industry'. *European Economic Review* 41: 1635–54.

Atkinson, S.E. and R. Halvorsen (1986) 'The Relative Efficiency of Public and Private Firms in a Regulated Environment: The Case of U.S. Electric Utilities.' *Journal of Public Economics* 29: 281–94.

Bailey, R.W. (1987) 'Uses and Misuses of Privatization'. In R.W. Bailey (ed.) *Privatization and Development*. New York: Academy of Political Science.

Bargeman, P. (1970) 'Heterogeneous Capital, the Production Function and the Theory of Distribution'. *Review of Economic Studies* 37: 407–36.

—— (1978) 'Notes on Consumption, Investment and Effective Demand: I'. *Cambridge Journal of Economics* 2(4): 335–53. Reprinted in J. Eatwell and M. Milgate (eds) *Keynes' Economics and the Theory of Value and Distribution*. London: Duckworth, 1983.

—— (1979a) 'Notes on Consumption, Investment and Effective Demand: II'. *Cambridge Journal of Economics* 3(1): 63–82. Reprinted in J. Eatwell and M. Milgate (eds) *Keynes' Economics and the Theory of Value and Distribution*. London: Duckworth, 1983.

—— (1979b) 'Notes on Consumption, Investment and Effective Demand: A Reply to Joan Robinson'. *Cambridge Journal of Economics* 3(2): 181–7. Reprinted in J. Eatwell and M. Milgate (eds) *Keynes' Economics and the Theory of Value and Distribution*. London: Duckworth, 1983.

Barnes, P.A. (1985) 'UK Building Societies: A Study of the Gains from Merger'. *Journal of Business Finance and Accounting* (Spring): 75–91.

Beesley, M.E. and S.C. Littlefield (1989) 'The Regulation of Privatized Monopolies in the United Kingdom'. *Rand Journal of Economics* 20: 454–73.

Bhaduri, A. and Robinson, J. (1980) 'Accumulation and Exploitation: An Analysis in the tradition of Marx, Sraffa and Kalecki'. *Cambridge Journal of Economics* 4(2): 103–15. Reprinted in A. Bhaduri *Unconventional Economic Essays*. Oxford: Oxford University Press, 1993.

Bishop, M. and J. Kay (1988) *Does Privatization Work? Lessons from the UK*. London: Centre for Business Strategy, London Business School.

—— (1989) 'Privatization in the United Kingdom: Lessons from Experience'. *World Development* 17: 643–57.

Bishop, M. and D. Thompson (1992) 'Regulatory Reform and Productivity Growth in the UK's Public Utilities'. *Applied Economics* 24(11) (November): 1181–90.

Blanchard, O. and P. Aghion (1996) 'On Insider Privatization'. *European Economic Review* 40: 759–66.
Blaug, M. (1974) *The Cambridge Revolution, Success or Failure? A Critical Analysis of Cambridge Theories of Value and Distribution*. London: Institute of Economic Affairs.
Bliss, C.J. (1968) *Rates of Return in a Linear Model*. Cambridge, mimeograph.
—— (1975) *Capital Theory and the Distribution of Income*. Amsterdam: North Holland; New York: American Elsevier.
Boardman, A. and A.R. Vining (1989) 'Ownership and Performance in Competitive Environments: A Comparison of the Performance of Private, Mixed, and State-owned Enterprises'. *Journal of Law and Economics* 32: 1–33.
Boardman, A.E. and A.R. Vining (1992) 'Ownership versus Competition – Efficiency in Public Enterprise'. *Public Choice* 73(2): 205–39.
Borcherding, T., W. Bush and R. Spann (1977) 'The Effects of Public Spending on the Divisibility of Public Outputs in Consumption'. In T.E. Borcherding (ed.) *Budgets and Bureaucrats: The Sources of Government Growth*. Durham, NC: Duke University Press.
Borcherding, T.E., B.C. Bunaby, W.W. Pommerehne and F. Schneider (1982) 'Comparing the Efficiency of Private and Public Production: the Evidence from Five Countries'. *Zeitschrift flier Nationaloekonomie*, Supplement 2.
Bortolotti, B., M. Fantini, D. Siniscalco and S. Vitalini (1998) 'Privatisation Processes in a Cross-section of Countries: An Empirical Analysis'. Working Paper. Italy: Universita di Torino.
Bos, D. (1991) *Privatization: A Theoretical Treatment*. Oxford: Clarendon Press.
Bothwell, J.L. (1980) 'Profitability, Risk, and the Separation of Ownership from Control'. *Journal of Industrial Economics* 28(3) (March): 303–11.
Bowen, S. (1997) 'Bolivian Watchdog Proud of its Teeth'. *Financial Times*, 27 July: 7.
Boycko, M., A. Shleifer, and R.W. Vishny (1994) 'Voucher Privatization'. *Journal of Financial Economics* 35: 249–66.
—— (1996) 'A Theory of Privatisation'. *Economic Journal* 106: 309–19.
Bryman, A. and D. Cramer (1999) *Quantitative Data Analysis with SPSS Release 8 for Windows: A Guide for Social Scientists*. London and New York: Routledge [1998].
Byatt, I. (1985) 'Market and Non-market Alternatives in the Public Supply of Public Services: British Experience with Privatisation'. In F. Forte and A. Peacock (eds) *Public Expenditure and Government Growth*. Oxford: Blackwell.
Campbell White, O. and A. Bhatia (1998) *Privatization in Africa*. Washington, DC: World Bank.
Cattell, R. B. (1966) *Handbook of Multivariate Experimental Psychology*. Chicago.
Caves, D.W. and L.R. Christensen (1980) 'The Relative Efficiency of Public and Private Firms in a Competitive Environment: The Case of Canadian Railroads'. *Journal of Political Economy* 88(5): 958–76.
Chang, H-J. and A. Singh (1992) *Public Enterprises in Developing Countries and Economic Efficiency*. Geneva: UNCTAD.
—— (1993) *Public Enterprise in Developing Countries and Economic Efficiency: A Critical Examination of Analytical, Empirical and Policy Issues*. UNCTAD Review 4. Geneva: UNCTAD.
—— (1997) 'Can Large Firms be Run Efficiently Without being Bureaucratic?' *Journal of International Development* 9(6) (September–October): 865–75.

Chen, E.K.Y. (1997) 'The Total Factor Productivity Debate: Determinants of Economic Growth in East Asia'. *Asian-Pacific Economic Literature* 11(1) (May).

Christensen, L.R. and D. Cummings (1975) 'Real Product, Real Factor Input, and Total Factor Productivity in the Republic of Korea, 1960–73'. Discussion Paper No. 7057, reprinted in *Journal of Development Economics* 8 [1981]: 285–302.

Christensen, L.R., D. Cummings and D.W. Jorgenson (1980) 'Economic Growth, 1947–73: An International Comparison'. In J.W. Kendrick and B.N. Vaccara (eds) *New Developments in Productivity Measurement and Analysis*. Chicago, IL: University of Chicago Press: 595–698.

Christensen, L.R., D.W. Jorgenson and L.J. Lau (1973) 'Transcendental Logarithmic Production Frontiers'. *Review of Economics and Statistics* 55(1): 28–45.

Clark, J.B. (1889) 'The Possibility of a Scientific Law of Wages'. *Publication of the American Economic Association*, Vol. IV, 39–63.

—— (1891) 'Distribution as Determined by a Law of Rent'. *Quarterly Journal of Economics*, Vol. V, 289–318.

Clarke, T. (1993) 'The Political Economy of the UK Privatization Programme: A Blueprint for Other Countries?' In T. Clarke and C. Pitelis (eds) *The Political Economy of Privatisation*. London and New York: Routledge.

Clarke, T. and C. Pitelis (eds) (1993) *The Political Economy of Privatisation*. London and New York: Routledge.

Conyon, M.J. (1995) 'Industry Profit Margins and Concentration: Evidence from UK Manufacturing'. *International Review of Applied Economics* 9(3): 275–90.

Conyon, M., P. Gregg and S. Machin (1995) 'Taking Care of Business: Executive Compensation in the UK'. *Economic Journal* 105(430) (May): 704–14.

Cook, P. and C. Kirkpatrick (1988a) 'Privatization in Less Developed Countries: An Overview'. In P. Cook and C. Kirkpatrick (eds) *Privatization in Less Developed Countries*. Brighton: Wheatsheaf.

—— (1988b) *Privatization in Less Developed Countries*. Brighton: Wheatsheaf.

—— (1988c) *Privatization, Enterprise Development and Economic Reform: Experiences of Developing and Transitional Economies*. Northampton, MA: Edward Elgar.

—— (1995) *Privatisation Policy and Performance: International Perspectives*. New York: Harvester Wheatsheaf.

Cosh, A.D., A. Hughes and A. Singh (1980) 'The Causes and Effects of Takeovers in the UK: An Empirical Investigation for the UK at the Micro Economic Level'. In D.C. Mueller (ed.) *The Determinants and Effects of Mergers: an International Comparison*. Cambridge, MA: Oelgeschlager, Gunn & Hain.

—— (1990) *Takeovers, Short-termism and Finance–Industry Relations in the UK Economy*. London: Institute for Public Policy Research.

Cowling, K. et al. (1980) *Mergers and Economic Performance*. Cambridge: Cambridge University Press.

Cram, W. and A. Zardkoohi (1978) 'A Test of the Property Rights Theory of the Firm: Water Utilities in the United States'. *Journal of Law and Economics* 21 (October): 395–408.

Creamer, R. (1972) 'Measuring Capital Input for Total Factor Productivity Analysis'. *Review of Income and Wealth* 18(1): 55–78.

Curwen, P. (ed.) (1992) *Understanding the U.K. Economy*. Basingstoke: Macmillan.

DataStream: www.datastream.com

De Alessi, L. (1969) 'Implications of Property Rights for Government Investment Choices'. *American Economic Review* 59(1) (March): 13–24.

Debreu, G. (1959) 'Theory of Value. An Axiomatic Analysis of Economic Equilibrium'. Cowles Foundation Monograph No. 17. New York: John Wiley and Son.

—— (1974) 'Excess Demand Functions'. *Journal of Mathematical Economics* 1(1): 15–21.

De Fraja, G. (1993) 'Productive Efficiency in Public and Private Firms'. *Journal of Public Economics* 50: 15–30.

Demsetz, H. (1967) 'Toward a Theory of Property Rights'. *American Economic Review* 57(2) (May): 347–49.

Denison, E.F. (1962) *The Sources of Economic Growth in the United States and the Alternatives Before Us*. New York: Committee for Economic Development.

Dertouzos, M., R. Lester and R. Solow (1989) *Made in America*. Cambridge, MA: MIT Press.

Dewenter, K. and P.H. Malatesta (1998) 'State-owned and Privately owned Firms: An Empirical Analysis of Profitability, Leverage, and Labour Intensity'. Working Paper. Washington, DC: University of Washington.

Djankov S., S. Classens and G. Pohl (1997) *Ownership and Corporate Governance: Evidence from the Czech Republic*. Washington, DC: World Bank, Office of the Regional Vice President, East Asia and Pacific, and Europe and Central Asia, and Middle East and North Africa Technical Department, Finance and Private Sector Development Division.

Dobb, M.H. (1973) *Theories of Value and Distribution since Adam Smith. Ideology and Economic Theory*. Cambridge: Cambridge University Press.

Downs, A. (1967) *Inside Bureaucracy*. Boston, MA: Little, Brown and Co.

Dunleavy, P. (1991) *Democracy, Bureaucracy, and Public Choice: Economic Explanations in Political Science*. London: Harvester.

Dunshire, A.K. Hartley and D. Parker (1991) 'Organizational Status and Performance – Summary of the Findings'. *Public Administration* 69(1) (Spring): 21–40.

Eatwell, J. and M. Milgate (eds) (1983) *Keynes' Economics and the Theory of Value and Distribution*. London: Duckworth.

*Economist, The* (1992a) 'Paying the Boss'. 1 February: 13.

*Economist, The* (1992b) 'Worthy of His Hire?' 1 February: 21.

Edwards, J., J.A. Kay and C.P. Mayer (1987) *The Economic Analysis of Accounting Profitability*. Oxford: Clarendon Press.

Ehrlich, I., G. Gallais-Hamonno, Z. Liu and R. Lutter (1994) 'Productivity Growth and Firm Ownership: An Empirical Investigation'. *Journal of Political Economy* 102: 1006–38.

Faere, R., S. Grosskopf and J. Logan (1985) 'The Relative Performance of Publicly Owned and Privately Owned Electric Utilities'. *Journal of Public Economics* 26: 89–106.

Fine, B. (1980) *Economic Theory and Ideology*. London: Edward Arnold.

—— (1982) *Theories of the Capitalist Economy*. New York: Holmes & Meier.

—— (1989) *Marx's Capital*. London: Macmillan.

—— (1993) *Marx's Capital*. London: Macmillan.

—— (1990) *The Coal Question*. London: Routledge.

Fine, B. (1992) 'Total Factor Productivity. Realism: The South African Coal Mining Industry'. *South African Journal of Economics* 60(3): 277–92.

—— (1995) 'Privatization and the RDP: A Critical Assessment'. *Transformation* 27: 1–23.

—— (1997a) 'Privatization and the Restructuring of State Assets in South Africa: A Strategic View'. Paper presented to COSATU workshop, Johannesburg, 17 March.

—— (1997b) 'Privatization: Theory and Lessons from the UK and South Africa'. *Seoul Journal of Economics* 10(4): 373–414.

Fine, B. and K. Bayliss (1998) 'Beyond Bureaucrats on Business: A Critical Review of the World Band Approach to Privatization and Public Sector Reform'. *Journal of International Development* 10: 841–55.

Fine, B. and L. Harris (1985) *The Peculiarities of the British Economy*. London: Lawrence & Wishart.

Finsinger, J. (1984) 'The Performance of Public Enterprises in Insurance Markets'. In M. Marchand, P. Pestieau and H. Tulkens (eds) *The Performance of Public Enterprises: Concept and Measurement*. Amsterdam: North Holland.

Fiorina, M.P. and R.G. Noll (1978) 'Voters, Bureaucrats, and Legalisators'. *Journal of Public Economics* 9(2): 239–54.

Fisher, F.M. (1971) 'The Existence of Aggregate Production Functions: Reply'. *Econometrica*, Vol. XXXIX, 405.

Foreman-Peck, J. and D. Manning (1988) 'How Well is BT performing? An International Comparison of Telecommunications Total Factor Productivity'. *Fiscal Studies* 9(3) (August): 54–67.

Foreman-Peck, J. and M. Waterson (1985) 'The Comparative Efficiency of Public and Private Enterprise in Britain: Electricity Generation Between the World Wars'. *Economic Journal* 95 (Supplement): 83–95.

Forsyth, P. and R. Hocking (1980) *Economic Efficiency and the Regulation of Air Transport*. Melbourne: Committee for Economic Development of Australia.

Frydman, R., C.W. Gray, M. Hessel, and A. Rapaczynski (1998a) 'When does Privatization Work? The impact of Private Ownership on Corporate Performance in Transition Economies'. Working Paper. New York: C.V. Starr Center for Applied Economics, New York University.

—— (1998b) *Capitalism with a Comrade's Face: Studies in the Postcommunist Transition*. Budapest: Central European University Press.

Furubotn, E.G. and S. Pejovich (1972) 'Property Rights and Economic Theory: A Survey of Recent Literature'. *The Journal of Economic Literature* 10(4) (December): 1137–62.

—— (1973) 'Property Rights, Economic Decentralization and the Evolution of the Yugoslav firm, 1965–1972'. *Journal of Law and Economics* 16(2) (October): 275–302.

—— (eds) (1974) *The Economics of Property Rights*. Cambridge, MA: Ballinger.

Galal, A., et al. (1994) *Welfare Consequences of Selling Public Enterprises: An Empirical Analysis*. New York: World Bank Oxford University Press.

Galal, A., L. Jones, P. Tandon and I. Vogelsang (1992) *Welfare Consequences of Selling Public Enterprises*. Washington DC: World Bank.

Gayle, D.J. and J.N. Goodrich (eds) (1990) *Privatization and Deregulation in Global Perspective*. London: Pinter.

Glassman, C.A. and S.A. Rhoades (1980) 'Owner vs. Manager Control Effects of Bank Performance'. *Review of Economics and Statistics* 2 (May): 263–70.

Goldring, M. (1993) 'Private Lives of Really Useful Companies'. *Independent*, 25 March.

Goodman, J.B. and G.W. Loveman (1991) 'Does Privatization Serve the Public Interest?' *Harvard Business Review* 69(6) (November–December): 26–39.

Gordon, R.J. (1990) *The Measurement of Durable Goods Prices*. Chicago, IL: University of Chicago Press.

Gorsuch, R.L. (1983) *Factor Analysis*. Hillsdale, NJ, and London: Lawrence Erlbaum.

Graham & Trotman (publisher) (1983) 'Major Companies of Europe'.

Griliches, Z. (1964) 'Research Expenditure, Education and the Aggregate Agricultural Production Function'. *American Economic Review* 54(6): 961–74.

—— (1970) 'Notes on the Role of Education in Production Functions and Growth Accounting'. In L. Hanson (ed.) *Education, Income and Human Capital*. New York: Columbia University Press: 71–115.

—— (1996) 'The Discovery of the Residual: A Historical Note'. *Journal of Economic Literature* 34(3) (September): 1324–30.

Griliches, Z. and D.W. Jorgenson (1962) 'Capital Theory: Technical Progress and Capital Structure, Sources of Measured Productivity Change: Capital Input'. *American Economic Review* 52(1): 50–61.

Grosfeld, I. (1990) 'Unusual Opportunities. The Mutual Impact on Each Other of Reform Economics and the Western Economic Theory'. *Kozgazdasagi szemle* XXXVII (January): 44–59.

Haggarty, L. and M.M. Shirley (1996) 'A New Database on State-owned Enterprises'. Working Paper. Washington, DC: World Bank.

Hague C. (1996) 'Introductory Texts on Urban and Regional Planning'. *Town Planning Review* 66(2) (April): 207–12.

Hahn, F.H. (1972a) *The Share of Wages in the National Income. An Enquiry into the Theory of Distribution*. London: Weidenfeld and Nicolson.

—— (1972b) *Notes on Vulgar Economy*. Cambridge, mimeograph.

—— (1973a) *On the Notion of Equilibrium in Economics: An Inaugural Lecture*. Cambridge: Cambridge University Press.

—— (1973b) 'The Winter of Our Discontent'. *Economica*, Vol. XL, 322–30.

Hahn, F.H. and J.A. Kenneth (1971) *General Competitive Analysis*. Amsterdam: North Holland.

Harcourt, G.C. (1973) 'The Rate of Profits in Equilibrium Growth Models: A Review Article'. *Journal of Political Economy*, LXXXI, 1261–77.

—— (1975) 'Capital Theory: Much Ado about Something'. *Thames Papers in Political Economics*.

—— (1976) 'The Cambridge Controversies: Old Ways and New Horizons or Dead End'. *Oxford Economic Papers* 28(1): 25–65.

Harcourt, G.C. and V. G. Massara (1964) 'Mr Sraffa's Production of Commodities'. *Economic Record* 40: 442–54. Reprinted in I. Bradley and M. Howard (eds) *Classical and Marxian Political Economy: Essays in Honour of Ronald L. Mee*. London: Macmillan, 1982.

Hart, O., A. Shleifer and R.W. Vishny (1997) 'The Proper Scope of Government: Theory and an Application to Prisons'. *Quarterly Journal of Economics* 112: 1127–61.

Hartley, K. and N. Hooper (1992) 'Industry and Policy.' In P. Curwen (ed.) *Understanding the U.K. Economy*. Basingstoke: Macmillan.

Haskel, J. and S. Szymanski (1993) 'Privatization, Liberalization, Wages and Employment – Theory and Evidence for the UK'. *Economica* 60(238) (May): 161–82.

Hayek, F.A. (1984) *The Essence of Hayek*. Edited by C. Nishiyama and K.R. Leubel. Foreword by W. Gienn Campbell. Stanford, CA: Hoover Institution Press, Stanford University.

—— (1989) 'Order With or Without Design?' In *Selections from F.A. Hayek's 'Contributions to the Theory and Application of Spontaneous Order'*. Compiled and introduced by Naomi Moldofsky; comment by Sudha R. Shenoy. London: Centre for Research into Communist Economies.

—— (1994) *The Road to Serfdom*. Chicago, IL: University of Chicago Press.

Heald, D. (1983) *Public Expenditure: Its Defence and Reform*. Oxford: Robertson.

Hemming, R. and A.M. Mansoor (1988) *Privatization and Public Enterprises*. Washington, DC: IMF.

Herman, E.S. (1981) *Corporate Control, Corporate Power*. Cambridge: Cambridge University Press.

Hicks, J.B. (1932) *The Theory of Wages*. London: Macmillan.

Hodgson, G. (1997) 'The Fate of the Cambridge Capital Controversy'. In M. Sawyer, P. Arestis and G. Palma (eds) *Capital Controversy, Post Keynesian Economics and the History of Economics: Essays in Honour of Geoff Harcourt*. Vol. 1. London: Routledge.

Hodgson, M. (1998) *Economics and Institutions*. Cambridge: Polity Press.

Iordanoglou, C.H. (2001) *Public Enterprise Revised. A Close Look at the 1954–79 UK Labour Productivity Record*. Aldershot: Edward Elgar.

Jasinski, A.H. (1991) 'Dilemmas of Public Innovation Policy in Poland in the Transition to a Market Economy'. *Science and Public Policy* 18(2): 131.

Johanson, H.G. (1971) *The Two-Sector Model of General Equilibrium*. London: Allen and Unwin.

—— (1973) *The Theory of Income Distribution*. London: Gray-Mills Publishing.

Jorgenson, D.W. (1966) 'The Embodiment Hypothesis'. *Journal of Political Economy* 74(1): 1–17.

Jorgenson, D.W. and Z. Griliches (1967) 'The Explanation of Productivity Change'. *Review of Economic Studies* 34(3) (July): 249–83.

Kaldor, N. (1972) 'The Irrelevance of Equilibrium Economics'. *Economic Journal*, Vol. LXXXII, 1237–55.

Kalecki, M. (1939) *Essays in the Theory of Economic Fluctuations*. London: Allen and Unwin.

Kay, J.A. and D.J. Thompson (1986) 'Privatisation: A Policy in Search of a Rationale'. *Economic Journal* 96: 18–32.

Kendrick, J.W. and D. Creamer (1961) *Measuring Company Productivity*. New York: National Industrial Conference Board.

Keynes, J.M. (1953) *The General Theory of Employment, Interest and Money*. San Diego, CA, and London: Harcourt Brace Jovanovich.

Kikeri, S., J. Nellis and M. Shirley (1992) *Privatization: The Lessons of Experience*. Washington, DC: World Bank.

Kirzner, I.M. (1976) 'Equilibrium versus Market Process'. In E.G. Dolan (ed.) *The Foundations of Modern Austrian Economics*. Mission, KS: Sheed & Ward.

Kole, S.R. and J.H. Mulherin (1997) 'The Government as a Shareholder: A Case from the United States'. *Journal of Law and Economics* 40: 1–22.

Kornai, J. (1988) 'Individual Freedom and Reform of the Socialist Economy'. *European Economic Review* 32(2–3) (March): 233–67.

Laffont, J-J. and J. Tirole (1991) 'Privatization and Incentives'. *Journal of Law, Economics and Organization* 7: 84–105.

Li, W. (1997) 'The Impact of Economic Reform on the Performance of Chinese State Enterprises, 1980–1989'. *Journal of Political Economy* 105: 1080–106.

Linowes, D.F. (1990) 'Privatization and Deregulation in the United States'. In D.J. Gayle (ed.) *Privatization and Deregulation in Global Perspective*. London: Pinter.

Littlechild, S.C. (1986a) *Economic Regulation of Privatised Water Authorities: A Report Submitted to the Department of the Environment*. London: HMSO.

—— (1986b) *The Fallacy of the Mixed Economy: An Austrian Critique of Recent Economic Thinking and Policy*. Second edition. London: Institute of Economic Affairs.

—— (1989) 'Three Types of Market Process'. In R.N. Langlois (ed.) *Economics as a Process*. Cambridge: Cambridge University Press.

—— (ed.) (1990) *Austrian Economics*. Aldershot: Edward Elgar.

—— (2000) *Privatization, Competition and Regulation*. London: Institute of Economic Affairs.

Maddison, A. (1972) 'Explaining Economic Growth'. *Banca Nazionale Del Lavoro Quarterly Review* 22(102): 211–51.

Mantel, R. (1974) 'On the Characterization of Aggregate Excess Demand'. *Journal of Economic Theory* 12(2): 348–53.

Marchand, M., P. Pestieau and H. Tulkens (eds) (1984a) *The Performance of Public Enterprises: Concept and Measurement*. Amsterdam: North Holland.

—— (1984b) 'The Performance of Public Enterprises: Normative, Positive, and Empirical Issues'. In M. Marchand et al. (eds) *The Performance of Public Enterprises: Concept and Measurement*. Amsterdam: North Holland.

Marsh, D. (1991) 'Privatisation under Mrs Thatcher: A Review of the Literature'. *Public Administration* 69 (Winter): 459–80.

Marshall, A. (1890) *Principles of Economics*. London: Macmillan.

Martin, S. and D. Parker (1995) 'Privatization and Economic Performance Throughout the UK Business Cycle'. *Managerial and Decision Economics* 16: 225–37.

—— (1997) *The Impact of Privatisation: Ownership and Corporate Performance in the UK*. London: Routledge.

Martinez-Vazquez, J. (1981) 'Selfishness versus Public "Regardingness" in Voting Behaviour'. *Journal of Public Economics* 15(3): 349–61.

Marwell, C. and R.E. Ames (1981) 'Economists Free Ride, Does Anyone Else?' *Journal of Public Economics* 15(3) (June): 295–310.

Marx, K. (1969a) *Theories of Surplus Value*. Part I. London: Lawrence and Wishart.

—— (1969b) *Theories of Surplus Value*. Part II. London: Lawrence and Wishart.

—— (1972) *Capital*. Vol. III. London: Lawrence and Wishart.

—— (1976) *Capital*. Vol. I. Harmondsworth: Penguin.

Matthews, K. and P. Minford (1987) 'Mrs Thatcher's Economic Policies 1979–87'. *Economic Policy* (October): 57–102.

Megginson, W.L., R.C. Nash and M. van Randenborgh (1994) 'The Financial and Operating Performance of Newly Privatized Firms: An International Empirical Analysis'. *Journal of Finance* 49: 403–52.

Megginson, W.L., R.C. Nash, J.M. Netter and A.L. Schwartz (1998) 'The Long Term Return to Investors in Share Issue Privatisations'. Working Paper. Athens, GA: University of Georgia.

Megginson, W.L. and J.M. Netter (1998) 'Equity to the People: The Record on Privatisation by Public Offers.' In *Privatisation Yearbook*. London: Privatisation International: 27–34.

Menyah, K. and K. Paudyal (1996) 'Share Issue Privatisations: The UK Experience'. In M. Levis (ed.) *Empirical Issues in Raising Equity Capital*. Amsterdam: Elsevier Science.

Millward, R. (1982) 'The Comparative Performance of Public and Private Ownership'. In Lord Roll (ed.) *The Mixed Economy: Proceedings of Section F (Economics) of the British Association for the Advancement of Science*. London: Macmillan Press.

—— (1988) 'Measured Sources of Inefficiency in the Performance of Private and Public Enterprises in LDCs'. In P. Cook and C. Kirkpatrick (eds) *Privatisation in Less Developed Countries*. Brighton: Wheatsheaf.

Millward, R. and D. Parker (1983) 'Public and Private Enterprise: Comparative Behaviour and Relative Efficiency.' In R. Millward, D. Parker, L. Rosenthal, M.T. Sumner and N. Toppham (eds) *Public Sector Economics*. London: Longman.

Moldofsky, N. (1989) 'The Problems Reconsidered, 1920–1989'. In F.A. Hayek (ed.) *Selections from F.A. Hayek's Contributions to the Theory and Application of Spontaneous Order*. Compiled and Introduced by Naomi Moldofsky; comment by Sudha R. Shenoy. London: Centre for Research.

Monsen, R.J., J.S.Y. Chiu and D.E. Cooley (1968) 'The Effect of Separation of Ownership and Control on the Performance of the Large Firm'. *Quarterly Journal of Economics* 83(3) (August): 435–51.

Morgan, W. (1977) 'Investor-Owned vs. Publicly-Owned Water Agencies'. *Water Resources Bulletin* 13.

Morishima, M. (1973) *Marx's Economics. A Dual Theory of Value and Growth*. Cambridge: Cambridge University Press.

Morris, J. and P. Blyton (eds) (1991) *A Flexible Future? Prospects for Employment and Organization*. Berlin: W. de Gruyter.

Nadiri, M.I. (1970) 'Some Approaches to the Theory and Measurement of Total Factor Productivity: A Survey'. *Journal of Economic Literature*, 8(4) (December): 1137–77.

Nelson, J.R. (1964) *Marginal Cost Pricing in Practice*. Englewood Cliffs, NJ, and London: Prentice-Hall.

Newberry, D. and M.G. Pollitt (1997) 'The Restructuring and Privatization of Britain's CEGB – Was it Worth It?' *Journal of Industrial Economics* 45: 269–303.

Niskanen, W. (1968) 'The Peculiar Economics of Bureaucracy'. *American Economic Review* 48(2) (May): 293–305.

Nuti, D.M. (1974) 'On the Rates of Return on Investment'. *Kyklos*, Vol. XXVII, 345–69.

Nutter, G. (1974) 'Markets Without Property: A Grand Illusion'. In E.G. Furubotn and S. Pejovich (eds) *The Economics of Property Rights*. Cambridge, MA: Ballinger.

O'Driscoll, G.P. and M.J. Rizzo (1985) *The Economics of Time and Ignorance*. Oxford: Blackwell.

Parker, D. (ed.) (1998) *Privatisation in the European Union: Theory and Policy Perspectives*. London and New York: Routledge.

Parker, D. and K. Hartley (1991) 'Privatization – A Conceptual Framework'. In A.F. Ott and K. Hartley (eds) *Privatization and Economic Efficiency: A Comparative Analysis of Developed and Developing Countries*. Aldershot: Edward Elgar: 11–25.

Parker, D. and S. Martin (1995) 'The Impact of UK Privatisation on Labour and Total Factor Productivity'. *Scottish Journal of Political Economy* 42(2) (May): 201–20.

Pasinetti, L.L. (ed.) (1974) *Growth and Income Distribution. Essays in Economic Theory*. Cambridge: Cambridge University Press.

Pejovich, S. (1990) *The Economics of Property Rights: Towards a Theory of Comparative Systems*. Dordrecht and Boston, MA: Kluwer Academic.

Pescatrice, D.R. and J.M.I. Trapani (1980) 'The Performance and Objectives of Public and Private Utilities Operating in the United States'. *Journal of Public Economics* 13(2): 259–76.

Phelps, B.E.H. (1962) *The Economics of Labour*. New Haven, CT, and London: Yale University Press.

Picot, A. and T. Kaulmann (1989) 'Comparative Performance of Government-owned and Privately-owned Industrial Corporations – Empirical Results from Six Countries'. *Journal of Institutional and Theoretical Economics* 145(2) (June): 298–316.

Pinto, B., M. Belka and S. Krajewski (1993) 'Transforming State Enterprises in Poland: Evidence on Adjustment by Manufacturing Firms'. *Brookings Papers on Economic Activity*: 213–61.

Pistor, K. and A. Spicer (1997) 'Investment Funds in Mass Privatization and Beyond: Evidence from the Czech Republic and Russian Private Sector'. *World Bank* (December): 33–6.

Pohl, G. et al. (1997) *Privatization and Restructuring in Central and Eastern Europe: Evidence and Policy Options*. Washington, DC: World Bank.

Prescott, E.C. (1997) 'Needed: A Theory of Total Factor Productivity'. Minneapolis, MN: Federal Reserve Bank of Minneapolis Research Department.

Ramanadham, V.V. (1993) *Constraints and Impacts of Privatization*. London and New York: Routledge.

Ramsey, F.P. (1928) 'A Mathematical Theory of Saving'. *Economic Journal*, Vol. XXXVIII, 543–59.

Rees, R. (1989) *Public Enterprise Economics*. Second edition. London: Weidenfeld and Nicolson.

Ricardo, D. (1992) *The Principles of Political Economy and Taxation*. London: Dent Rutland.

Rizvi, S.A.T. (1994a) 'The Microfoundations Project in General Equilibrium Theory'. *Cambridge Journal of Economics* 18(4): 357–77.

—— (1994b) 'Game Theory to the Rescue'. *Contributions to Political Economy* 13: 1–28.

Robinson, J. (1953) 'The Production Function and the Theory of Capital'. *Review of Economic Studies*, Vol. XXI: 81–106.

—— (1971a) 'The Existence of Aggregate Production Functions: Comment'. *Econometrica*, Vol. XXXIX: 405.

—— (1971b) *Economic Heresies: Some Old-fashioned Questions in Economic Theory*. New York: Basic Books.

—— (1973) *Collected Economic Papers*. Vol. IV. Oxford: Blackwell.

—— (1974) *History Versus Equilibrium*. London: Thames Polytechnic.

Robinson, J. (1975a) 'Introduction, 1974. Comments and Explanations'. In *Collected Economic Papers*, Vol. III. Second edition. Oxford: Blackwell: iii–xiv.
—— (1975b) 'Letter to Editor'. *Cambridge Review*, Vol. XCVI: 91–2.
—— (1975c) 'Review of L.L. Pasinetti, Growth and Income Distribution. Essays in Economic Theory, 1974.' *Economic Journal*, Vol. LXXXV, 397–9.
—— (1975d) 'The Unimportance of Reswitching'. *Quarterly Journal of Economics*, Vol. LXXXIX, 32–9.
—— (1975e) *Collected Economic Papers*. Vol. 3. Second edition. Oxford: Blackwell.
—— (1979) 'Garegnani on Effective Demand'. *Cambridge Journal of Economics* 3(2): 179–80. Reprinted in J. Eatwell and M. Milgate (eds) *Keynes' Economics and the Theory of Value and Distribution*. London: Duckworth, 1983.
—— (1980) *Further Contributions to Modern Economics*. Oxford: Blackwell.
Romer, P.M. (1986) 'Increasing Returns and Long-run Growth'. *Journal of Political Economy* 94(5): 1002–38.
Rowthorn, B.E. (1974) 'Neo-classicism, Neo-Ricardianism and Marxism'. *New Left Review* 86: 63–87.
Rowthorn, B. and H-J. Chang (1991) 'Public Ownership and the Theory of the State'. Paper presented to the Conference on International Privatisation, Strategies and Practices, St Andrews University, Scotland, 12–14 September.
Samuelson, P.A. (1962) 'Parable and Realism in Capital Theory: The Surrogate Production Function'. *Review of Economic Studies*, Vol. XXIX: 193–206.
—— (1966) 'A Summing Up'. *Quarterly Journal of Economics*, Vol. LXXX: 568–83.
—— (1971) 'Understanding the Marxian Notion of Exploitation: A Summary of the So-called Transformation Problem between Marxian Values and Competitive Prices'. *Journal of Economic Literature*, Vol. IX: 399–431.
—— (1972) 'The Economics of Marx: An Ecumenical Reply'. *Journal of Economic Literature*, Vol. X: 51–7.
—— (1973) 'Samuelson's "Reply on Marxian Matters"'. *Journal of Economic Literature*, Vol. XI: 64–8.
—— (1974) *Interest Rate Determinations and Oversimplifying Parables: A Summing Up*. Buffalo, NY, mimeograph.
Samuelson, P.A. and C.C. Von Weizsäcker (1971) 'A New Labour Theory of Value for Rational Planning Through Use of the Bourgeois Profit Rate'. *Proceedings of the National Academy of Science*, USA, Vol. LXVIII: 1192–4.
Sappington, D.E.M. and J.E. Stiglitz (1987) 'Privatization, Information and Incentives'. *Journal of Policy Analysis and Management* 6(4) (Summer): 567–82.
Schmalansee, R. (1989) 'Industrial Economics: An Overview'. *Economic Journal* 98 (September): 643–81.
Sen, A. (1974) 'On Some Debates in Capital Theory'. *Economica*, Vol. XLI: 328–35.
Shapiro, C. and R.D. Wright (1990) 'Economic Rationales for the Scope of Privatisation'. In E.N. Suleiman and J. Waterbury (eds) *The Political Economy of Public Sector Reform and Privatisation*. Boulder, CO: Westview Press.
Simonetti, R. et al. (1998) *Understanding Economic Behaviour: Firms*. Buckingham: Open University Press.
Singh, A. (1971) *Takeovers: Their Reference to the Stock Market and the Theory of the Firm*. London: Cambridge University Press.
—— (1992a) 'Mental Health in Profit and Loss Making Public and Private Sector Industries'. *Indian Journal of Social Work*, Vol. LIII (4) (October): 637.

—— (1992b) 'Industrial Policy in the Third World in the 1990s – Alternative Perspectives and Current Issues in Industrial Economic Strategy'. Manchester and New York: Manchester University Press: 123–44.

Solow, B.M. (1957) 'Technical Change and the Aggregate Production Function'. *Review of Economics and Statistics*, Vol. XXXIX: 312–20.

—— (1963) *Capital Theory and the Rate of Return*. Amsterdam: North Holland.

Sonnenschein, H. (1972) 'Market Excess Demand Functions'. *Econometrica* 40(3): 549–63.

—— (1973a) 'Do Walras's Identity and Continuity Characterize the Class of Community Excess Demand Functions?' *Journal of Economic Theory* 6(4): 345–54.

—— (1973b) 'The Utility Hypothesis and Market Demand Theory'. *Western Economic Journal* 11(4): 404–10.

Sraffa, P. (1960) *Production of Commodities by Means of Commodities. Prelude to a Critique of Economic Theory*. Cambridge: Cambridge University Press.

Starr, P. (1987) 'The Limits of Privatization'. In S. Hanke (ed.) *Privatization and Development*. San Francisco: Institute for Contemporary Studies.

—— (1989) 'The Meaning of Privatization'. In S.B. Kamerman and A.J. Kahn (eds) *Privatisation and Welfare State*. Princeton, NJ: Princeton University Press.

—— (1990) 'The Limits to Privatization'. In D.J. Gayle and J.N. Goodrich (eds) *Privatization and Deregulation in Global Perspective*. London: Pinter.

Statistic Sweden: www.scb.se

Steegman, I. (1975) 'Critique of the Critic'. *Times Higher Educational Supplement*, 31 January.

Stevens, J. (1996) *Applied Multivariate Statistics for the Social Sciences*. Third edition. Hillsdale, NJ: Lawrence Erlbaum.

Stiglitz, J.E. (1974) 'The Cambridge–Cambridge Controversy in the Theory of Capital: A View from New Haven: A Review Article'. *Journal of Political Economy*, Vol. LXXXII, 893–903.

—— (1985) 'Credit Markets and the Control of Capital.' *Journal of Money, Credit and Banking* 17(2) (May): 133–52.

Sunstein, C.R. (1990) *After the Rights Revolution: Reconceiving the Regulatory State*. Cambridge, MA: Harvard University Press.

Tanoira, M. (1987) 'Privatization as Politics'. In: Hanke, ed.

Thackray, J. (1983) 'America's Amazing Executive Wealth'. *Management Today*, July.

Thirlwall, A.P. (1972) *Growth and Development: With Special Reference to Developing Economies*. London: Macmillan.

Thurstone, L.L. (1931) *The Measurement of Social Attitudes*. Chicago.

Tittenbrun, J. (1996) *Private Versus Public Enterprise: In Search of the Economic Rationale for Privatization*. London: Janus.

Tobin, J. (1973) 'Cambridge (U.K.) *v.* Cambridge (Mass.)'. *The Public Interest*, Vol. XXXI (Spring): 102–9.

Van de Walle, D. and K. Nead (eds) (1995) *Public Spending and the Poor: Theory and Evidence*. Baltimore, MD: Johns Hopkins University Press.

Veblen, T.B. (1919) *The Place of Science in Modern Civilisation and Other Essays*. New York: Huebsch. Reprinted with a new introduction by W.J. Samuels, New Brunswick, NJ: Transaction, 1990.

Veljanovski, C. (1987) *Selling the State: Privatisation in Britain.* London: Weidenfeld and Nicolson.

—— (1990) 'Privatization: Progress, Issues and Problems'. In D.J Gayle and J.N. Goodrich (eds) *Privatization and Deregulation in Global Perspective.* London: Pinter.

Vernon, R. (1981a) 'State-owned Enterprises in Latin American Exports'. *Quarterly Review of Economics and Business* 21(2): 98–114.

—— (1981b) 'International Economic Relations in Transition'. *World Economy* 4 (1) (March): 17–28.

Vickers, J. and V. Wright (1989) *The Politics of Privatisation in Western Europe.* London: Cass.

Vickers, J. and G. Yarrow (1991a) 'Economic Perspectives on Privatisation'. *Journal of Economic Perspectives* 5: 111–32.

—— (1991b) 'The British Electricity Experiment'. *Economic Policy* 12 (April): 187–232.

—— (1988) *Privatization: An Economic Analysis.* Cambridge, MA, and London: MIT Press.

Vining, A.R. and A.E. Boardman (1992) 'Ownership versus Competition: Efficiency in Public Enterprise'. *Public Choice* 73: 205–39.

Von Weizaäcker, C.C (1971) 'Ende einer Wachstumstheorie? Zu Hajo Rieses Missverständnissen über die "neoklassiche" Theorie'. *Kyklos*, Vol. XXIV, 97–101.

Walras, L. (1954) *Elements of Pure Economics.* Homewood, IL: Richard D. Irwin.

Weeks, J. (1981) *Capital and Exploitation.* Princeton: Princeton University Press.

—— (1989) *A Critique of Neoclassical Macroeconomics.* London: Macmillan.

—— (1993) 'Competition and Technical Change in an Aggregate Circulation Framework'. In G. Liodakis (ed.) *Society Technology & Restructuring of Production.* Athens: V. Papazissis: 131–44.

Wickens, M.R. (1970) 'A Theory of the Labour Market'. *Discussion Papers in Economics*, No. 36.

Williamson, O. (1970) *Corporate Control and Business Behaviour.* Englewood Cliffs, NJ: Prentice-Hall.

Wiltshire, K. (1987) 'Privatisation – The British Experience'. In K. Wiltshire (ed.) *Privatisation – The British Experience.* Melbourne: Committee for Economic Development of Australia/Longman Cheshire.

World Bank (1992) *Privatization: The Lessons of Experience.* Report. Washington, DC: World Bank.

—— (1995) *Bureaucrats in Business: The Economics and Politics of Government Ownership.* Oxford: Oxford University Press.

—— (1998) *Deininger and Squire Data Set.* Washington, DC: World Bank.

—— (1985a) 'Welfare Losses in Oligopoly and Monopolistic Competition'. *Journal of Industrial Economics* 33(4) (June): 515–29.

Yarrow, G. (1985b) 'Shareholder Protection, Compulsory Acquisition and the Efficiency of the Takeover Process'. *Journal of Industrial Economics* 34(1) (September): 3–16.

—— (1986) 'Privatization in Theory and Practice'. *Economic Policy* 2: 324–64.

—— (1989) 'Privatization and Economic Performance in Britain'. In K. Brunner and A.H. Meltzer (eds) *IMF Policy Advice, Marker Volatility, Commodity Price Rules and other Essays.* Amsterdam: North Holland: 303–44.

Yergin, D. and J. Stanislaw (1998) *The Commanding Heights: The Battle Between Government and the Marketplace that is Remaking the Modern World*. New York: Simon & Schuster.

Zeckhauser, R.J. and M. Horn (1989) 'The Control and Performance of State-Owned Enterprises'. In P.W. MacAvoy (ed.) *Deregulation and Privatization in the United States*. Edinburgh: Edinburgh University Press.

# Index

*Compiled by Sue Carlton*


Aharoni, Y. 42
airline industry 61, 75–6
Alchian, A.A. 16, 18
Amadeus 98, 140, 142
Ames, R.E. 27
Anders, C. 21
Anderson, S. 53, 70
asymmetric information 11, 22, 40, 44, 45, 50
Austria 26, 27, 40
  type-one factor analysis 101–3
Austrian school of economics 28–34, 48, 49–50, 165
  critical assessment of 31–4

Bailey, R.W. 22
bankruptcy, threat of 35, 37, 42, 52, 78
Barnes, P.A. 22
Beesley, M.E. 60
Belgium 40
  type-one factor analysis 104–6
Bhaduri, A. 90
Bishop, M. 53, 60, 68, 71–2, 79
Bliss, C.J. 88
Boardman, A. 53, 63, 64–5, 67–8
Borcherding, T.E. 38, 53, 63, 64, 65–7
Bortolotti, B. 57
Bos, D. 21–2
Bothwell, L.L. 19
Boycko, M. 53, 63
Brazil 57
Britain *see* UK
British Aerospace (BAe) 69
British Airways 69, 84
British Steel 84
British Telecommunications 56
Bulgaria, type-one factor analysis 106–8

Cambridge classical critique 82, 84, 89–91, 96
Canada 57
capital
  depreciation 87
  measurement of 88–90
  and technological change 88–9
  utilisation of 87
Cattell, R.B. 95
Caves, D.W. 37, 60
Central Electricity Board, UK 70
CES (constant elasticity of substitution) 86
Chang, H.-J. 34, 43, 81
Chen, E.K.Y. 86
Chile 57, 74
China 57
  public sector reform 68
Chirac, Jacques 57
Christensen, L.R. 37, 60, 86
Clarke, T. 57, 76–7, 80, 164
Cobb-Douglas function 86
competition 30–1, 34
  and equilibrium 46, 47
  and performance 2, 11, 12, 13, 15, 37, 49, 163, 167
  quantity theory of 46
contracting-out 1, 64
contracts, incomplete 63
Conyon, M.J. 6
Cook, P. 25, 27–8
corporate performance
  measuring 2, 11, 12, 13, 23, 28, 34, 44, 48, 51, 54, 55, 68–9, 77–9, 165
    factor analysis 82, 83, 84, 92–6, 97, 166–7
    neo-classical approach 82–3, 84, 85–92, 166
Cosh, A.D. 40, 43
Cowling, K. 22, 40
Creamer, D. 87
Czech Republic 70–1, 84

DataStream 98, 140, 141–2
De Alessi, L. 64

De Fraja, G. 53, 62
Demsetz, H. 17–18
Denison, E.F. 87, 88
Denmark, type-one factor analysis 109–11
deregulation 1, 68
Dertouzos, M. 43
Dewenter, K. 53, 70
dividends 19
Djankov, S. 84
Dunleavy, P. 27
Dunshire, A. 53, 69

*The Economist* 20, 21
efficiency
  allocative 37, 84
  dynamic 84
  internal 37
  and ownership 12, 64–7, 163
  productive 84
Ehrlich, I. 53, 73, 75–6
electrical utility sector 38, 61
empirical studies
  critical assessment of 76–9
  performance of privatised enterprises 53, 55, 68–76, 80, 83–4
  relative performance of public and private sector 53–4, 60–8, 79–80, 81, 97, 99, 100–42
  *see also* factor analysis; neo-classical approach
entrepreneurship 12, 13, 30, 31, 33
  characteristics of entrepreneurs 33–4
'exit' system 43

factor analysis 82, 83, 84–5, 92–6, 97, 166–8
  practical procedure 93–6
    correlation matrix 94
    extraction of factors 95
    principal components 94–5, 97
    rotation of factors 95–6, 97
    sample size 94
  type-one (comparing private, mixed and state-owned companies) 97, 99, 100–42, 166
    Austria 101–3
    Belgium 104–6
    Bulgaria 106–8
    Denmark 109–11
    France 113–17
    Germany 117–20
    Netherlands 121–3
    Norway 123–6
    Poland 126–8
    Portugal 128–31
    Sweden 131
    total-country analysis 99, 101, 135–8
    UK 131–5
  type-two (privatisation performance) 98, 143, 145, 146–8, 161–2, 166–7
  type-three (characteristics of ownership) 98, 143–5, 148–58, 162, 167
  type-four (effect of concentration on corporate performance) 98, 143, 145, 158–61, 162, 167
Faere, R. 53, 60, 61, 63
Fine, B. 7–8, 11–12, 44, 52, 91–2, 164
Finland 26
  type-one factor analysis 111–13
Finsinger, J. 53, 61
Fiorina, M.P. 24
Foreman-Peck, J. 53, 61
Forsyth, P. 53, 61
France 26, 27, 40, 57
  type-one factor analysis 113–17
French Telecom 57
Frydman, R. 53, 70–1
Furubotn, E.G. 14

Galal, A. 53, 73, 74
Germany 21, 26, 27, 40, 56, 57
  life insurance companies 61
  type-one factor analysis 117–20
Glassman, C.A. 19
golden shares 21, 39
Goldring, M. 28
Goodman, J.B. 58
Gordon, R.J. 88
Gorsuch, R.L. 93
government
  intervention in economy 2, 23, 26–7, 29, 44–5, 46, 50

government – *continued*
  role in public enterprises 18, 24–5, 35–6
Griliches, Z. 87, 88, 89

Hague, C. 6
Hart, O. 53, 63
Hartley, K. 53, 62
Haskel, J. 53, 72
Hayek, F.A. 28–9, 30, 31, 32, 61
Heald, D. 6
Herman, E.S. 21
Hicks, J.B. 72–3
Hocking, R. 53, 61
Hodgson, G. 32–3
Hooper, N. 53, 62
Hungary 70–1, 84

India 57
individualism 28–9, 32–3
Indonesia 74
inflation 91–2
innovation 30–1
Iordanoglou, C.H. 41
Italy 57

Japan 21, 40, 57
Jasinski, A.H. 33
Jorgenson, D.W. 87, 89
Joseph, Keith 61

Kaiser criterion 95
Kay, J.A. 53, 60, 68, 71
Kendrick, J.W. 87
Keynesianism 7
Kikeri, S. 53, 57
Kirkpatrick, C. 25, 27–8
Kirzner, I.M. 31
Kole, S.R. 63
Korea 43
Kornai, J. 61

labour market, capital–labour relationship 7
Laffont, J.-J. 53, 62
Leyland 78
Li, W. 68
life insurance companies, Germany 61
Linowes, D.F. 23
Littlechild, S.C. 31, 43, 60
Loveman, G.W. 58

'Major Companies of Europe' 98, 140
Malatesta, P.H. 53, 70
Malaysia 74
managers
  compensation/incentive payments 15, 17, 19–21, 22, 35, 38
  competition among 15, 16–17, 21
  controlling behaviour of 15–17, 19–22, 35
  distribution of duties 15–16
  in public enterprises 24, 26–7
  and risk-taking 40–1
  and threat of takeover 21–2, 35
marginal productivity of labour 92
market failure 2, 23, 41, 44
Marsh, D. 76
Martin, S. 53, 60, 72–3
Martinez-Vazquez, J. 26–7
Marwel, C. 27
Matthews, K. 77
Megginson, W.L. 53, 58, 73, 83
Mexico 57, 74
Millward, R. 39, 53, 63, 67
Minford, P. 77
Moldofsky, N. 31
Monsen, R.J. 19
Morgan, W. 38–9
Mulherin, J.H. 63

National Freight 69
nationalisation 3–4, 23, 25, 30, 78
neo-Austrian school of economics 8, 12, 13, 44, 45–6, 48, 50, 165, 168
neo-classical approach 82–3, 84, 85–92, 166
  Cambridge critique 82, 84, 89–91, 96
  critiques of 86–92
  *see also* total factor productivity (TFP)
Netherlands 57
  type-one factor analysis 121–3
Netter, J.M. 58
new industrial economics 8, 47

new institutional economics 12, 13, 44, 45, 46, 48, 165
new political economy 8, 12, 44–5, 46, 48, 50, 165
'new synthesis' 12, 13, 44–8, 165
  critical assessment of 46–8
Newberry, D. 53, 70
Noll, R.G. 24
Norway, type-one factor analysis 123–6
Nutter, G. 18

oblique rotation 96
O'Driscoll, G.P. 29, 32
OECD countries 57–8
orthogonal rotation method 96
ownership
  characteristics of 98, 143–5, 148–58, 162, 167
  common 33
  concept of public ownership 18–19
  and corporate performance 2, 11, 13–14, 16–17, 19, 22, 83, 166, 167, 168
  and efficiency 12, 64–7, 163
  and factor analysis 98, 99–100, 101, 135, 140, 167
  *see also* property rights theory; shareholders

Parker, D. 26, 39, 53, 60, 63, 67, 72–3, 81
Pejovich, S. 14, 16
performance *see* corporate performance
Pescatrice, D.R. 38
Phelps, B.E.H. 88
Pinto, B. 68
Poland 70–1, 84
  public sector reform 68
  type-one factor analysis 126–8
Pollitt, M.G. 53, 70
Portugal, type-one factor analysis 128–31
prices, as product of competition 30, 31, 34
principal components analysis 94–5, 97
principal–agent theory 12, 13, 34–44, 48, 50, 62, 165
  critical assessment of 38–44
principal–axis factoring 94–5
private sector
  and diversification of risk 19
  and efficiency 6, 52–3, 60
  and market discipline 12, 13, 43
  performance *see* factor analysis, type-one
  and social welfare 62
  and threat of bankruptcy 35, 37, 78
  and threat of takeover 21–2, 35, 39–40, 52
privatisation
  and concentration of corporate ownership 4–5
    *see also* factor analysis, type-four
  and continued state intervention 28, 165
  cost-benefit analysis 70, 74–5, 83
  covering range of policies 1, 6
  and directors' salaries 6
  and economic efficiency 52, 80, 83
  economic theories of 11–13
  and expansion in share ownership 4–5
  explanations for 7–8, 58, 164–5
  and globalisation 7
  historical overview 56–9
  and ideology 6
  and labour force reduction 83, 84
  manager–workforce relationship 72
  performance *see* factor analysis, type-two
  and prices 5, 70, 76
  and profitability 3, 49, 74, 76–7
  and quality of service 5
  and reduction in levels of delegation 42–3
  and regulation 5, 37–8
  and restrictions on foreign investment 39–40
  and sale of assets 5
  and social outcomes 47–8, 70, 74, 76–7, 80, 83, 164
  and technological progress 6, 7
  theoretical literature on 7–8

profit maximisation 30, 37, 49
profit-sharing systems 20
profitability 3, 66, 74, 75, 76, 77–9
property rights theory 12, 13–23, 48–9, 63, 64, 65, 165
  critical assessment of 17–23
public choice theory 12, 23–8, 48, 49, 63, 64, 165
  critical assessment of 26–8
public sector
  and competition 30, 60
  and delegation 42–3
  and diversification of risk 19
  and entrepreneurship 30
  and excess of input 27
  and freeriders/self-interested managers 26–7, 41, 43, 50, 52, 64
  and higher costs 64
  history of 163
  and inefficiency 4, 12, 23, 24, 25, 27, 35, 39, 49, 50, 52, 63
  and innovation 30
  lack of financial discipline 61
  monitoring of 42
  objectives of state enterprises 26
  ownership 16–17, 18–19, 33, 36
  performance *see* factor analysis, type-one
  and profitability 6, 76–8
  and reform 4, 68
  and social welfare 62
  and threat of bankruptcy 42, 52
  and threat of privatisation 168

Ramanadham, V.V. 53
Reaganism 7
Rees, R. 25
rent-seeking 24, 44–5, 50, 168
Rhoades, S.A. 19
Rizzo, M.J. 29, 32
Robinson, J. 90
Rolls-Royce 69
Rowthorn, B. 34
Royal Ordnance Factories 69

Sappington, D.E.M. 19, 53, 62
Scandinavian countries 57
Scree test 95
share options 19–20
share prices
  as disciplinary mechanism 43
  tool for monitoring efficiency 22
shareholders 15, 16
  and decision-making/control 17, 19, 36–7, 49, 50
  and dividends 19
  as investors 18
  and ownership 17–18
Singh, A. 39, 43, 81
Solow, B.M. 86, 87, 88
South Africa 57
Soviet bloc 57
Spain 57
Sraffa, P. 89–90
Stanislaw, J. 61
Starr, P. 22–3, 27
Statistical Package for the Social Sciences (SPSS) 94–5, 97, 135, 146
Statistics Sweden 98–9, 140
Stiglitz, J.E. 19, 53, 62
structure conduct-performance (SCP) 47
Sub-Saharan Africa 57
subjectivism 29–30, 31–2
Sunstein, C.R. 24
Sweden 26, 27, 40
  Concentration 159–61, 162, 167
  type-one factor analysis 131
Szymanski, S. 53, 72

Taiwan 43
takeover
  and efficiency improvement 22, 40, 43
  threat of 21–2, 35, 37, 39–40, 43–4, 52
Tanoira, M. 28
Thatcher, Margaret 56, 60, 61, 69
Thatcherism 7, 165
Thirlwall, A.P. 87, 88
Thompson, D. 53, 60, 71–2, 79
Thurstone, L.L 92
Tirole, J. 53, 62
Tittenbrun, J. 33
Tonqvist productivity index 71–2
total factor productivity (TFP) 74–6, 82–3, 84, 86, 93, 96, 166
  critiques of 86–92

trade unions 3, 24
transaction costs 43, 44, 62
translog production function 86–7
Trapani, J.M.I. 38

UK 26, 40, 52, 56–7, 69
  empirical studies 53, 71–3, 74
  type-one factor analysis 131–5

VEBA 56
Veljanovski, C. 58
VES (variable elasticity of substitution) 86
Vickers, J. 3, 5, 22, 60, 61, 68, 164
Vining, A.R. 53, 63, 64–5, 67–8
'voice' system 43
Volkswagen 56, 78

water utility sector 38–9
Waterson, M. 53, 61
Weeks, J. 46
Whiteside, R.M. 66
World Bank 68
  1992 report 69–70
  listing of privatised firms 74
Wright, V. 3, 5, 60, 61, 68

Yarrow, G. 22, 60, 68, 164
Yergin, D. 61